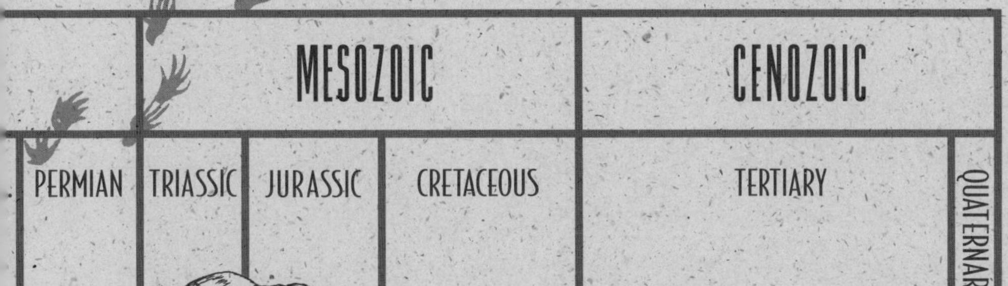

| MESOZOIC | | | | CENOZOIC | |
|---|---|---|---|---|---|
| PERMIAN | TRIASSIC | JURASSIC | CRETACEOUS | TERTIARY | QUATERNARY |

EARLY
MAMMALS

AGE OF
MAMMALS

EARLY
REPTILES

AGE OF
DINOSAURS

| 280 | 230 | 195 | 141 | 65 | 1.8 |

# EARTH'S
# FIRST
# STEPS

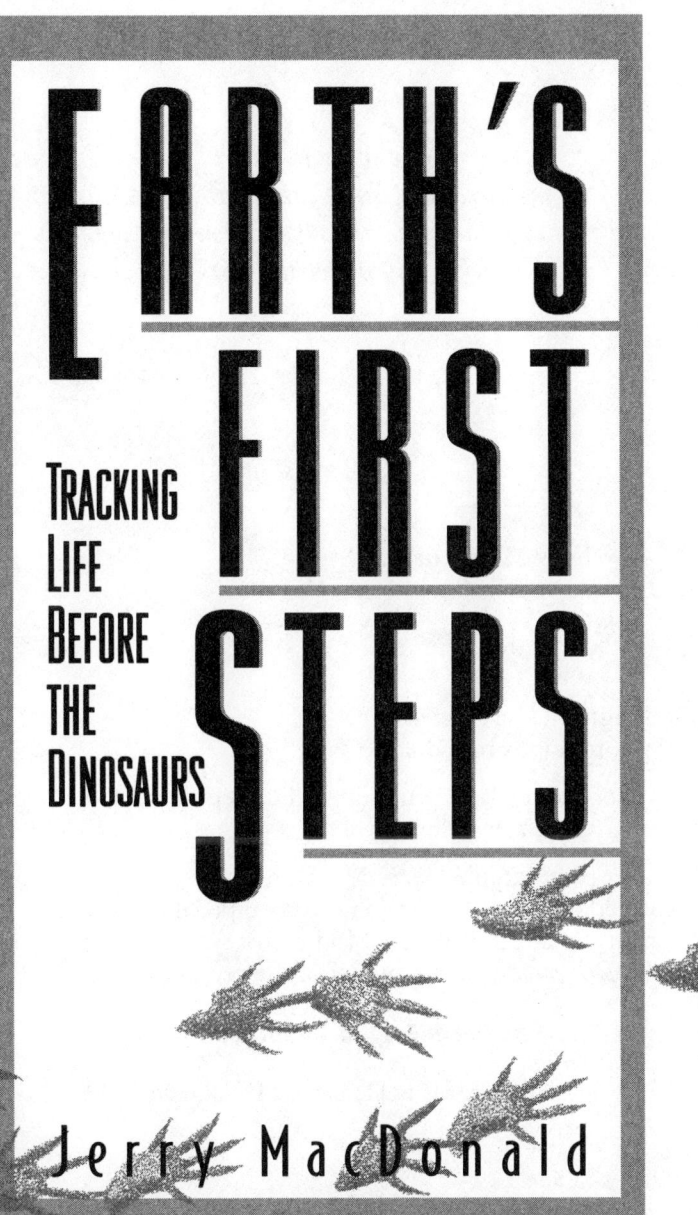

# EARTH'S FIRST STEPS

## TRACKING LIFE BEFORE THE DINOSAURS

### Jerry MacDonald

FRANKLIN PIERCE
COLLEGE LIBRARY
RINDGE, N.H. 03461

Foreword by Martin Lockley
Introduction by Nicholas Hotton III

*To my wife, Pearl,*
*and my three children, Noah, Justin, and Hannah.*
*I know that these last seven years have often been tough for you all.*
*I just hope this book makes up for the years the locusts have eaten.*
*I love you all.*

© 1994 by Jerry MacDonald
All rights reserved.

9  8  7  6  5  4  3  2  1

Book design by Margaret Donharl
Cover photographs by Eduardo Fuss

Front cover photograph: An unidentified reptile track discovered near Las Cruces, New Mexico.

Back cover photographs: Jerry MacDonald brushes off some unidentified prints that appear curiously bipedal at the main excavation site in the Robledo Mountains. Also pictured is the skull of a *Dimetrodon* and a model of the reptile. Cast by J. Fischner.

**Library of Congress Cataloging-in-Publication Data**
MacDonald, Jerry
    Earth's first steps : tracking life before the dinosaur / Jerry MacDonald.
      p.    cm.
    Includes Index.
    ISBN 1-55566-119-X
    1. Footprints, Fossil—New Mexico—Robledo Mountains.
2. Paleontology—Permian.   3. Animals, Fossil—New Mexico—Robledo Mountains.   I. Title.
QE845.M23    1994
560'.1729—dc20
                                    94-32303
                                     CIP

QE
845
M23
1994

Printed in the United States by
Johnson Printing
1880 South 57th Court
Boulder, Colorado 80301

FRANKLIN PIERCE
COLLEGE LIBRARY
RINDGE, N.H. 03461

# Contents

# ILLUSTRATIONS

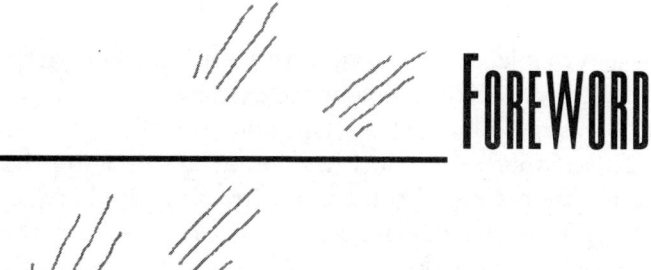# FOREWORD

*"Hallo!" said Piglet, "what are you doing?" "Tracking something," said Winnie-the-Pooh very mysteriously. "Tracking what?" said Piglet, coming closer. "That's just what I ask myself. I ask myself, What?"*

—A.A. Milne

When Jerry MacDonald telephoned to tell me his book about fossil footprint discoveries in New Mexico's Robledo Mountains had been accepted for publication, my first reaction was "Wow! another book on tracks." Until recently, books on fossil footprints have been both rare and specialized. But no longer. Especially on the subject of dinosaur tracks, there has been a recent rash of books, magazine articles, TV documentaries, and a remarkable resurgence of interest on the whole subject of fossil footprints.

As far as Jerry's work was concerned, I knew that for over half a decade he had been digging tracks and getting good coverage in the local, national, and even international press. Why were these tracks so newsworthy? From the published accounts, and my one trip to look at the main discovery site, I knew that he had uncovered a rich treasure trove of predinosaurian footprints from the Paleozoic era which had been touted as the "best in the world." This alone was newsworthy and had sparked widespread discussion about the tracks.

As a tracker, what could I write in my foreword on this esoteric subject? I don't know much about Paleozoic or predinosaurian tracks—for that matter hardly anybody knows much about predinosaurian tracks, especially in North America. Mostly we know that, whereas we once thought such ancient tracks were rare, they are now turning out to be incredibly abundant. As Jerry's discovery proves, there is a veritable embarrassment of fossil footprint riches out there and the Robledo tracks are a prime example.

Fortunately, I was saved by the bell. This book is really not about tracks in a specific scientific sense. So I have no need to try to make educated pronouncements on who made the tracks and what they really mean—though clearly they are very important. Rather, this book turns out to be about the process of the discovery and the subsequent reaction of the local community, the paleontological fraternity, politicians, and land management authorities. More than anything the story is about Jerry's often strenuous and always persistent efforts to find and excavate the trackway motherlode, and how he always believed it was there. Like a man half-crazed with gold fever, Jerry roamed the Robledo Hills, mumbling to himself, all the time convinced that the big discovery lay just around the corner. And sure enough, it did.

On June 6, 1987, Jerry hit pay dirt and opened a Paleozoic Pandora's box—the best fossil footprint discovery in North America from this era, and possibly the best in the world. It was a discovery that would stir deep feelings in many people at a time when paleontology is riding a wave of extreme popularity. Paradoxically, this timely footprint discovery story also comes at a time when paleontology is chronically under-staffed, under-funded, and inextricably caught up in widespread societal controversy about the value of fossils and who should have legal access and jurisdiction over such valuable, non-renewable resources.

In many ways Jerry MacDonald's story is a classic tale of frontier hardship and stubborn persistence in the face of adversity and skepticism. But Jerry's struggle has not been so much on the frontiers of intricate specialized science, but more on the frontiers of popular scientific credibility and dedication to personal academic goals. Until recently, the study of fossil footprints has been considered, at best, a highly specialized field, but more often it has been viewed as the lunatic fringe of paleontology, a field best suited to cranks. Students of tracks were taken about as seriously as Winnie-the-Pooh, that familiar bear of "very little brain," tracking a woozle. Trackers had a hard time convincing colleagues of the validity of the subject, let alone convincing the scientific and administrative establishments of the need to fund serious research.

But a growing number of fringe specialists have "believed" sufficiently in the value of tracks—as Jerry did—to establish the study of fossil footprints as a respectable interdisciplinary science forging a new niche on the frontier between paleontology and sedimentary geology. Getting tracks accepted by the mainstream has never been easy, even in this new era of footprint respectability. Jerry's story of faith in tracks and the uphill road to acceptance and credibility is therefore reminiscent of the experiences of many professionals.

One of the reasons that tracks have rarely been found in such abundance in the past is that no one really looked very hard. But the motto is "seek and thou shalt find," sometimes paraphrased in paleontology and science as "you find what you're looking for." This is what Jerry did so persistently, and then once he had found the sites, he did something trackers rarely do, he started digging. Ridiculous as it might seem—for paleontologists are always asked what they are "digging up"—trackers rarely dig for tracks. There have been only a couple of major tracks excavations in the entire history of research of fossil footprints. Jerry's strenuous digging activities must certainly rank as the largest single-handed excavation of fossil footprints ever undertaken.

Surprise, surprise! Digging produces tracks, just as it does bones and archaeological artifacts. Jerry either arrived at this obvious conclusion a lot quicker than most trackers, or he was just too darn obsessed to stop digging until he had torn into the mountain and laid open the fossil footprint motherlode. Like many a colorful character in paleontology, Jerry MacDonald did not lack imagination, and the proof that his wild dreams of trackway motherlodes and his vision of track heaven were not crazy was best proved simply by exposing the evidence.

Jerry did more than just expose tracks. In this highly candid and personal story he has also exposed his very soul. Through his blunt, chatty, and folksy style, we are exposed to his moments of elation and of disappointment, his determination, his self doubt, and his search for the holy grail of acceptance in the scientific community. We are also exposed to the world of paleontological politics where academia, officialdom, commercial enterprise, para-professionals, amateurs, politicians, and even track thieves cross paths, often on shaky ground.

Despite a degree in earth science, Jerry's discovery led him not into a world of rocks and fossils, but into a world of politics and policy decisions. Who would be responsible for the development of the site? Who would validate the find? Who would fund the project? Would it even be funded? Who would conduct the scientific investigations? Where would the tracks find a permanent home? A degree in earth science does not necessarily equip one to understand such politics. Jerry, however, had switched from earth science to sociology as he entered graduate school. This fortuitous change of direction gave Jerry a new perspective, allowing him to look at the discovery in the context of its sociological impact on the local and paleontological communities. In a surprising change of gears in the book's later chapters, the story switches from the reminiscences of a persistent rock hound to an objective sociological analysis of the discovery, legitimization, politicization, and enculturation phases of the Robledo's footprint saga. This phase of the saga takes us from the desert world of Robledo rocks and rattlesnakes to the corridors of power. Here the currency is no longer rocks and fossils, but instead revolves around the impact of expert testimony, congressional records, six- and seven-figure appropriations, and the 1990s political future of fossils with a quarter of a billion years of history.

Paleozoic tracks are without a doubt some of the most difficult to interpret. In this respect, Jerry MacDonald opened a scientific Pandora's box, a discovery of such sufficient magnitude that it will probably not begin to be adequately understood without three to five years of serious study. Despite inevitable setbacks, local politics, lack of adequate funding, and lack of policy precedents for handling such a "discovery," Jerry MacDonald has succeeded in three things: First, he has convinced the paleontological world that the fossil footprints of the Robledo Mountains are a world-class find. Second, he has derived some measure of personal satisfaction in his quest by proving that, all along, he was on the right track with a worthy cause. And, third, Jerry has assured his place in tracking history as the man behind the Robledo trackways discovery. Here then is his remarkably personal story.

*Martin Lockley, Ph.D.,*
*Professor of Geology*
*University of Colorado at Denver*
*Author of* Tracking Dinosaurs

# Acknowledgments

First, my thanks go to all of my early supporters: Dr. Thom Votaw, for his infectious enthusiasm and scientific openness; Dr. Brad Blake, for his brave support of my work when it was not fashionable to do so; Gene and Peggy Elliot—I could not have weathered the storms without them; Oscar and Maretha Branson, for their kindness and pep talks; Betty Lady, for singing the praises of the tracks everywhere she went; Keith Whelpley, for his unbiased reporting; Harold "Buz" Walker, for his open mind and commitment to the truth; Paul and Yoli Bardwell, for keeping the shrine alive; Mike and Helen Royal, for their generosity; and the legions of people that made up an exciting groundswell of community support.

My thanks also go to my paleontological friends who believed in me from the beginning: Dr. Nicholas Hotton III of the Smithsonian Institute, for his uncompromising support, encouragment, and overflowing generosity; Dr. David S. Berman and Dr. Mary Dawson of the Carnegie Museum of Natural History in Pittsburgh, for their rave reviews on the Robledo material and the Carnegie's early financial support; Dr. Craig Black of the Natural History Museum of Los Angeles County, for early generous financial support; Dr. Don Wolberg, for aiding in the formation of a scientific consortium to ensure the success of the Trackways Project.

Where would I have been without my incredible field men: Doug Wood and Dave Slagle—would that every paleontological project was so blessed with talent like you; my graduate assistants, Gary Olmstead and Chris Whitman; my annual one-day workers from Dr. Scotty MacNeish's archeological excavations; and my visitors from the Potomac Museum group, including Jon Kramer and Hal

Halverson. Also, Pat Beckett, for a shoulder to cry on; Mark Schult, for two summers of research; Dr. James Farlow, for his visit and written evaluation of the Robledos; Dr. Steve Buchmann, for peeking at the invertebrates; and Glen Kuban, for cosmological discussions, cast-making, and a view of the Robledo "man tracks"; and Dr. Harold Alexander.

To the 1994 trackways team which, in addition to Nicholas Hotton, include Dr. Spencer Lucas, Gary Morgan, and Pete Reser of the New Mexico Museum of Natural History; and Dr. Adrian Hunt and Dr. Martin Lockley of the University of Colorado at Denver; thanks for putting meat on the bones.

To New Mexico Senators Jeff Bingaman and Pete Domenici, New Mexico Congressman Joe Skeen, Arkansas Senator Dale Bumpers, and their assistants, who are responsible for giving the trackway discovery its latest political successes.

To all of the United States Bureau of Land Management officials and employees who supported my work from the beginning and never waivered, even in the midst of controversy: Mike Mallouf, Tim Salt, Scott Florence, Jim Fox, Stephanie Hargrove, Linda Rundell, Ted Barr, Mark Hakela, Diana "Punky" Garretson, Larry Woodard, Robert Salas, Pam Smith, Steve Fosberg, Jon Josephs, Bob Calkins, and Dewayne Sikes. Also thanks to Jack Quaintance (I will always remember Jack, who recently passed away), Don Couchman, and Mike O'Neill.

To all of those at Johnson Books who have given of their time and talents on this book; managing editor Walt Borneman, editorial assistant Theresa Duggan, and copy editor Sheila Berg.

My greatest debt is to Martin Lockley and Nick Hotton. Not only did they generously agree to respectively write the foreword and introduction, but also Nick and Martin painstakingly reviewed two drafts of the entire manuscript for scientific accuracy and perspective. Clearly, the responsibility for any errors which remain is mine alone.

Finally, my thanks to those early track hunters, fossil hunters, and quarrymen whose recollections and experiences were so helpful in cracking the case.

# INTRODUCTION

Jerry MacDonald has written an exciting tale about the remarkable deposit of fossil footprints in the Robledo Hills near Las Cruces, New Mexico. The trackmakers were land animals of the Early Permian, a time more than 270 million years ago, when vertebrates first established themselves firmly in terrestrial environments. Better than most books of its genre, this one catches the human element of paleontology, the drama, excitement, and thrill of the scientific chase—yes, and the blood, sweat, tears, and politics as well—recounted by one who has experienced it all.

Early Permian fossil bones are fun because they tell us what the animals looked like, how they were put together, and how they came to be preserved. Fossil trackways, however, provide a more immediate experience because they tell us what these long-extinct animals were doing with their machinery at a specific instant in time 270 million years ago.

The Robledo Hills deposits include one of the world's greatest accumulations of fossil trackways of Early Permian age and show the dramatic diversity of four-footed vertebrates and their multi-footed arthropod prey. The footprints are so clear that they look almost as though they had been made after yesterday's thunderstorm. The mud and silt into which the trackways were impressed was deposited along the shores of a shallow inland sea and is now consolidated into reddish layers which record the ebb and flow of tides in that sea. The layers, like sequential photographs each preserving an instant of time, repeatedly record the activity of foraging vertebrates and invertebrates whose adventures began (and often ended) at low tide.

The variety of traces of living things preserved is comprehensive, including giant Permian amphibians and predatory synapsids as well

as small amphibians that looked like living salamanders and small reptiles that looked like lizards. Nearly every major taxonomic group
known from bones is represented here by clear and extensive tracks,
and numerous forms, both vertebrate and invertebrate, are unknown
elsewhere. These include, in addition to small amphibians and reptiles,
a variety of arthropods: scorpions, giant centipedes and millipedes,
horseshoe crabs, and dragonflies and other insects. Several insect
trackways also show the prints of tetrapod insectivores that may well
have been hunting them down, some of them ending under the heavy
print of a reptile's foot. Finally, the picture is completed by the occurrence of plant fossils within the trackway layers, in particular early
conifers. Even the weather has been fossilized, with 270 million-year-
old rain prints, mud cracks, and ripple marks decorating the surfaces
of many layers.

An unusual and refreshing aspect of this book is that, although it is
about vertebrate paleontology, it is not about dinosaurs. The Early
Permian was about 70 million years *before* the oldest dinosaurs and represents a world much stranger than that of dinosaurs. Despite all the
palaver of the last thirty years, it is still not popularly recognized that
what made their world so exotic was primarily the dinosaurs themselves, together with their spectacular collapse. Otherwise, the world of
dinosaurs was populated by such commonplace animals as mammals,
birds, crocodiles, turtles, lizards, and snakes. Before dinosaurs became
extinct, the plants on which they fed would have been almost as familiar to us as the flora of the present-day Everglades. In the Early
Permian, by contrast, there were not only no dinosaurs, but no mammals, birds, crocodiles, turtles, lizards, or snakes, and no flowering
plants. The plants of the time looked more like those of the coal forests
than those of our day.

In the Early Permian we can identify the remote ancestors of animals of the age of dinosaurs, but few of them looked at all like what
they were later to become. The Early Permian ancestors of mammals,
for example, were synapsids of the order Pelycosauria, which included
the biggest animals of their time, about the size of a large crocodile.
Some of the big synapsids, such as *Dimetrodon* and *Sphenacodon*, were
also the nastiest predators of their time. Others, such as *Edaphosaurus*,
were among the first tetrapods to be identifiable as plant eaters.
Ironically, the Early Permian ancestors of all the other reptiles, including dinosaurs and crocodiles, were generally much smaller than synapsids, ranging in size from a fence lizard to a tree iguana, and were
of very lizard-like appearance. Most of them were also rarer than

synapsids, and most probably fed chiefly on insects and other arthropods. Synapsids and reptiles, however, comprised only about half of the tetrapod population of the Early Permian. The other half consisted of amphibians, many of them distantly related to living frogs, toads, and salamanders but a significant component unrelated to anything living today. Early Permian amphibians ranged from animals of the size and appearance of living salamanders to animals six to eight feet long, with enormous froglike heads, stout limbs, and short tails. Living amphibians (the word means "both lives") hatch from fishlike eggs and spend part of their life in water as larvae, with gills as well as lungs; some, in fact, never come out of the water and follow a fishlike mode for their whole lives. So also must it have been with Early Permian amphibians, but a significant number of them became highly terrestrialized as adults, so much so that they gave synapsids and reptiles a good run for their money in competition for terrestrial niches.

Momentary activities of this whole De Millean cast of characters are probably represented in the Robledo Hills trackways and, thanks to Jerry MacDonald's persistent efforts, are now available to be sorted out. But don't take my word for it—read on.

*Dr. Nicholas Hotton III*
*Research Paleontologist Emeritus*
*National Museum of Natural History*
*Smithsonian Institution*

# CHAPTER ONE

## Needle in a Haystack: On the Trail of Fossil Footprints

Approaching Las Cruces from the west on Interstate 10 in the late summer of 1983, I was struck by the majesty of the mountains that lie just to the east. The Organs, named after rugged peaks that resemble organ pipes, form the southern end of the Rocky Mountains, which stretch all the way from Canada to west Texas. Rising almost nine thousand feet above sea level, the Organs may seem insignificant when compared to the Colorado Rockies, but since the first Spanish colonists passed through the area in 1550, travelers have been awed by their sudden appearance in the middle of the Chihuahuan high desert.

About five miles before reaching the city, the interstate plunges hundreds of feet within a little more than a mile before leveling off on the vast floodplain of the legendary Rio Grande. Las Cruces is a sleepy city cradled for ten miles within the Rio Grande Valley. Mesilla, a historic Spanish settlement, sprang up over three hundred years earlier only miles to the west of the heart of Las Cruces, and the area is more popularly called the Mesilla Valley.

Legend has it that Billy the Kid was gunned down in Mesilla over one hundred years ago, and Pat Garrett, the man who shot Billy, was himself the victim of gunplay just east of Las Cruces along what is now New Mexico 70. Continuing on this highway eastward, the ground again rises several hundred feet before butting up against the steep wall of the Organs.

Nestled just to the west of Las Cruces are the Robledo Mountains. Running north and south along the western edge of the harnessed Rio Grande, this unassuming range is entirely overshadowed by the Organs. In fact, it is barely seen by motorists traveling east on Interstate 10 until they look back west after entering Las Cruces.

The Robledos were named after Pedro Robledo, who, along with a large caravan of Spanish settlers, traveled north from Chihuahua, Mexico, into the heart of the New Mexico territories. Robledo was among Juan de Oñate's colonists who were sent to take possession of New Mexico after Oñate claimed it for Spain. Robledo was the first settler to die, and he was buried at the foot of the range.

The contrast between the Organs and the Robledos is dramatic. From a distance the Robledos appear plain and desolate. No greenery can be seen along the hillsides, and the tops of the mountains have long been worn flat. Still, the Robledos offer a variety of outdoor activities, from rabbit hunting and target shooting to hiking and off-roading.

In contrast, the Organs cannot be penetrated by vehicle, and only a few strenuous trails lead accomplished hikers to the other side. These mountains have claimed more than their share of lives from a never-ending stream of rock climbers who want to add them to their lists of conquests.

Both ranges have seen considerable scientific work by various types of geologists—in particular, a cadre of sedimentologists, stratigraphers, and earth science students from New Mexico State University, just a few miles away in Las Cruces. It is in this area that the differences begin to favor the Robledos for local interest.

The Organs are an ancient batholith, the igneous core of a long gone mountain range that once rose nearly twenty thousand feet. Millions of years of erosion from rains and winds ground away the softer outer shroud, depositing vast amounts of loose sediment both east and west of the range and eventually exposing the hard igneous core that can be observed today. This igneous rock was rich in minerals and over a dozen mine shafts are scattered along the lower slopes of the range. According to old-timers, the Organs also hide at least one "lost" gold mine, and some of the abandoned mines are still searched by rock and gem hunters in what is a very dangerous, but fairly common practice. The Organs, however, are entirely devoid of fossils. By contrast, the Robledo range has always been popular among fossil hunters and collectors and has consistently guaranteed a wonderful and abundant variety of invertebrate marine fossils, too, both old and young.

When I descended into the Mesilla Valley for the first time, I had only two things on my mind—college and fossils. I could not have imagined then that my life would soon become so intertwined with the Robledo Mountains.

Las Cruces was the perfect place for me. The view from virtually any spot was breathtaking. All around, as far as the eye could see, were wonderful exposures of sediment—the perfect hunting ground for fossils and the perfect place for a fossil lover.

I have a fascination with fossils for several reasons. For one thing, they were once alive. The dramatic transformation from living creature to something that looks like rock has always amazed me. Fossils are geometric wonders. The frozen spiral of an ammonite, the perfect sutures of a nautiloid, the glossy scales of a fish, and the miracle of a dragonfly's remains preserved in hardened mudstone all fascinate me. It seems to me that the earth doesn't want any of its life-forms to be lost as it spins out its existence, and so it preserves a record of them all. Fossils display an unceasing progression, a continuity that sets my imagination on fire.

I have to admit that I also like fossils because I like old things. I would rather pass the time with a box of unsorted fossils than a new video machine and a dozen game cartridges. Actually, I have never been much of a risk taker, and when one of my newfound friends in Las Cruces invited me to go rappelling off a three-hundred-foot cliff in the Organ Mountains, I told him "no way" unless there was a fossil protruding from the face halfway down. The old Camel cigarette slogan can likewise be used as the fossil lover's motto: "I'd walk a mile for a [fossil]."

Fossil hunters love desolation. The more desolate an area, the better, because vast eroded exposures have the best chance of yielding abundant fossils. But the rock exposures in southern New Mexico consist primarily of limestone, marine (water-laid) sediments. Though there may be some scattered shark teeth or even spines in these rocks, the vast majority of fossils are of marine invertebrates (animals without a backbone), including a rich variety of seashells, snails, nautiloids, coral, and other kinds of sea life.

Many of the marine fossils found in the Las Cruces area have relatives that still live in earth's oceans today, indicating that something dramatic has happened to this whole section of earth. I had already traveled eight hundred miles from San Diego's beautiful shores, climbing steadily in altitude all the while. By the time I drove into Las Cruces, I had already reached an altitude of 4,500 feet in the heart of the southwestern desert. Sometime in the past, about 270 million years ago, this high desert community was shoreline. The marine fossils are the proof. Something significant apparently thrust this whole area nearly a mile into the sky.

We find further evidence of profound changes in elevation and environment one hundred miles to the east of Las Cruces in the Sacramento Mountains. The southern end of the range, called the Guadalupe Mountains, is composed entirely of limestone. The Guadalupes preserve is the world's largest fossil reef, which rivals in size and majesty the world's largest living reef, the Great Barrier Reef, off the eastern coast of Australia. When alive, this fossil reef lies 150 miles off the coast of present-day Las Cruces. Now, this area is eight hundred miles from the Pacific and nearly one thousand miles from the Gulf of Mexico. The nearest shoreline is on the eastern coast of Baja, California, about six hundred miles away.

There is much more evidence that the New Mexico of today is remarkably different from what it was in the past. Scientists have established that in the Paleozoic era, before the age of the dinosaurs, southern New Mexico was a migrating shoreline at sea level and was located near the equator. Portions of New Mexico were semi-tropical, and vast stretches of land near the coast were populated by beautiful conifers up to fifty feet high. Today Las Cruces is an arid desert at 32 degrees north latitude, nearly three thousand miles from the present location of the equator.

All around is evidence of the constant geological and ecological change that characterizes the history of the earth. Such change probably contributed to the wholesale demise of both terrestrial and marine fauna, creating vacant ecological niches that would later be filled by legions of different plants and animals, ushering in the Mesozoic era, the age of the dinosaurs.

The old floodplain of the once-mighty Rio Grande preserves additional evidence of relentless change. A rich mammal fauna, which in its variety resembles mammals that currently exist in the savannas of Africa, is a testimony to the age of mammals that followed the age of dinosaurs. Near Las Cruces, paleontologists have found the remains of prehistoric elephants like the mammoth and its smaller cousin, the mastodon, as well as dire wolves, cave bears, saber-toothed tigers, camels, zebras, ground sloths, large birds of prey, and at least three species of giant tortoise.

It is well known that the present river sands often yield scattered mammal bones and petrified wood that are anywhere from ten thousand to three million years old. But this is the extent of the fossils that can be found in southern New Mexico. Fossil collectors have an interesting choice: marine fossils nearly three hundred million years old, or mammal bones and wood no older than three million years. There is little in between. What happened to 250 million years of biological pre-history? In southern New Mexico it is missing virtually everywhere.

Sediments from the age of dinosaurs end about eighty-five miles to the north of Las Cruces, near the present town of Truth or Consequences, and sediments from the next age, the Tertiary, are mostly volcanic and void of fossils. But there is one other kind of fossil that can be found in southern New Mexico: prehistoric footprints that were made when Las Cruces was a coastal plain, when the ancient reef flourished, and sea clams and snails lived in abundance. These fossil footprints were made by a menagerie of four-footed animals that prowled the shores of the ancient sea more than a quarter of a billion years ago, nearly fifty million years before dinosaurs roamed the earth.

Most of these footprints are concentrated in the Robledo Mountains, but they were unobtrusive and virtually ignored. Though everyone knew of the rich deposits of marine fossils in the hills, the Robledos were much more secretive about revealing their terrestrial bounty. Although the scattered footprints found loose in the maze of arroyos that make up much of the Robledos were known for nearly fifty years, they were never examined collectively as evidence of a coherent prehistoric story of trackways buried just below the surface. This was to change in 1987, but the story really begins in 1983, when I first drove my family down the west mesa and into Las Cruces.

## Setting the Stage

You would think that my first exposure to fossil footprints would have been in some fossil collector's field guide, but, like nearly all other collectors, fossil footprints were not in my vocabulary. When I thought of fossil footprints, I envisioned dinosaur tracks, big ones, perhaps in a block of rock weighing at least five hundred pounds, certainly not collector size.

Collectors prefer their fossils to be manageable, hand size to field-pack size at best. I never dreamed that fossil footprints could be small and in rock of a manageable size. However, that perception changed when I walked into the Earth Science Department at New Mexico State University (NMSU) to register for geology classes.

As at any university, the Earth Science Department had rows of display cases full of gems, minerals, and fossils, most of which came from the local area. Some of the most impressive fossils were those of Pleistocene times, around twelve thousand to twenty thousand years ago, of mammoth and mastodon bones. Significantly overshadowed in the collection were three small red slabs preserving what appeared to be tiny footprints. The slabs, placed on the top shelf of a display case in the hall, had no accompanying data whatsoever—no locality, no identification, no explanation.

I wasn't immediately enraptured by them. Tiny, half-inch footprints certainly don't capture one's attention like the two-and-a-half-foot-long femur of an elephant, especially an extinct elephant found in the high desert sands half a world away from where their only remaining relatives live today. I was also more interested in the marine fossils in another case. Nearly all the fossils came from NMSU's "backyard." The university's geology program had an excellent reputation, not just for its faculty and classwork but also for providing exceptional field experience to its earth science students.

To become familiar with my new surroundings, I spent much of my free time hiking all over the open desert, and I climbed to the top of the Robledo, Doña Ana, and Organ mountain ranges to get a bird's-eye view of the land. I was also a participant in several guided outings to see everything from fascinating archaeological sites to impressive volcanic cones and lava flows, all sponsored throughout the year by NMSU's Kent Hall Museum.

My first field trips were during an earth science class in spring 1984: one was to Bishops Cap, a hat-shaped mountain about twelve miles south of the university which is very rich in marine invertebrate fossils, and the other to the Robledos. During the field trip to the Robledos, we hiked up a broad, steep canyon until we came to a large outcrop of layered red sandstone. The focus of the field trip was an outcrop of spectacular magma intrusions about a mile farther up the canyon, but on our way back down we were told that this monstrous red bed had previously yielded a rare footprint or two.

When our primary work was done, we spent some of our free time combing the extensive debris looking for footprints. None of us really knew what we were looking for, but we scrutinized every crack or indentation in search of the elusive tracks. A few students thought they found something, but no one was equipped to verify whether the little scratchings were actually footprints or some other sedimentary feature.

One student did indeed find something that we all agreed had to be the small trail of some tiny animal, and we were all very envious. But that was the end of the story. Again, no one could identify the trail, explain its origin, or place it in a paleontological context.

None of us considered that these bits and pieces of track-bearing rock could be of great scientific value. The tracks that we did find were destined to be a small trophy in a student's fossil collection, where they would rest, unstudied and unknown. And try as we might, nobody else found anything more that day. Nobody that is, but me. I discovered a fascination with fossil footprints.

Back in Breland Hall the next day, I looked again at the specimens exhibited in the hall cabinets. What the student found the day before was just as good as what was displayed, and I was impressed. Probably like everybody else, I assumed that I was staring at the best footprints that could be found in the area. I did not entertain the idea that better fossil animal trails could be found in the mountains, or even that other places in the Robledos could also yield such tracks. Two years passed with no more footprint encounters, and I soon lost interest in looking for them.

## Building an Intellectual "Tractor"

My next exposure to fossil footprints was in 1986, but I must digress a bit to put this encounter into focus. I had received my bachelor's degree in earth science in 1985, at the age of thirty-two. I graduated with honors and was quite proud because my first attempt at college thirteen years earlier had been unsuccessful.

In 1971, fresh out of high school, I had enrolled at the University of Wisconsin at Madison. My major was geology, a subject I had loved since early childhood when my desert-loving father introduced me to it. But things went wrong from the beginning. An accident during my first semester caused my attendance and coursework to suffer. I did no better during the second semester. After admitting that I did not want to be in college, I packed up and left.

My problem then, as now, was that I excel only in classes that I like. It would be ten years before I realized that I had made a mistake. I moved to Norman, Oklahoma, to raise a family and start a non-academic career. After employment as a baker, carpenter, and school bus driver, I began my own cabinet-making business. Running my own business eventually wore me down, and I sold out and moved to San Diego, California.

Faced with big family responsibilities but very few opportunities, I eventually decided, like the prodigal son, to go back to school. I had toyed with the idea for a couple of years, but I finally committed myself, thanks to marvelous advice from a friend I had recently met.

I had always dabbled in science, even after leaving the University of Wisconsin for Oklahoma in 1972. During my ten years away from school, I worked in my spare time on research interests in seismology, anthropology, and paleontology. My friend, a Ph.D. with a thriving professional career, knew of my self-education program and had read much of my research. He finally couldn't contain himself anymore and broached the subject of college. "Jerry, you have a good mind. It's like a farmer's field, but you're using a hoe on it," he said, as he put his hands on each side of my head. "Imagine what you could do with a tractor. A college education is that tractor."

His argument was convincing, but I was scared to death. I was married and had three children. Going back to school would be a very big step that wouldn't pay off for several years. But being a baker or carpenter didn't pay off either, and I really did want to pursue my research interests. I had completed one semester of acceptable college work which was now ten years old. I didn't know if I could compete with students who were fresh out of high school and familiar with the basic education requirements for college. There was only one way to find out.

In the fall of 1982, I enrolled as a freshman at Southwestern Community College in San Diego. Again my major was geology. This time I was determined not to leave school until I got my degree, no matter what. But I surprised myself. I loved college. I loved all my classes. Knowing what I wanted to do with my life really made a difference. I excelled. In my second semester, I won a schoolwide competition for an academic scholarship and my extra-curricular research in paleobiology won the Biology Department's sponsorship in a national research competition held at the University of Santa Clara. I was also on the dean's list both semesters. After one year at Southwestern Community College, I was ready to try for a bachelor's degree at a four-year university.

I desperately wanted to go to San Diego State University. I talked to the Earth Science Department head and showed him my work on earthquakes. He was impressed. For obvious reasons, I thought that southern California was the perfect place to study earthquakes, and I was planning to enroll in fall 1983. It never happened.

However, I wasn't the only one who wanted to go back to school. My wife, Pearl, also yearned to finish her degree. As we talked together, we felt that the best college for both of us was New Mexico State University in Las Cruces, a college Pearl had attended in 1971, but left after her sophomore year.

I made some phone calls to get information about NMSU's geology program, and then immediately found out the bad news. The department did not offer any coursework in seismology or an advanced degree. Unless I wanted to enroll at New Mexico Technical Institute, 140 miles away in Socorro where the New Mexico Bureau of Mines is also located, and be separated from my family while my wife attended NMSU, I would have to consider a degree in some other area of geology.

I decided that I wanted to pursue an emphasis in historical geology and paleontology. I was satisfied that at least initially I could make progress, so I enrolled in the Geology Department at NMSU in fall 1983. It helped that a phone friend suggested that there were numerous extra-curricular activities in paleontology and enough fossils around to make any fossil lover happy.

Two semesters later I began to exhaust the classes I was interested in, and I began to take issue with departmental requirements. I did not want a job with an oil company or as a geological engineer, or something else very specialized, and the Geology Department at NMSU was moving away from classical geology toward applied geology and geological engineering. I wanted to be as broadly educated as possible, and the program at NMSU was too restrictive. I wanted to play the field.

## A Big Heart for Science

Although most of my humanities requirements had been met at Southwestern Community College and during my first year at NMSU, there were still many other courses I wanted to take, and the geology program simply had no room for electives. I was like a kid in a candy store. My mind had awakened, and my insatiable desire for education was quite literally driving me mad. The question was how could I continue my geology education while still taking classes from other disciplines?

I soon found the answer. I could take many of the same geology courses required for the geology degree and still have room for other courses if I enrolled in the earth science/education program. Being in the honors program from the beginning helped, as I was allowed to be fairly creative in structuring my undergraduate program. I had always loved teaching, so the switch into science education came easily.

This move proved to be very important, because it introduced me to Professor Thom Votaw. He was my science education advisor and we soon became very good friends. We both fancied ourselves Renaissance men despite the academic pressures to adopt a "career-oriented" education; we loved knowledge and loved to follow our intellectual curiosity wherever it took us, even if that pursuit involved spending our own money. Thom had an undergraduate degree in biology, and was broadly educated through independent studies for his master's and doctoral degrees. Though he was a small-framed man, he had a big heart for science.

To say that meeting Thom was providential is to understate the matter. Had we not met, my first encounter with fossil footprints two years earlier, subsequently forgotten, would not have resurfaced. Thom was intellectually innocent when it came to fossil footprints, but that was about to change.

Thom had numerous extra-university endeavors going on at the same time. The one he enjoyed most involved the creation of a natural history museum in Las Cruces. The project was spearheaded by the New Mexico Museum of Natural History (NMMNH) in Albuquerque, 240 miles to the north. Thom was the local director of this pilot project. He loved it. The idea of a local museum soon took off. Many collectors in the area were pleased with the possibility of having their own museum in Las Cruces and began to donate fossils.

In short order, I became involved. Thom already had a couple of assistants, but I still wanted to participate. We were soon involved in the field, as Thom and I, and sometimes another friend, collected fossils from several localities around southern New Mexico. We often contributed to the modest collections of this fledgling museum. In time, I was working as a volunteer paleontologist for the new Las Cruces Natural History Museum. This became both a blessing and a curse. It was fun while it lasted, but the museum soon got into trouble.

Since the Las Cruces museum was under the wing of the state in terms of both sponsorship and funding, it had no authority to establish a collection on its own. When the director of the New Mexico Museum of Natural History came for a visit, Thom showed him some of the donated material. Included in the collection were mammoth molars and bones, a few dinosaur bone fragments, fossilized leaves and plants, numerous invertebrate fossils, and the fossilized track of a camel, supposedly found close to Las Cruces.

Much to Thom's surprise, the director was not pleased. He insisted that all specimens donated to the Las Cruces museum be sent to Albuquerque, including the camel track. (Thom said that particular specimen was the "straw that broke the camel's back.") The state museum would then decide if the specimens were significant enough to add to its own collection. What it didn't want, the director would return to Las Cruces.

This arrangement was certainly not agreeable to Thom or the other local supporters. Many locals donated material because they expected it would be exhibited in Las Cruces, not Albuquerque. An uneasy relationship became increasingly so, and both museums realized that there would soon be a parting of the ways. When locals came in to donate fossils, they were informed that their donations would first have to go to the state museum in Albuquerque and that they would be housed locally only if the former didn't want them. Nobody wanted to take that chance, and the number of donations immediately dropped off.

It's curious how such things happen in life, how seemingly insignificant encounters or unrelated events can later loom large. This was just such an event. This little disagreement would increase in significance when my search for footprints finally began. If this incident had not occurred, Thom and I would probably have continued to work with our local NMMNH branch museum. We would probably have glided into a joint research program by the time I finally hit trackway paydirt. As it was, things did not work out that way.

## A Fossil-filled Day

In the midst of this battle over turf, the local natural history museum decided to go ahead with its advertised and greatly anticipated "bring in your fossils" day one weekend in the spring of 1987. Thom and I promised that we would do everything we could to identify each collector's finds. Such a goal was certainly too ambitious, but we did the best we could.

Very interesting material was brought in by the public for identification, and for a day Thom and I were in fossil lover's heaven. We waded through mountains of literature in an effort to make the correct identification.

One big rock really caught Thom's eye. A member of our local museum's board of directors, Mark Torres, brought in a forty-pound slab with what appeared to be several small fossil tracks on it. Thom showed it to me immediately. It certainly appeared to be covered with footprints, but there was no discernible trackway preserved. Instead, the rock was covered with tracks going in all directions.

My mind flashed back to my first footprint encounter years earlier. I remembered the field trip, and I remembered the slabs in Breland Hall at NMSU. If my memory served me right, it was obvious that this one slab preserved tracks a whole lot better than the university specimens. I waited to hear where it had been found. I had already guessed—the Robledos. But it had been found in a wash, so no one knew exactly where it had originated.

We had no idea of what paleontologists call taphonomic history: How were the footprints made in the first place; how were they fossilized; and how were they preserved intact for umpteen millions of years from the Paleozoic era until 1987. We couldn't identify what animal made the tracks, nor could we place a definitive age on the rock. We knew that most of the Robledos were made up of Permian sediments that were at least 250 million years old, so we tentatively ascribed that age to the tracks.

Even though I couldn't prove it, even to myself, I had a feeling that this slab was better than *any* previously collected. That did it. The search was on. Thom and I, being hopeless dreamers, believed that there had to be a lot more where that came from. But where exactly did it come from? I was determined to find out.

The fragile association between the museum in Las Cruces and Albuquerque collapsed. Thom resigned and the local museum changed hands. I was advised that if I wanted the fossils I found to stay in Las Cruces, I would have to hunt for them on my own.

## A Bug in the Brain: The Search Begins

The Robledos—the name burned on my brain. When conditions are right, the arroyos in the Robledos can turn angry very quickly. Rains of just an inch can start a flash flood that can do a great deal of damage. These floods can easily transport forty-pound blocks around as though they were grains of sand. But I knew two things: flash floods can't move a rock from one arroyo to another unconnected one, and material is always washed downstream. An arroyo in the Robledos was all I had to go on. But if I could locate the right one, and I started at its mouth and worked up into the mountains, sooner or later—if providence smiled—I would discover the origin of the slab.

As I walked the Robledos, I hunted for the kind of rocks that would produce fossil tracks. The Torres slab was over eight inches thick and composed of heavy reddish gray siltstone. The three small university specimens, however, were impressed in a brittle red mudstone.

Every arroyo and wash (smaller than an arroyo) was covered with material of every kind and shape that could have come from virtually anywhere upstream. Even the little sandstone fragments I found in the arroyo were overwhelmed with river rock and by the monstrous gray blocks of marine limestone that had slid down into the canyons from layers up above. No matter where I looked, the material was almost always the same, a jumbled mess.

When I did find something, it seemed to me that I could explain the impressions as some other kind of sedimentary feature, not a footprint. There was never a specimen that I could identify conclusively as a footprint.

A few weeks later, the local natural history museum sponsored a field trip into the Robledos to hunt for fossil invertebrates. We took a group of thirty to an area around a mountain that was slowly being whittled down by a large quarrying operation. While everybody was looking for fossil seashells, Thom and I started looking for fossil tracks in endless red debris high above the quarry.

As I look back on it now, that was the least likely place in the entire range to find tracks. No wonder it seemed like a waste of time. I don't know why we didn't look at the red beds at the bottom of the mountain. In any case, I was about to give up my hunt.

The museum slab forced me to ask some hard questions. I began to wonder in just how extensive an area fossil footprints could be found. Mexican rock workers excavating inside the quarry pit itself sometimes found little tracks, but were not sure what they were. Yet, when I first walked through the area, I didn't find a thing other than some scratchings and an occasional feature that may or may not have been a track made by an animal.

It appeared that finding a no-doubt-about-it footprint was more a case of luck than expertise. I needed one more encounter to cement my determination to find the elusive fossilized footprints. This encounter was entirely serendipitous. I was reading the monthly real estate magazine for the southern New Mexico area and dreaming about what it would be like to own a nice adobe house with a lot of land out in the desert somewhere. I thumbed through the magazine and came across a full-page ad for a beautiful adobe home in Las Cruces. Since it was way out of our price range (they were asking $375,000 and I couldn't afford even $30,000), I was about to turn the page when I noticed one of the selling points: "Many of the floors are made up of flagstone, preserving beautiful specimens of fossilized ferns." I just had to see it.

Since the home was being shown by appointment only, we had to devise a strategy. My wife and I scheduled an appointment and then arrived in proper attire—Pearl in a Spanish-style dress and I in a pinstriped suit. It was indeed a beautiful adobe home, certainly worthy of the price tag. While Pearl followed the owner around the house, I got on my hands and knees to study the floors. Everywhere were specimens of exquisite beauty. These were without a doubt the best dendrites I had ever seen. But the ad was wrong in one respect: dendrites are not fossils. Dendrites are pseudo-fossils, formed when water that is rich in magnesium and iron seeps between small fractures in lithified sediments. The result is often spectacular red or black fern-like traces that permanently stain the rock. This house had the best examples I had ever seen.

I did find several fossil plants, but what was odd was that if the dendrites had been correctly identified in the first place, the ad would not have used them as a selling point and I would have never come to the house. I would have missed the hidden prize.

In the living room, far away from the dendrites, was another stone floor. At first I thought I was seeing things to compensate for the great disappointment of finding mostly pseudo-fossils. But there were indeed trackways on the floor. Several trails preserved tail drag as well as tracks. Unfortunately, the floor was heavily varnished and the resultant glare from the lights in the house made good viewing very difficult. But they *were* there.

The owner, soured by my declaration that the floors were made up mostly of pseudo-fossils, perked up again as I studied the living room floor. I asked the $64,000 question: "Where did these rocks come from?" The Robledo Mountains would be the obvious answer, and that was the answer she gave.

## Tracks, Tracks Everywhere

At the time, Las Cruces was the second fastest growing city in the nation, behind Fort Meyers, Florida. Increased construction resulted in an ever-growing need for building stone for walls, floors, and fireplaces. The Robledos quarry was opened to help fill that need.

Years later I would see that nearly every house that was built with rock from the Robledos quarry had fossils and trackways slabs built into it somewhere, but at the time it certainly seemed rare. I've often wondered what I would have done if I had learned that finding tracks and plants on building stone from the Robledos was a common occurrence. Like everybody else, I may have assumed that the fossils were commonplace and therefore not very significant.

After all, it was inconceivable to me that the fossil beds in the Robledo quarry could continue to be worked by bulldozers day after day without some preliminary paleontological assessment of the site. Somebody must have concluded that a quarry could be safely operated there without damaging any significant fossil beds.

Unfortunately, none of the collectors or scientists who knew the history of the area voiced concern when the quarry began operation. Perhaps they didn't know how many tracks were being unearthed. The paleontological significance of the Robledo range was evidently based entirely upon its invertebrate marine fossils, which were considered to be so abundant as to be almost inexhaustible. Armed with these environmental assessments, the Bureau of Land Management (BLM) allowed several quarrying contracts to be filed and worked.

Tragically, the fact that fossils found in the *terrestrial* sediments of the Robledos were never reported to the BLM resulted in significant scientific losses. The quarry was allowed to operate virtually in the heart of track-bearing red bed sediments and unknowingly destroyed hundreds of tons of fossil-bearing sediment. A few of the quarry contractors recognized the beauty of the fossil plant material and stockpiled them for eventual use in floors, walls, and fireplaces. In time, New Mexico State University became the biggest buyer of flagstone from the quarry, and tracks, ripples, and small plants can be seen on some of the rock walls in and around the university.

All I knew the day I saw the tracks on the living room floor, however, was that it was another curious piece of the puzzle. I placed it in the back of my mind with the Breland Hall specimens and the Torres slab. All the evidence indicated to me that there could be lots of good plants and tracks out there, but again, the nagging question was, where?

I was faced with a contradiction. The museum specimens were entirely overshadowed by the much bigger specimens on the floor of a local house. It just didn't make sense to me. I had never heard anyone suggest that plant fossils could be found in the Robledos. There were no plant fossils displayed in Breland Hall alongside the footprint slabs. I considered the few specimens I found in the area nothing more than plant debris, fossil junk, but now I was looking at a floor full of the stuff.

As I tried to narrow down the origin of the Robledo plant material I started to get a terrible feeling that maybe the layer had been destroyed by earthmovers in the quarry, broken up over the years by contractors for use as building stone. I was beside myself. I imagined an entire city built from precious fossil plant and track material. This point was graphically brought home to me when I went to eat lunch at Guacomole's Pick-up Patio, a Mexican restaurant just south of the

Robledos. As I was ordering, I chanced to look at the floor. There at my feet was a rock slab full of footprints. I counted a dozen more slabs preserving footprints that made up the patio floor. All had come from the Robledos quarry.

My interest in the terrestrial fossils of the Robledo Range soon became driven by concern and worry as much as by curiosity. The disparate information and evidence I had been gathering began to fit together. For the first time, I considered undertaking a serious and intensive search. The research question in a nutshell was this: If the tracks and plants from the quarry had been virtually destroyed, were any left? Or did the Robledos harbor other specimens, just as good or better? I had to know.

## A Shoreline in the Desert

I received my bachelors degree in the fall of 1985, and I wanted to keep going all the way to my Ph.D. But I was sandbagged. At the time, the Earth Science Department at NMSU did not offer a graduate degree program and even planned on eliminating its only course in paleontology once the invertebrate paleontology professor retired. I did not have enough of the undergraduate requirements to transfer to graduate-level work in biology, so I was stuck.

I finally decided to enter the graduate program in the Sociology/ Anthropology Department. I loved anthropology and sociology, and, having taken several courses as an undergraduate, I could enter with no undergraduate deficiencies. Best of all, my classes met at night, which left me free to hunt fossil footprints during the day.

My footprint quest began auspiciously enough: armed with numerous leads from local fossil collectors, hikers, and Mexican quarrymen, as well as my little box of broken-up footprint junk, I set out to the mountains in search of the "motherlode." I determined to search the Robledo red beds until I satisfied my own curiosity that the sediments were adequately explored and evaluated.

On the surface, it certainly seemed strange that I would be hunting for fossil footprints in a range predominately comprised of marine sediments which were exceedingly rich in fossilized water-dwelling invertebrates. But my undergraduate geology classes taught me much about the Robledos. Sandwiched between these thick marine layers were small seams of terrestrial sediments. Research indicated that the Robledo sediments preserve a series of shifting depositional boundaries that represent at least seven transgressions and regressions of the sea.

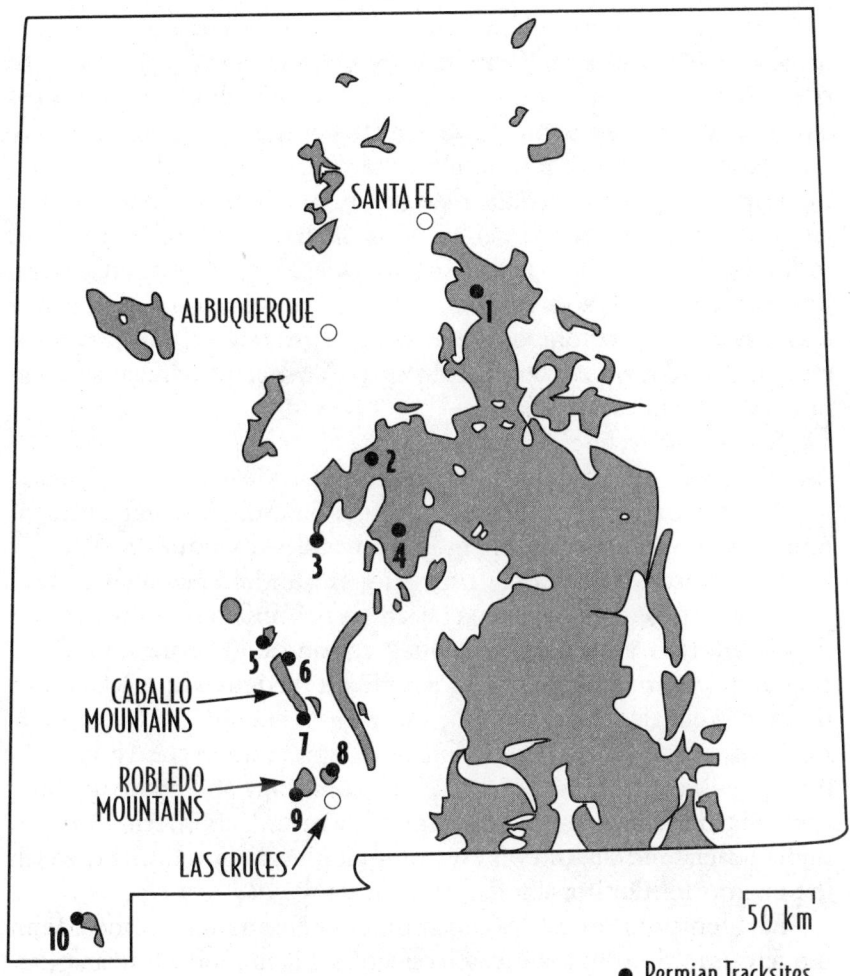

• Permian Tracksites

## THE PERMIAN OF NEW MEXICO

*Most of south-central New Mexico, indicated by shaded areas, is composed of Permian sediments. All of the areas producing fossil trackways, indicated by closed and numbered circles, are located along the western flank of these sediments, and the best trackway localities are found in tiny exposures to the northwest of Las Cruces. Numbered areas are:*

> *1. San Miguel; 2. Abo Pass; 3. east of Socorro; 4. Bingham; 5. Fra Cristobal Mountains; 6. Caballo Mountains; 7. McLeod Hills; 8. Dona Ana Mountains; 9. Robledo Mountains; 10. Big Hatchet Mountains.*

After Barry Kues, *Fossils of New Mexico,* University of New Mexico Press, 1982; and MacDonald, "Footprints from the Dawn of Time," *Science Probe,* July 1992.

No shoreline stretches on forever. Eventually a fine-grained mud gives way to coarser sands and silts which may in turn give way to even coarser sand dune deposits. As you follow a shoreline, you usually observe that one setting gives way to another. For example, there are some localities along a shoreline that seem to be made up entirely of shells, while other sections of shoreline may preserve mud flats or rocks and pebbles. Still other sections of shore may be made up of well-scoured cliffs and promontories where there seems to be no beach at all. Those of us who live near the ocean know of these places and may choose any one of these spots for recreation. But for swimming and wading, we would doubtless pick a section of shoreline that preserves the finest (and softest) beach sands.

Just as a shoreline can subtly change as we walk parallel to it, the shoreline will also change as we walk perpendicular to it. Walking inland from the shore, the beach changes from finely sifted sands or muds, to coarser sand and then, in many cases, to small dunes.

But imagine if you could drill a hole a hundred feet deep to take a core sample of any section of beach you choose—perhaps the section of shore made up of shell-enriched sands. Since the top of the core is the youngest, the core is read from the top down. We notice that the skeletal-rich sands end eight feet down and give way to terrigenous (earth-born) sands and silts. This terrestial sediment in turn gives way to terrigenous mud, which in turn gives way to a section of pebble-rich sands. Still lower, we find another section of shelly beach, and on and on the core sample changes until we reach the bottom of the bore hole.

Such changes in the composition of the sediments of the shore are due to changes in the environment and the rate of deposition. You observed such a change of composition as you walked along the shore. The core sample tells you that the beach has been changing over and over again for at least as long as it took to deposit one hundred feet of sediment along the shoreline.

Certain layers of rock, called facies, are like still photographs representing the types of deposition within a particular local environment. When the "photograph" changes from one type of deposition to another, we call that a facies change.

Facies changes are important for a paleontologist to note, because these changes may often represent boundaries within ecological worlds. When depositional environments migrate laterally, sediments of one environment come to lie on top of those from an adjacent environment. Earth scientists call this principle Walther's Law.

Shorelines can be viewed as a never-ending frontier dispute between two distinct environments, the terrestrial and the marine. Sometimes, when sea levels rise, the sea wins and covers large areas of land that had previously basked in the sun away from the sea. These terrestrial sediments are therefore covered by marine sediments. Sometimes, when sea levels lower, the land wins, and terrestrial sediments cover up areas that were previously entirely under water.

When a sandy shoreline progrades over muddy sediments offshore, the shoreline moves further seaward as the sea level drops. This seaward migration of the shore is known as a regressive depositional cycle. When a sandy shoreline is covered over by offshore muds as sea level rises, the sea moves further inland, and this landward movement of the shore is called a transgressive depositional cycle. Often, there may be several transgressive and regressive cycles within the same rock formation, and such cycles would indicate that the water levels were constantly adjusting to either drought or flood, as in a lake or shallow sea. A shoreline, then, is the meeting of two depositional environments, sea and land. The contact between these two environments is the beach you sunbathe on.

What I had found in the Robledos was just such a depositional battle. The sea often overran the shore in pre-Las Cruces, and when it did, it deposited limey mud, sometimes chock full of shells and other sea-dwelling animals, as well as sea plants and coral. Yet still other sections of limestone are nearly devoid of shells and clams, just like what we saw when we walked along our hypothetical shoreline.

The Robledo red beds, however, are as different from the marine deposits as different can get. First, there are not a lot of red beds preserved in the range. The red beds occur as little wedges within vast, thick layers of limestone. They also contain no marine fossils at all, and give the appearance—at least from a distance—of being as sterile of life as the moon. But close examination of the red beds shows a remarkable series of sedimentary "photographs" that provide the key to understanding sedimentary cycles within the Robledos. It seemed to me that the red beds were as understudied as the marine sediments were overstudied. The question which nagged at my brain was an intriguing one. Could the Robledo red beds hide secrets about life 280 million years ago, almost fifty million years before the emergence of dinosaurs? I was determined to find the answer.

# Chapter Two

## Following the Footprints:
## They Must Lead Somewhere

In the spring of 1987 I was in the final semester of coursework for my master's degree in sociology and anthropology and had begun work on my thesis. I applied to the doctoral program in sociology at the University of Virginia and was accepted with full funding, contingent on satisfactory completion of my remaining courses and successful defense of my thesis. Everything was set for me to leave Las Cruces. But I had the nagging feeling that something big had been left undone.

During this time Thom called. He had found a fossil collector who was willing to show us some possible footprint outcrops that he had looked at years ago. I called him immediately, and we arranged to meet on a Saturday afternoon. At the last minute Thom had to cancel.

Ron Ratkevitch met me just outside Las Cruces at the Cattlemen's Steakhouse at noon on April 21, 1987, and we set out. It was no surprise that he drove straight to the huge community quarry. It seemed that everything concerning footprints centered around that pit. Here I was again.

"There are occasional tracks in the quarry," Ratkevitch noted, "but I think the good material we used to poke around in has been all but destroyed." Where had I heard that before?

He pointed out a place where beautiful carbonized Permian plants had been found in the late 1970s, a location that was without question the source of the carbonized plant slabs I had seen on the living room floor. That location no longer existed, having been long since bulldozed. It would have been over one hundred feet away from the present side of the quarry. "Were there lots of plants, or just a few here and there?" I asked painfully.

"They were everywhere," Ron answered, "but they were concentrated in a narrow seam of yellow rock." Ron was clearly disappointed. I was discouraged.

We weaved our way through rocky arroyos that fed into the quarry, stopping here and there to check out red debris. Some of the hillsides were covered with limestone slabs that weighed more than one thousand pounds. The rest of the mountains were covered with red and yellow rock. Mesquite bushes and an occasional prickly pear cactus punctuated the landscape. Nothing new here.

Occasionally, we saw small holes in the hillsides, dug fairly recently by collectors or at the turn of the century by prospectors. The Robledos were once extensively explored for minerals and a few mines, rusted tramway cables, tailings piles, and pack trails, which are now trails for cattle and deer, can still be seen in the area. The little exploratory pits were not very big and were widely separated. Some of them were dug by sedimentologists who wanted to analyze the vertical sequence of strata in the area.

In order for a sedimentologist or stratigrapher to understand the origins of the sediments he or she is studying within a given formation, it is necessary to analyze the processes of deposition and the resultant accumulation of layers. Often, the products of ancient depositional processes, the layers themselves, are hidden from the trained eye of the investigator. In such cases, scientists drill deep into the earth to pull up a core of sediments, which reveals both composition and thickness of the unknown layers deep below the surface.

Sometimes the scientist does not have to drill, as the layers may be exposed on the sides of canyons, mountain slopes, or valleys. One rule earth scientists always keep in mind when studying layered sediments is that all strata, no matter how dipped or tilted they are now, were originally formed more or less horizontally. Geologists call this rule the principle of original horizontality.

When a sedimentologist or a stratigrapher wants to study the composition and thickness of sedimentary rock from a given formation and measure facies changes, he or she will take samples of a multitude of layers at several different points, sometimes miles apart. These layers are then studied vertically by taking samples from each. Digging a vertical trench twenty feet deep may yield more than one hundred subsamples representing as many as one hundred layers in that section.

Each of these vertical sequences is like a slice that enables scientists to see and compare a cross-section of sediments. They are looking for subtle changes in the composition and thickness of the sediments, as well as for evidence of erosion and deposition. There are several such trenches dug in the slopes of Robledos.

As Ron and I walked further into the mountains, I chanced to look down in the arroyo bottom and spied a rock that grabbed my attention. It was a footprint—a very big one. I picked it up and measured it. It was over eight inches long.

"Did you just find that track?" Ron asked. "That's the biggest footprint I've ever seen from the Robledos."

The print had obviously lain exposed and broken in the wash for a considerable period of time. It was in three pieces. The action of flash floods and rain had eroded the clarity of the print, but it was still a beauty. This was my first honest-to-goodness footprint, and it was a real winner.

I don't know what excited me more, the footprint or the material it was on. The print was impressed in a smooth mudstone, and from the way the mudstone was broken, it was obvious that it was part of a trackway. It was not a happenstance step by a reptile into a pool of mud. It was one of a series of steps on a mud flat. But where did it come from?

Needless to say, my blood was up, and so was Ron's. We poked around on a few hillsides for two hours, but found nothing to match the size or quality of that chance print I had found. Was it just another lucky find or did it lead somewhere?

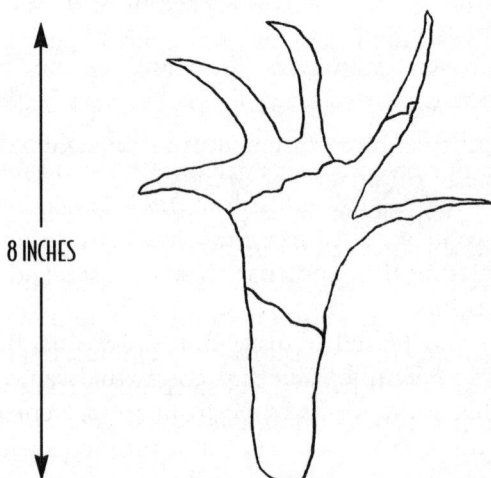

8 INCHES

*A diagram of the first track found. It is of a pelycosaur, like* Dimetrodon.

## Collecting Fossils: Science or Obsession?

Many fossil collectors have a bad habit. They have a myopia that comes with the territory. My wife is a psychotherapist and she jokingly refers to them with what psychologists call an "obsessive disorder NOS (not otherwise specified)." It may be stating the obvious to point out that for a collector, collecting fossils is the ultimate goal. But fossil collectors are not necessarily scientists. Collectors are looking for a product. A scientist, on the other hand, certainly knows how important collecting a fossil is, but he or she employs the scientific method to gather it and interpret the area where the fossil is found. To a collector, the fossil is everything; but to a scientist, the fossil is a means to further scientific investigation and paint a larger picture.

Collectors searched for Robledo tracks like they searched for virtually every other kind of fossil. When I first went with fossil collectors to find marine fossils, our "science" ended when we were able to find a productive outcrop (I'll talk more about productive outcrops later). We didn't care about why the fossils were there, or what they meant, or even if they were significant. We simply wanted fossils, and certain hillsides produced them.

After locating a good site, the science of collecting fossils consisted of climbing a hillside, sitting on the ground, and pulling out the loose layers. We would clean dirt off the surface, split a rock or two, and then throw them down to the floor of the canyon if we found nothing. Everybody would poke around in a spot for five minutes or so and then get tired of it and move up or down the hill a few feet, or maybe cross-slope for twenty feet or more. Then we'd do the same thing all over again. And our rock-hound methodology worked. We ended up with a lot of fossils but very little data.

Now, there is nothing wrong with this kind of collecting. Although I haven't surveyed every paleontologist, I think it is safe to say that we all started collecting fossils in this manner. I think it is also safe to say that we may still collect a few fossils this way. But at some point, we began to understand that the fossils we had found really belong to the world.

The hillsides may be full of many kinds of fossils. But fossils not only have intrinsic scientific value but contextual value as well. The area and layer that some fossils come from are extremely important to science. And this is where one runs into problems with the collector mentality.

Most collectors use the same procedures that I have described when hunting for even the most important kinds of fossils, primarily vertebrate fossils. While the paleontologist knows that the specimen is just one part of the picture, the collector gathers up the specimen as a trophy, ignorant of or just disinterested in the valuable data that surrounds the fossil in the ground. This can create problems, especially when bones are removed from their place of repose. Paleontologists agree that a tremendous amount of information is lost every year when well-meaning, but ignorant collectors remove fossil bone from the ground.

Presently, there are dozens of collectors (maybe hundreds?) roaming the hills hoping to retrieve fossil dinosaur bone. It brings the highest prices and is the easiest to sell to the public. These collectors are after bones on the surface and are generally not interested in excavating any additional bones of the animal below the surface. This is troubling to professionals as well as to conscientious collectors.

Evidence of fossil bone at the surface is the only sure way paleontologists can find promising excavation sites. Surface bone serves as a red flag or field marker. If the surface bones are removed, these promising sites are lost until years of erosion exposes (and destroys) more of the skeleton. Unfortunately, most surface collectors make no attempt to inform paleontologists of their finds, even though the possibility is great that more of the skeleton is hidden from view just below the surface. Valuable data is irretrievably lost.

Many collectors think that it is more advantageous to spend months picking up hundreds of surface bones than it would be to take months to excavate (sometimes illegally) what may be only a few more bones of one skeleton. A paleontologist excavates no matter how long it takes. An unscrupulous collector scavenges to the detriment of science.

Some collectors are like fast-food junkies. They want an immediate return. Work yields product; the quicker, the better. If they don't find something in five minutes, they give up and move somewhere else. But the earth rarely rewards the casual explorer. If you're methodical and take your time, and if you're patient, the earth will often grant you riches beyond belief.

I was not just after scattered, disconnected footprints here or there. I wanted layers of footprints. I wanted continuity. I wanted the motherlode. Others were happy to pull out one piece of the puzzle. I wanted the whole puzzle.

## A Flirtation with Prehistoric Worlds

As you must realize by now, I am a paleontological romantic. I've always navigated by the star of my imagination. As a result, I've had many disappointments, but I've also had my share of fulfillment. My house is chock full of prehistoric memorabilia (it's also full of old comic books, but that's another story). One of my great loves is collecting paleontological art—posters and portraits of dinosaurs and other prehistoric animals that are pictured in the environments in which the artist thinks they lived.

Naturally, the primary focus of this art is the fleshing out of these long-extinct creatures. One is really looking into the imagination of the artist, which can provide a jumping-off place for the viewer's imagination. The art captures these animals in various active poses. But there is another, subtler revelation—the earth beneath their feet. Imagine the tracks these animals would make as they went about their daily activities. What kind of signature would an animal leave when it chases its prey? Or stalks it? What kind of prints would it leave when it's eating? Or resting? Except for aquatic or flying beasts, I've yet to see any prehistoric art in which the animals are not in constant contact with the ground.

It is important to understand how footprint evidence is a reflection of living activities, and as such, it is an extremely important clue in the re-creation of these animals. In fact, their re-creation is the universal goal of paleontology. It doesn't end when the skeleton is put together.

Scientists who study prehistoric footprints are ichnologists, (after the Greek word *ichnos*, meaning track), and the science of trackway study is ichnology. Footprints preserve, sometimes in great detail, evidence of how the track maker and others of its kind lived, whereas bone discoveries generally preserve what the animal looked like and where it was buried. They seldom indicate where and how it died.

Today, humans can stand next to one of the most spectacular fossil trackway sites in the world, near Glen Rose, Texas. Clearly etched in stone is the trail of a large sauropod dinosaur (like *Brontosaurus*) and a second trackway from a carnivorous two-footed dinosaur (like *Allosaurus*) that are over 110 million years old.

Such physical evidence of the life patterns of extinct animals is tremendously exciting and elicits all kinds of questions. Is this four-footed dinosaur being stalked by this giant meat-eater? Are they both walking alongside an ancient seashore? Trackway localities often provide paleontologists with the best opportunities to re-create the environments in which these animals existed.

It is true that trackways often provide the only record of many kinds of animals. The great variety of trackways from the Jurassic period of the Connecticut Valley is a record of numerous kinds of dinosaurs known only from tracks. Good trackway sites with a great variety of footprints allow paleontologists to learn a great deal about the habits of the animals represented as well as to understand their manner of locomotion and the ancient environment in which they lived.

Truly excellent trackway sites are quite rare, for a number of very specific conditions must be met for trackway preservation to take place. First, the sediments must be fine-grained, with granule size ranging from silt to fine sand. Second, they must have been laid down in an environment of continuous but episodic deposition. Third, they must have been subject to alternate wetting and drying out—wetting to record the tracks in the first place, and drying out to preserve them momentarily until they are safely buried by the next episode of deposition. Fourth, there must have been a next episode of deposition to preserve tracks over the longer term. It definitely helps if the tracks were lightly dusted with dry wind-blown clay or silt while they were still fresh and before they were buried. This dusting keeps the layers from sticking together during burial, and makes it possible to split the rocks along the planes of footprints.

So where do paleontologists look for surviving trackways? The foregoing knowledge enables us to narrow our search significantly, and my search was centered on the right kinds of rocks in a mountain range no more than eight miles long and two to three miles wide. Most of the reports of tracks seemed to have been concentrated in the southern half of the range.

Ron Ratkevitch had originally collected footprint debris in the Robledos in the late 1970s, but in the course of my search I found others who had the footprint bug at about the same time as Ron. The places they took me were all geographically related to the community quarry; none were far from "civilization." Later, I discovered a similar period of interest in Robledo footprints in the early 1960s. Undoubtedly, the area was known locally for much longer than that.

The record notation for a New Mexico trackway occurrence is much older. Kelly Conrad, a student working with trackway specialist Martin Lockley at the University of Colorado at Denver, found mention of the discovery of fossilized tracks in Oiva, New Mexico, in an 1840 German scientific journal by Dr. K.C. von Leonard and Dr. H.G. Bronn, of the University of Heidelberg.

The oldest report of Paleozoic fossil footprints in North America, the classic description of dinosaur tracks, was made by the Reverend Edward Hitchcock in 1836 in the now-world-famous Connecticut Valley fossil assemblage. He initially called them "bird tracks."

The New Mexico report of von Leonard and Bronn came only sixteen years after the first printed reference to fossil footprints ever published, those discovered in Scotland in 1824 in the old red sandstone, which are clearly predinosaurian sediments. Those footprints are close in age to the Robledo footprints, dating back to around three hundred million years before the present.

The trouble with the von Leonard and Bronn report is that in 1840 New Mexico was three times as large as it is today. It encompassed a large part of western Texas, southern Colorado, nearly half of Arizona, and part of Utah. So we do not know the location of Oiva, New Mexico. As it was, I had trouble just trying to make sense out of an eight-square-mile area within the Robledo Mountains. I didn't need to add another 250,000 square miles to my search.

## Open Doors, Closed Minds

During the years that I was amassing information about footprints in the Robledos, it was inevitable that I was also being exposed to a variety of interpretations of that information. I began to acquire assumptions and biases that subtly eroded the fresh perspective I held as a result of being new to the field.

While I was a paleontologist by day, I was a sociologist by night. I was also occasionally a guest lecturer in sociology and psychology classes at NMSU. I was offered a position as summer faculty in the honors program there. I accepted and began teaching a sociology course, "Thought Reform and Brainwashing: Manipulative Techniques of Social Influence." The first thing I did on the first day of class was engage in an experiment with my new students.

The experiment was simple enough. I pretended to be a student—an older returning student—and on the first day of class I sat just outside the closed door to my classroom. I said nothing and did nothing. I just sat with a notebook and a backpack and waited. A few students came and sat down beside me and also waited. As we got closer to the beginning of class, more and more students sat down outside the door.

When it was time for class to begin, I got up, opened the unlocked door, and waited for my bewildered students to file in. No one had bothered to try the door. Why? Because everybody assumed that one of those who had gotten there earlier had already done so. No one dared to think that we were all sitting out in the hall for no good reason. As more and more students came and sat in the hall, the assumption became more and more credible. "All of us can't be that dumb."

After the embarrassed students were seated, I asked if anyone had wanted to check the door for themselves. A couple of hands were raised. When I asked why they didn't do it, the answer was always the same. They felt they were in a double bind: they wanted to check the door because they would have looked foolish if the door was unlocked the whole time; they didn't want to check the door because they would have looked foolish if they had found that the door was indeed locked.

Everybody agreed that just the simple act of checking the door knob in front of the rest of us would imply that we had been too foolish to check for ourselves. No one wanted to take the risk. So there we sat. Quiet. For ten minutes. Thirty college students and one college professor neutralized in the hall.

By the spring of 1987, I had successfully worked myself into just such a bind. Was the doorway to the Robledo fossil footprints locked, making a search for it sheer foolishness, or was it unlocked, just waiting for someone to open it? I was to experience a lesson both in looking foolish and in taking things for granted.

There seemed to be a million reasons why the Robledo footprint door was closed, and those reasons were very logical. But I wanted to try the door myself, in spite of the collected wisdom of all who went before me. I was torn between what I felt to be correct and what was believed to be so.

It is true that I could not have been any more enthusiastic about fossil footprints. But I sometimes wondered, as others admitted to me later, if my unwarranted enthusiasm was because the tracks were such a curiosity.

While one collector had built a fireplace wall out of tracks he found in the Robledos, another was concerned that my intensive search for tracks might exhaust the tiny supply remaining on the hillsides. He emphasized that these tracks were very rare and hard to find, so I needed to make sure that I left some for other collectors. It was apparent to me that nobody really knew what was going on in the Robledos with regard to the abundance or scarcity of tracks to be found. The trackway gospel was simple and well known: "If you sift through the red beds long and hard enough you might chance upon a track."

## The Collection History of the Robledos

Over decades, all of the facts, opinions, and biases surrounding Robledo tracks were subtly merged into a collection history. Such an informed history results any time collectors, hikers, and scientists begin to share their findings and experiences in a particular geographic area. Information about the scientific productivity of an area is based in large part on the accumulated history of the work done and the material collected there.

There are numerous research papers on the Robledo Mountains. It may be one of the most studied areas in New Mexico. The strata, elevations, and lay of the land are so well known that there are "right" and "wrong" answers that geology students are tested on as they interpret the geology of the Robledos to their professors at New Mexico State University.

Yet not one of these papers focused on fossil plants and footprints from the area. Outside of a gallant effort by Ron Ratkevitch to describe his fossil collecting in the Robledos in the 1980 amateur collectors magazine *Rocks and Minerals*, there was virtually no work devoted to the tracks of the Robledos.

One reason there was nothing written on the trackways is that there was never a sizable collection to describe in the first place. Three badly weathered slabs with a few small prints do not command much attention among professionals. Nor does the paleontological study of someone's fireplace or living room floor constitute a major research area. More to the point, however, was that sedimentologists and stratigraphers never brought their observations to the attention of qualified trackway specialists, or vertebrate paleontologists specializing in life before the dinosaurs. If the tracks were mentioned at all in the scientific literature, it was only in footnotes and asides in papers on unrelated subjects.

Part of the problem is that education itself has become too compartmentalized. Professionals in one area may feel that they are not qualified to look into information that is not directly related to their area of expertise. By the time one becomes established in a given field, he or she has generated enough commitments to last the rest of his or her career. One may feel it unprofitable to take the time to become conversant with another discipline. But to ignore particular geological data because one is not a trained specialist in that discipline seems like scientific shortsightedness that may lead to a tragic loss of data.

Such omitted data has been a long-standing problem for paleontologists when they consult sedimentological and stratigraphical research for clues that would suggest promising paleontological endeavors. To many paleontologists, an analysis of a sedimentary deposit is only complete when equal attention has been given to both fossils and rock particles.

Often, research by sedimentologists on the paleoclimate, paleo-geography, and stratigraphy of specific regions is done with only pass-ing reference to the kinds of fossils found in the area. For example, many plant species can only exist in extremely restrictive ecological niches, and a thorough knowledge of the kinds of fossil plants found in a given area is crucial to an accurate understanding of the ancient climate there. The same is true of the kinds of animals that are known to have existed in an area undergoing such research.

Research in the Robledos has suffered in this way. Terrestrial paleontology of the region was not given much attention by geolo-gists conducting research in other disciplines. As a result, the main problem was the inability of professionals to place the trackway debris into any kind of broad scientific perspective.

How did fossil footprints from the area compare to similar fossil footprint regions for significance and abundance? How important are the trackways to an overall understanding of Permian life, and how indicative are they of the climate and topography of the area? What were the conditions necessary for the preservation of footprints, and why were they concentrated in the Robledos? Questions on the kinds of plants that existed in the area or the proportion of tracks of rep-tiles relative to amphibians (a generally broad distinction in trackway research) were never asked.

To be fair, however, I really don't think anyone seriously consid-ered a comparative study involving the Robledo tracks, in part because the handful of Paleozoic trackway sites that were known to exist in the United States had been so underpublished that only a select few knew of their existence. These Paleozoic sites were entirely overshadowed by the descriptions and general excitement surround-ing quite a number of excellent dinosaur track localities.

But there were tantalizing teasers. The Robledos were used for field training of students in earth science at New Mexico State University. In any given year, numerous students were in the hills, mapping, surveying, and sampling the same arroyos. Despite the vol-ume of material these efforts produced, however, it was largely repet-itive and conducted within very specific parameters. The scant footprint material that had been collected before 1987 showed that in nearly every case, the tracks that were found were approximately a quarter-inch to a half-inch long. If trackways (that is, several consec-utive footprints) were found, they were always of small animals and the trackways were of short length, at the most four or five consecu-tive footprints on a slab eight to ten inches long.

The quality of the trackways was almost always poor, primarily because the specimens lay exposed and broken on the hillsides for years and years until someone had the good fortune to see them. Because the tracks were often obscured by years of exposure, poor preservation often masked the anatomical uniqueness of the print, and it was commonly assumed that the trackmakers could not be identified. All the tracks were believed to have been made by reptiles, specifically "lacertoids" (lizards).

There is a world of difference in significance between good-sized faunules and hit-and-miss debris on a hillside. Debris, though valuable in confirming that there was terrestrial life in the area at one time, tells us little about the world in which the track maker existed. If it was assumed that finding a significant concentration of tracks was impossible, it is entirely understandable that scattered trackway debris was given little attention. An isolated track tells very little and therefore has limited scientific value. The real value of tracks is often contextual rather than intrinsic. Though the "quick fix" for a collector may simply be to pull as many tracks out of a hillside as possible, a scientist has to take a methodical approach and slowly and carefully excavate the fossil material. But slow and careful methodologies often create problems. Sometimes great discoveries occur late in a paleontologist's field season. There is nothing that frustrates a paleontologist more than finding a skeleton embedded in the rocks when there is no time left to excavate it. The desire to gather as much data as possible will often require, however, that the scientist leave much of the skeleton in the ground, to await a more careful excavation the next year.

By contrast, collecting trackways in the Early Permian red beds is often done piecemeal. The red beds are too broken up to yield the kind of continuity one hopes for. But even here, the careful collecting and diagramming of tracks is extremely useful for research purposes. While the collector may only be interested in collecting, the scientist is interested in the data that can be obtained from the fossils. It is only by comparing, analyzing, and evaluating that the significance of any fossil collection can be determined.

The productivity of fossil occurrences like the Robledo trackways can be evaluated through what I call a product/effort equation. Such an equation is simply a function of the amount of significant material relative to the effort exerted to find the material. The higher the productivity number, the better the site.

If one were to look for good marine invertebrate fossils from the Robledos, for example, there are a number of sites that are excellent producers. One site I found while hunting for fossil footprints produces pelecypods (clams) at a rate of about 80 per hour. The equation for that spot would be 80/1. Some other sites produce brachiopods at a rate of well over 100 per hour.

I have found this equation useful in ranking sites against each other. The equation can also be used to rank not just the number of specimens found in a given area but also the number of quality specimens found in a given area. The equation would be expressed as the number of specimens collected in an hour over the number of significant specimens found among them. For example, if I found 80 pelecypods in an hour, but only 20 of those were perfectly preserved, the equation would be 80/20, meaning that 25 percent of the pelecypods found in the area will be significant. Obviously, the closer to 100 percent, the better.

The productivity of bone beds can be ranked the same way. There is a bone site that I work occasionally when I need a respite from fossil footprints. The area can yield bones at a rate of about twenty per hour. But most of these are fragments with very little paleontological value.

What keeps me interested is the fact that out of one hundred bones found over the course of a five-hour search, I will generally find ten of significance, ten diagnostic specimens: a portion of a jaw, some good fossil teeth, a partial pelvis or rib, an antler or a toe bone, a turtle scute, or a large mastodon leg bone, sometimes even a nice piece of petrified wood.

*Significance* is the important word here. Good product/effort equations must include the variable of significance. And there can be no declaration of significance without good background research. Collecting the fossil is certainly not the end of the game. It's only the beginning. All fossils should be viewed as possessing potential significance. After research, the scientist may find that the fossils have very little significance. In fact, this may happen more often than not. But even if a fossil is found to be significant just one time out of ten, the scientist cannot ignore the odds. Those odds are good enough to make the scientific game worth the effort.

Many fossils were collected half a century ago or more. Even though they may not have seemed significant at the time, as the knowledge base within paleontology increases, earlier collections may suddenly gain in significance. This is constantly happening. Museum curators all agree that there is more than just one career to be made in the bone rooms of the world's museums.

In addition to significance, one must take into consideration the ability of the fossil hunter to recognize finds in the field. Good fossil hunters may often achieve excellent product/effort equations while others with less experience will achieve poorer results even though hunting in the same spot at the same time. It takes a great deal of field experience to recognize a fossil in the field. Most people are used to seeing a fossil after it has been cleaned up and prepared for exhibition, but in the field, most fossils are embedded in rock that in many cases hides all but 5 or 10 percent of the specimen.

Collectors and hikers in the Robledos were significantly handicapped in recognizing trackways in the field and in ascertaining their significance once they were found. There are virtually no fossil footprint panels found in the standard fossil reference guides that have become so invaluable to fossil hunters. Furthermore, there were essentially no hands-on examples of tracks that people could look at to better aid them in their hunt for specimens. Undoubtedly much trackway material was completely overlooked simply because it was not recognized in the field. Finally, the time of day one searches for fossils in the field is very important to the success or failure of a field scientist.

In any event, for whatever reason, collectors who roamed the Robledos in the past had commented that a considerable effort was needed to find just a few specimens. I think some may have thought that there was good material hidden away somewhere in the range, but just making the effort to find it was daunting. Finding the source beds was difficult; excavating them was nearly impossible. The product/effort equation was very low and scared off all but the most persistent researchers.

This lore surrounding the Robledo tracks resulted in psychological uniformitarianism: what had been found in the area was representative of what would be found there in the future and adequately represented the parameters of both abundance and significance. Since nothing of major significance was ever found, and no sites produced significant finds in an "acceptable" amount of time, minds were closed and expectations were low. This mindset was the basis for the low general opinion of the importance and extent of the Robledo footprints. Doubtless, all these factors discouraged any attempt to systematically and methodically explore the beds.

As a result, collecting in the Robledos prior to 1987 was haphazard. There was never any concentrated search designed and carried out to answer once and for all just how extensive and significant the footprints were.

## A Stranger in a Strange Land

At least in the beginning, my quest was largely unbridled because I had little familiarity with the area and very little idea of the biases with which the footprints were viewed. Many important discoveries are made by "foreigners," those who unabashedly march into an area with a simple expectation of success. Often, however, discoveries may come about through a research bias that the hopeful discoverer acquires as he or she interprets the facts. The Robledo track evidence could have been interpreted as a glass half empty. I saw it as a glass half full.

Like any profession, paleontology has its own set of rules of thumb that the initiated quickly learn. For example, Rule 1: Just because one kind of fossil appears to be locally abundant, abundance does not mean insignificance. A particular fossil, plentiful as it is, may be unique to a given area, which in fact may be the only place on earth where this fossil is found.

Rule 2 is closely related: When it comes to fossils, take nothing for granted. Local fossil abundance can have a neutralizing effect on the researcher, deluding him or her from further investigations. Curiously, the opposite is also true. Assumptions of the rarity of some fossils can be just as neutralizing as many researchers do not invest the time looking for a needle in a haystack. I was about to be reminded of both of these rules.

I tried not to become preoccupied with the apparent impossibility of finding long trackways even though none had been found in the Robledos before. I was obsessed with finding something out of the ordinary. And, although the history of past discoveries was not in my favor, I was willing to spend days in the hot desert sun looking for them.

Scientists much more highly trained than I had been exploring the Robledos, sometimes for decades, but they weren't looking for footprints. To me it seemed obvious that no one ever went into the Robledos to *discover* the footprint motherlode. This brings us to Paleontological Rule of Thumb 3: When you go into the field, expect to discover something great.

Surely the energy to maintain a scientific quest comes partly through the exhilarating expectation of discovery itself. There might be something found in every shovelful of dirt, on every rock one picks up, in every canyon one hikes, and on every layer one uncovers. Every morning I woke with the thought that today was the day I might discover something totally new. Enter Paleontological Rule of Thumb 4: Don't expect to find anything if you don't cover a lot of ground.

My expectations were such a powerful driving force in my life that I never dreaded continuing the search. As a result, I felt compelled to look for discovery every free moment I had. As I was poking around in the vast debris fields on the slopes of several mountains, I began to assume, like everybody else, that even if I dug deep into the mountains, I would find a geological record that would be difficult to sort out. Throughout the entire range were thrusts and folds and faults that clearly implied that the strata in the range had been subjected to Nature's vegamatic. Yet I was still fascinated by the sparse and mostly erroneous descriptions of Robledo footprints. Such information seemed to beckon and haunt me.

The key to the whole thing was twofold: take all of the varied information, testimonials, and experiences and synthesize them into a solid research question, and then utilize opportunity and time. Time was exactly what I had. The search would not be easy. Fifty years is a long time. I had five months—five months to prove my theory. At the end of that time, if I came up empty, it was over. I would be leaving in August for the University of Virginia to begin my Ph.D. program. I had no plans to return to Las Cruces.

# CHAPTER THREE

## Footprints from the Dawn of Time

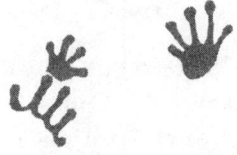

Fossil tracks exist from nearly every period in the history of life on earth, although vertebrate tracks are known only from the Devonian onward. Trackways, like all fossils, become rarer the farther back in time we go, but there are estimated to be several thousand dinosaur trackway localities around the world from the Triassic, Jurassic, and Cretaceous periods. Tracks are more plentiful than dinosaur remains, and there are about five hundred localities in the United States where tracks are abundant. The Connecticut Valley dinosaur footprint assemblage, the Glen Rose dinosaur trackways in central Texas, and the Colorado Plateau tracksite region are three well-known examples.

Although non-dinosaur and pre-dinosaur tracks are less well known, there are several good localities in North America, including sites in Mississippi, Nova Scotia, Alabama, Arizona, Utah, and Colorado. They are good sites, but they do not offer the kind of rich deposits a paleontologist dreams of.

Trackways become rarer in older rocks for two reasons. First, older deposits have been subjected to erosion for a longer time and are thus more likely to have been destroyed. Second, older rocks that have survived erosion have done so because they were buried under younger deposits and so remain hidden from our view. Finding good trackway sites from the Paleozoic era, a time tens of millions of years before the dinosaurs, is often difficult.

If there are locations that preserve tracks from the Paleozoic era—tracks older than 225 million years—we must look for them in areas that have been subjected to erosion of the younger, overlying sediments, exposing ancient sediments at or near the surface. There is no better place on earth to see the result of such a process than in the Grand Canyon of Arizona.

Indeed, such ancient footprints are preserved in the Paleozoic Coconino sandstone of the Grand Canyon in abundance. These long-buried fossil trackways were first discovered in 1915 by Professor Charles Schuchert and reported by Dr. R. S. Lull in 1918. Further collecting in the area was done by Dr. John Merriam, president of the Carnegie Institute. Merriam was so impressed with what he saw that he proposed exposing large areas of trackways for both research and public viewing. In 1924, Smithsonian paleontologist Charles W. Gilmore was asked by Stephen T. Mather, director of the National Park Service, to study and prepare such an exhibit. Gilmore began collecting representative footprint material from a section of the canyon that was frequently visited by tourists. As he did so, he hoped to ascertain the feasibility of exposing extensive footprints for an open-air exhibit.

The area Gilmore worked was about one thousand feet below the rim of the canyon, alongside the famous Hermit Trail. All of the trackways were found in the Coconino formation, a sandstone seam of Early Permian age, a time approximately 280 million years before the present and a full sixty million years before the emergence of dinosaurs.

The Coconino consists of a series of cross-bedded sands and one strata of massive thickness and uniform fineness. The beds form irregular wedges with numerous thin sublayers. It was on the upper surfaces of these sublayers that the majority of the tracks were preserved. The Coconino has a thickness of about 350 feet, and the footprints are found in the lower half of the seam. Gilmore believed that there could be abundant traces from about twenty feet above the base of the formation to about 150 feet above the base. Lateral continuity of the beds suggested that these tracks could be found over a wide area.

Gilmore brought back to the Smithsonian about seventeen hundred pounds of rock revealing a great variety of excellently preserved imprints. He was excited about the abundant variety of animal trails and was struck by the potential on-site lessons concerning not only the great age of the earth but also the perceived diversity of animals that could be deduced from the fossils.

My tactics were quite similar to Gilmore's. Once he identified an area yielding tracks, he began to remove overburden and debris until he came to a trackway layer retaining enough resilience and continuity to allow it to be exposed for a great distance. Gilmore's first tracksite was eight feet wide and twenty-five feet long. He continued to work around this initial exposure until he had an area of several hundred square feet that preserved a variety of tracks and trails.

It is clear that Gilmore considered widely exposed trackways the big prize. His strategy was twofold: find good footprints to expose, and find as many different kinds of trails as possible. Gilmore found the well-preserved footprints of trackmakers assigned to a variety of reptiles and amphibians, many of which were previously unknown. He also found several trails of desert-dwelling invertebrates, such as spiders and centipedes, and other more problematic traces.

Subsequent research has reinforced earlier evidence that the Coconino trackways were preserved in sediment of wind-blown origin. The formation apparently preserves series after series of shifting sand dunes, and nearly all the trails appear to be made by animals moving upslope.

Curiously, there appears to be a dearth of trails made by animals moving downslope. All the trails have significant sand mounds behind the heel end of the tracks. Another interesting observation was that many of the trails seemed to be oriented in the same direction. Do they show well-established trails to water, or large migratory movements of groups of these animals?

Gilmore also noticed that some species seemed to be confined to particular layers, and others, particularly *Laoporus*, seemed to be abundant everywhere. In one wonderful discovery, Gilmore observed that one track maker had an injured toe that made a dramatically different track on the right side as opposed to the normal left side.

There is still considerable debate over the formation of the trails. Their preservation is still hotly debated even after experiments have been conducted on the observed characteristics of footprints formed on dunes by present-day animals. Moreover, no skeletons have been found in the Coconino, so no direct evidence can be found linking a set of tracks to an animal known from bones.

From 1926 to 1928, Gilmore wrote three annual reports on the collections of tracks and trails that he had amassed, as well as his observations about the context of the fossils. He felt reasonably certain that there were about seventeen different species represented in the census, mostly vertebrates, but also including a handful of invertebrates. Today, after further study, ichologists believe that the trackways represent a much smaller number of species.

Gilmore recognized that these trackways would be valuable in correlating widely separated formations within the Paleozoic of North America. In particular, he felt comfortable relating the

Coconino formation to the Lyons sandstone formation of Colorado, on the basis of the preserved footprints found in the Lyons sediment.

When Gilmore was done working the Coconino, he had excavated the best trackway specimens from the Paleozoic found anywhere in the world. Pioneering trackway excavation methodologies, Gilmore had perceived the value of the fossils both intrinsically and contextually. Gilmore's footprint collections are currently housed at the Smithsonian's Natural History Museum for study and display.

## Footprints in a Coal Mine?

About the same time that Gilmore was writing his research on the Grand Canyon's Paleozoic trackways, a curious phenomenon was reported nearly two thousand miles to the east. Miners working a coal seam near Carbon Hill, Alabama, reported seeing what appeared to be animal tracks in the rock just above the coal. The occurrence seemed to be isolated in Mine 11 of the Galloway Coal Company.

The general manager of the mine, W. F. Cobb, and the chief engineer, A. P. MacIntosh, were informed of the phenomenon. MacIntosh mentioned the occurrence to Arthur Blair, a geologist for the Tennessee Coal, Iron, and Railway Company of Birmingham. Blair was skeptical but felt the reports were significant enough to warrant investigation. When he neared Mine 11, Blair was stunned to see a forty-foot trackway proceeding along the top of the mine slope and disappearing into solid rock. Blair became a believer on the spot. He took sample of the trail and returned to his Alabama office to research the occurrence. The fossilized tracks were entirely unique to the geology of Alabama.

In short order, several scientists went to the mine to obtain as many good specimens as they could to build a census for the Alabama Museum of Natural History. Assistant Curator David DeJarnette obtained splendid material, both of the discovery tracks and additional varieties. A year later, in December 1929, geologist Walter Jones of the Alabama Geological Survey visited the site to begin work on a report of the occurrence. Like everyone who had seen the trackway for the first time, Jones was quite taken by what he saw. He subsequently noted in his report that the "diversity of the fauna was most surprising."

The scientists were able to work out a research agreement with the Galloway Coal Company whereby they could study the occurrence with a minimum of interference from the mining operation.

Under the supervision of H. M. Johnstone, the superintendent of Mine 11, the material was excavated at significant expense to the mining company. Geologists noted, "The Company has fostered a notable contribution to science. Without this cooperation, the discovery could never have received the attention warranted by its importance."

The trackways occurred in the coal seams of the Upper Carboniferous Pottsville formation, which were laid down about three hundred million years ago, making them a little older than the Coconino trackways Gilmore was excavating. It seems that Permian track beds are not represented in the geology of Alabama.

The Pottsville formation is composed of shales, sandstones, conglomerates and, infrequently, thin limestone layers. The sediments were laid down in a constantly shifting shoreline, which alternately expanded and swamped lush freshwater marshes along the margins of the sea.

Fossil plant material is most commonly associated with coal seams (coal being entirely made up of plant material), so the occurrence of trackways was considered exceptional. While there were other scattered reports of the same phenomenon in coal seams in Pennsylvania and Kansas, they apparently were not to this extent.

The abundant vegetation supported a wealth of both marine and terrestrial invertebrates, which were the primary consumers in a food pyramid that ultimately supported a good variety of larger vertebrate animals. Since the dominant land animals of the Upper Carboniferous were amphibians, it is believed that many of the tracks were made by amphibians, although it is argued that reptiles were probably represented in this locality as well. Structurally, reptiles would have appeared quite similar to amphibians at this time.

Although there appeared to be perhaps a half-dozen different varieties of tracks represented in the coal shale, they were still treated as a curiosity with very little significance. At the end of his analysis of the tracks, Jones noted that the "tracks of these ancient animals have been of very little benefit to the anatomists and morphologists of the United States." This opinion, widely held in the first two decades of the twentieth century, would remain virtually unchallenged for another sixty years.

## From Sand to Mud: Dunes to Tidal Flats

While the Coconino trackway sediments in the Grand Canyon are composed almost entirely of sand dune deposits, and trackways from the Pottsville formation of Alabama are from a swamp-forest shore-line, the Robledos trackways were formed on a muddy plain, an almost perfectly level shoreline that gently oscillated back and forth. The Coconino and Pottsville trackways each represent specific ecological habitats, but the vast extent of the New Mexican mud flat may have included a number of local ecological habitats.

Although primarily mud flat, along this shoreline were localized lagoons and swamps, forested and non-forested shorelines, estuaries and ponds, and even occasional sandy shores and dunes. This mixture broke up the monotony of the mud flat and nurtured the formation of a number of small ecological habitats close to one another.

Not only were the Robledo habitats more diverse, but the nature of the muddy substrate was optimum for the preservation of nearly all the fauna groups represented by these localized habitats. A finely sorted mud retains both firm consistency as well as near-perfect deformability, allowing for the trace of a tiny bug or beetle to be preserved alongside the trace of a twelve-foot-long reptile. In the sandy deposits of the Grand Canyon, only the largest and heaviest invertebrates have been preserved.

For example, vertebrate tracks less than an inch in length are rare in the Coconino, but vertebrate tracks as small as one-eighth of an inch have been clearly recorded in the Robledo muds, as well as the faint traces of invertebrates which themselves were no larger than one-eighth of an inch and couldn't have weighed much more than a feather or a pin.

The Robledo mud flats contrast with the Coconino sandstones and the Pottsville shales in other ways. The Robledo muds preserve a variety of sedimentary features that are not represented in other trackway deposits. The flats, though almost perfectly horizontal, preserve slight undulations here and there. These low spots dried last when the mud baked in the sun. As a result, in addition to wonderfully preserved mud cracks, shrinkage lines marking the rates of dessication of the low spots are also preserved.

Sole marks are locally preserved in the sedimentary layers of southern New Mexico. Sole marks (or scour marks) are preserved when sediment-laden water moves fast over mud. First, the water erodes gouges in the substrate, streamlined in the direction of flow. Then, as water velocity declines progressively, sediment is dropped onto the gouged mud, preserving the gouges and other marks, until the water is moving so slowly that the last sediment to be dropped is perfectly smooth. When these layers are excavated, the top may be so

*In the Robledos, large mud-filled ponds often form after heavy rains. The mud is essentially identical to the type of mud laid down during Permian times. As the mud dries, large macro mud cracks form, making numerous plates (top). The mud, still moist, can record footprints but is also vulnerable to wind-blown debris (bottom photo), which sticks to the surface and damages the trackways. By the time micro mud cracks form (smaller plates inside the macro mud cracks) the mud is no longer impressionable and total dessication of the pond destroys any footprints made on the surface before the mud dried out.* Photos by Jerry MacDonald.

smooth as to reveal faint mud cracks, but the underside reveals a different story of deep and beautiful scour marks and sole marks.

The Robledo muds show abundant evidence of the natural sorting that takes place when sediments are gently deposited. The coarser particulates are dropped first and so find their way to the bottom of the mud, while the finest end up at the top. This explains the layering of perhaps 10 percent of the mudstones of the Robledos. Most of the preserved layers, however, are fine grained and thinly bedded, and represent repeated cycles of deposition.

While the Coconino tracks were preserved in a predominantly arid environment, where the mode of formation were winds and rains, the Robledo muds were largely water-laid. Tides may account for the cyclical nature of the Robledo muds. The often-wetted surface provided a frequently repeated substrate on which tracks were made. In fact, in the present-day muds (made up of 280-year-old sediments) that can be found in some areas of the Robledos after a good rain, tracks can often be observed under water where, for example, a lizard scurried across a mud puddle and left its tracks. This phenomenon was somewhat surprising to me, and calls into question any assertions that the mud was free of water when particular fossil tracks were made. I have observed the trail of present-day centipedes in the mud, a good two inches below the surface of the water. When the puddle dries, the tracks made underwater are virtually identical to those made on wet but not water-covered mud.

Finally, observing the drying-out process of present-day muds shows that this fine-grained mud desiccates first into macro mud cracks, where there are very large sections of mud (about a square foot) that split from the rest into a jigsaw of island-like plates, and then in time these large plates form micro cracks. The curious thing about this, however, is that the surface of these plates is still very impressionable, and a lizard running across the broken-up surface still leaves its tracks across all the plates that it scurries over. I now see that many fossil trails were made when the surface was well along in the desiccation process.

The window of opportunity for the preservation of present-day trackways in the muds of the Robledos (after all water has evaporated from the surface) is about two to three days in warm temperatures and clear skies. The high spots dry first, and the mud cracks move from highest to lowest levels. The preservation window increases significantly in cooler, overcast skies, in some cases doubling the time available for track making and track preservation.

Once the surface is fully dried, no footprints are preserved, and in fact the surface of the hardened mud cracks is slightly broken when an animal scurries past. Heavy animals today—such as cows—can leave evidence of their passing in the hardened mud, but even so the "tracks" show more mud crack damage than they do anatomical trackway preservation.

Now for the problem. It is very true that when the mud is still saturated, it is the most impressionable. As it dries, however, it is still subject to wind damage. The wind blows twigs, coarser sands, and other debris over the mud. So when the mud is finally dry, it is covered with a dirty surface that creates havoc with the fine tracks on the original surface.

In other words, the process of destroying the tracks begins while the tracks are being made. As the mud desiccates, the tracks are shrunken and broken in spots. As the wind blows over the still moist tracks, new debris adheres to the surface, partially covering other tracks. And when the mud finally dries, the layers become so brittle that the slightest winds and rains destroy them.

So what does this mean? The study of present-day muds suggests that the window of impressionability is best when the muds are saturated or even submerged, and this window decreases rapidly as the muds desiccate. Small tracks are the first to be lost, and as the moist mud lies drying in the sun, the continued preservation of these small tracks depends on how much or how little wind disturbs the mud.

## Making Footprints

To further understand the differences between the track-bearing sediments found in the Coconino formation of the Grand Canyon, the Pottsville formation of Alabama, and the Abo formation of the Robledo Mountains, it is helpful to think about how and when footprints are made in a variety of situations. We are all familiar with footprints. As kids we made them in mud all the time—age has made us more discreet—especially without shoes, or perhaps on our mother's freshly waxed floor. Sometimes, if we were very lucky, we would chance on some wet concrete. Making footprints was part of growing up. We would make them everywhere—in sand as well as in mud, along the seashore or along the sidewalk. We would make them in snow or at the municipal pool. We loved to leave footprints everywhere we went.

Yet our footprints eventually vanished. In time the sea rushed over them along the shore, the wind blew away our prints in the sand, the heat evaporated those along the pool, the sun melted our tracks in the snow. Even our prints in the mud dissolved in the next good rain. In short, all traces that we were ever in those places vanished forever. Except one.

I can still go back to the sidewalk and see the footprint and initials that I left twenty-eight years ago in Kenosha, Wisconsin. It stands as an enduring monument to my mischievous childhood. Yet it is obvious from such childhood experiences that only certain kinds of situations were conducive to preserving footprints. Some, like water prints, were extremely transitory, while others, like those made in mud and concrete, could survive for a while longer.

How is it possible to have preserved the footprints of dinosaurs and other prehistoric animals? The initial character of the sediment preserving fossil footprints is crucial for trackway preservation. It seems logical that a good impressionable surface would be characterized by fine-grained, wet, and stable sediment. Yet paleontologically speaking, many of the fossil trackways preserved, especially those of dinosaurs, are preserved in sediment too coarse to leave good anatomical detail.

Many dinosaur track sites simply consist of indistinct circular depressions, preserving virtually no detail at all. Such surfaces were probably very wet so that the mud forced upward on the sides of the print by the weight of the dinosaur collapsed into the tracks right after formation—like stepping in concrete too wet to retain the shape of the foot. In contrast, if the sediment lacks cohesion because the substrate is not only loosely packed but very dry, the tracks that are formed will lack the "cement" necessary to keep their shape (like the tracks made on a sand dune). The first winds and rains will destroy them.

My favorite dinosaur art poster is from Germany. It's of a full-sized *Brontosaurus* (*Apatosaurus* is more accurate) crossing the Autobahn. There are footprints in a farmers field made by this curious creature as it wandered toward the highway. But once it reached the pavement, its tracks disappear altogether. This illustrates an important lesson. There must be a good deformable (impressionable) surface for there to be footprints. A farmer's field is good. A superhighway is bad. Yet deformable surfaces must be stable enough to allow the tracks to remain for a considerable period of time. A farmer's field is good, but a frequently plowed field is bad. If the area is constantly affected by water, tracks would naturally break up by the force of tides, waves, and floods. A farmer's field is good, but daily irrigation is bad. Ideally, good sites should be only occasionally wetted and then allowed to harden, and then they should be gently buried by sediments somewhat dissimilar to the track-bearing surface.

If the composition of the sediment is too similar to the track surface, the two surfaces may bond together, making them virtually impossible to separate. Remember my footprint in the cement? If the workers poured more cement into my hardened footprint, not only would it disappear from view, but even if I knew the exact location of my print, I would be unable to uncover it again. Another factor in footprint preservation is size. A twenty-ton sauropod walking alongside a shoreline is going to leave tracks the size of a large bird bath or a bathtub. The prints would not only be wide but very deep as well. Even though we know that small animals are much more abundant than large ones, the chances of preservation of dinosaur tracks this large are infinitely greater than the preservation of a five-ounce, five-inch (sparrow-size) hatchling.

One advantage we have in our hunt for good fossil tracks is that many animals must seek water, and as a result an incredible number of footprints have been left along the shores of lakes, rivers, and seas. If the area was subject to frequent wetting and subsequent burial, whether from seasonal floods or tidal cycles and/or fluctuations in sea level, such large tracks could be preserved.

Many of the giant dinosaur tracks that the public is familiar with were made in limey mud, which hardened very quickly on the surface, forming a rock-like crust. When softer sediments flooded the area, the tracks were buried. As more and more sediment accumulated over the track layer, the weight lithified the layer, permanently preserving the imprints.

Thus we begin to see that the chance of one of our footprints surviving the forces of nature for a few hours, never mind days, months, or years, is very small. Indeed, fossilized footprints of humans are extremely rare, which is why the discovery of humanlike tracks on the Laetoli plain in Tanzania is so exciting. They were made in a fresh fall of volcanic ash by an adult and a child (or a man and a woman) over three million years ago, and are the only known footprints of such three-million-year-old prehistoric human ancestors.

## Tracking Today's Animals

There is an entire discipline devoted to tracking both humans and animals. The police employ trackers to hunt down criminals. Search and rescue teams employ trackers to find lost hikers. The

Bureau of Land Management and the National Park Service frequently employ trackers to hunt down rogue animals. Armies often employ trackers to seek out the enemy. These trackers can tell how many men they are following, how heavy their equipment is, whether they are retreating or advancing, and whether they are an enemy or friendly force.

In nineteenth-century America, tracking was a well-known art. Good tracking skills immeasurably increased one's chances of survival. Today, tracking is a dying art. Those of us who hike with any frequency pride ourselves in our ability to recognize the tracks of rabbits, deer, coyotes, or squirrels. But there are hundreds of animals that leave trails on the ground, and experienced trackers can recognize them all.

There is much more to tracking than just identifying the track maker. Where did the animal come from? We know that for a moment an animal crossed our path, but where did it go? We might follow the tracks off the hiking trail for a few feet or so, but inevitably we lose the trail in the leaves and brush of the forest floor. The trackway seems to disappear into thin air, and we think that the trail is irretrievably lost to the forest. But this is where the novice quits and the professional begins. A professional can follow a trail for days over virtually any kind of terrain.

There are only a handful of schools that train newcomers in the art of "reading the ground." They not only teach recognition of track makers from their footprints but also how to glean a remarkable variety of seemingly unrelated information from a trail. When carefully observed, footprints can reveal the sex of the track maker, as well as its speed of travel and what it is doing as it travels along. Experienced trackers claim that after a few hours of tracking, they can not only recognize the species, but the individual. They can gauge height and weight and whether the animal stopped to sniff the air or cock its ear.

A lot of tricks of the tracking trade have to do with what experts call pressure ridges, discs, and waves. For example, human footprints made during a leisurely walk have a clear wave that rises from toe to ball, then drops from ball to the beginning of the arch, and then rises at the arch and drops at the heel. If the track maker looks off to the side, pressure ridges on the outside of the footprint show it. If the track maker points off to the left or right with its arm, pressure ridges on the opposite side of the track show it.

When an individual runs, the nature of the wave changes dramatically. The toe digs in, the pressure wave moves back on the foot, and the heel print is faint to non-existent. If someone has an ambling gait, his or her tracks become even and flat. Serious running kicks up material explosively and leaves half-moon shapes in front.

The only way to really become fluent in reading the ground is through spending a great deal of time following tracks. Experienced trackers call it "dirt time." An added dose of experience comes if the tracker follows a trail right after it is made. A key to success is in the imagination, for often tracking seems to border on clairvoyance. Trackers must train themselves to "see" the track maker, to imagine its movements. In time an expert learns to anticipate the next few steps and can locate the spot where the next track should be.

I have spent a lot of time training myself in the art of tracking, and I have seen substantial improvement in my skills. One of my strategies is to make fifty prints or more among the rocks and sands of an arroyo, doing a variety of activities as I walk, such as pointing, stopping, even sneezing. These activities really do show up in the trail. The hardest thing I have had to learn is to not focus on one single print and then focus on the next. Tracking just doesn't work that way. You have to make your vision general, rather than specific.

The best way I can describe it is through the new "picture within a picture" posters. There is one poster that has five big dinosaurs in it, but you can't see them if you look at it normally. You have to kind of disengage your eyes and then, poof! there they are. By training yourself to look at the ground as a succession of tracks rather than as one after another, you can see the tracks for quite a distance.

But what does this mean for the paleontologist? I can't go somewhere and follow a *Dimetrodon* and observe the different kinds of tracks it makes. Or can I? I think that we can get close. But it's going to take many experiments with living reptiles to do this. For now, I follow the trails of these extinct beasts through solid rock, and I often notice tracks with slightly different shapes, sequences, or depths. These changes obviously mean something. Stay tuned.

## Face to Face with "Shake and Bake" Geology

The red beds of New Mexico began to be deposited in the Carboniferous (Pennsylvanian) and continued well into the Permian. Tranquil conditions persisted for millions of years. During this time, a large seaway existed that included wide areas of the southwestern United States. As a result, hundreds of miles of shoreline was created throughout much of south-central New Mexico. The pre-Las Cruces area became part of the western edge of the seaway that trended from north/northwest to south/southeast. The eastern edge included portions of southwestern Oklahoma and western Texas.

Much of the seaway was shallow in south-central New Mexico, and a far-reaching mud flat formed that was intermittently up to two hundred miles long. Large areas of nearly continuous mud flats occurred in the southern New Mexico area, from the present Mexican border to the Caballo Mountains, 120 miles away, and represented passive margins of the shoreline. The present-day Robledos are approximately in the middle of this mud flat that locally trended from southwest to northeast.

Two hundred eighty million years ago, as this mud flat emerged and developed, extensive coastal sedimentation—possibly in part from the seaward end of a large drainage basin—and a slowly rising ocean began to cover the mud flat with more and more layers until the lowland topography changed and the coastal environments disappeared altogether. Soon episodes of significant tectonic activity returned, forming new rifts which trended from southeast to northwest in New Mexico, and even continued into northern New Mexico. This rift activity separated the lithified Paleozoic sediments into a number of basins, bounded on each side by a mountain range. Geologists call this geomorphic phenomenon basin and range topography. The Robledo Mountains occur along the western edge of the Mesilla Basin, which also includes portions of northwest Texas and northern Mexico.

Were it not for the extensive rifting that took place in New Mexico beginning in the Late Permian, this lowland environment, tracks and all, would be thousands of feet below the surface, forever hidden. But the rifting caused the uplifting of the Lower Permian beds as a series of mountain-building events took place. The Paleozoic layers, once thousands of feet below the surface, were bent upwards, bringing parts of them close to the surface.

What Mother Nature did for paleontologists in southern New Mexico was to sink the middle of large horizontal sections of strata and upturn the edges; the strata were squeezed into a bowl-shaped basin. The edges of these broken sections, which included deep Paleozoic layers, were thrust up on either side, exposing them at or near the surface with the younger layers facing in and the old layers facing out. The younger layers were subsequently eroded and the loose sediment was deposited in the middle of the "bowl," leaving the most resistant Paleozoic layers to make up the sides. At the bottom of the "bowl" are the Paleozoic sediments as they

## BASIN AND RANGE PROVINCE

**FIGURE 1**

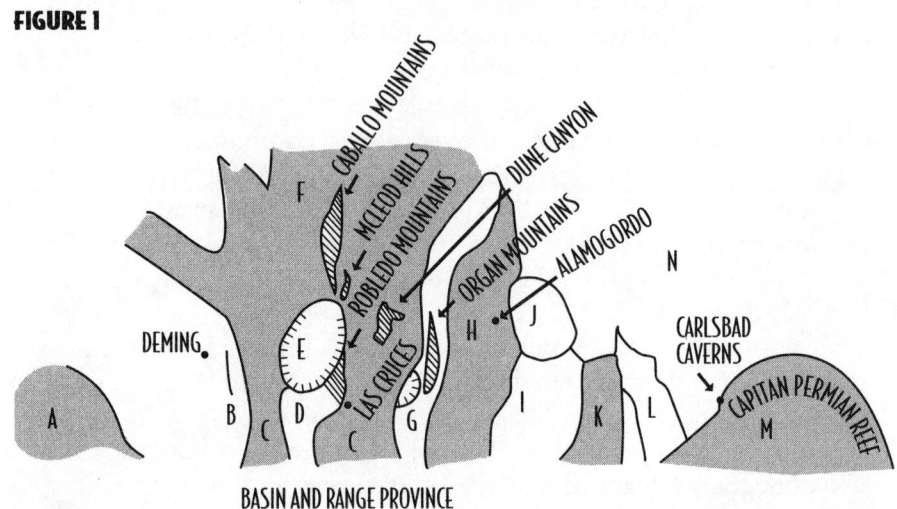

BASIN AND RANGE PROVINCE

**FIGURE 2**

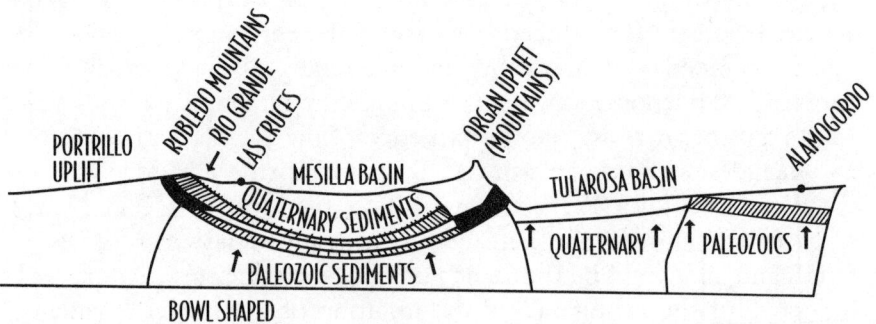

*The topography in southern New Mexico is broken into numerous areas of low relief or basins (shaded areas in figure 1) bordered on either side by uplifts or ranges. This alternating topography, caused by both volcanic and earthquake activity millions of years ago, has succeeded in exposing Paleozoic sediments (darkened levels in figure 2) that would otherwise be thousands of feet below the surface. The trackways are located along the contacts between these broad basins and high ranges. Lettered areas are:*

*A. Hacita Basin*
*B. Florida Uplift*          *G. Organ Uplift*              *L. Guadalupe Uplift*
*C. Mesilla Basin*          *H. Tularosa Basin*           *M. Delaware Basin*
*D. Potrillo Uplift*          *I. Otero Uplift*                *N. Pecos Slope*
*E. Volcanic depression*  *J. Sacramento Uplift*
*F. Caballo Mountains*    *K. Salt Basin*

Adapted from New Mexico Highway Geological Map, 1981.

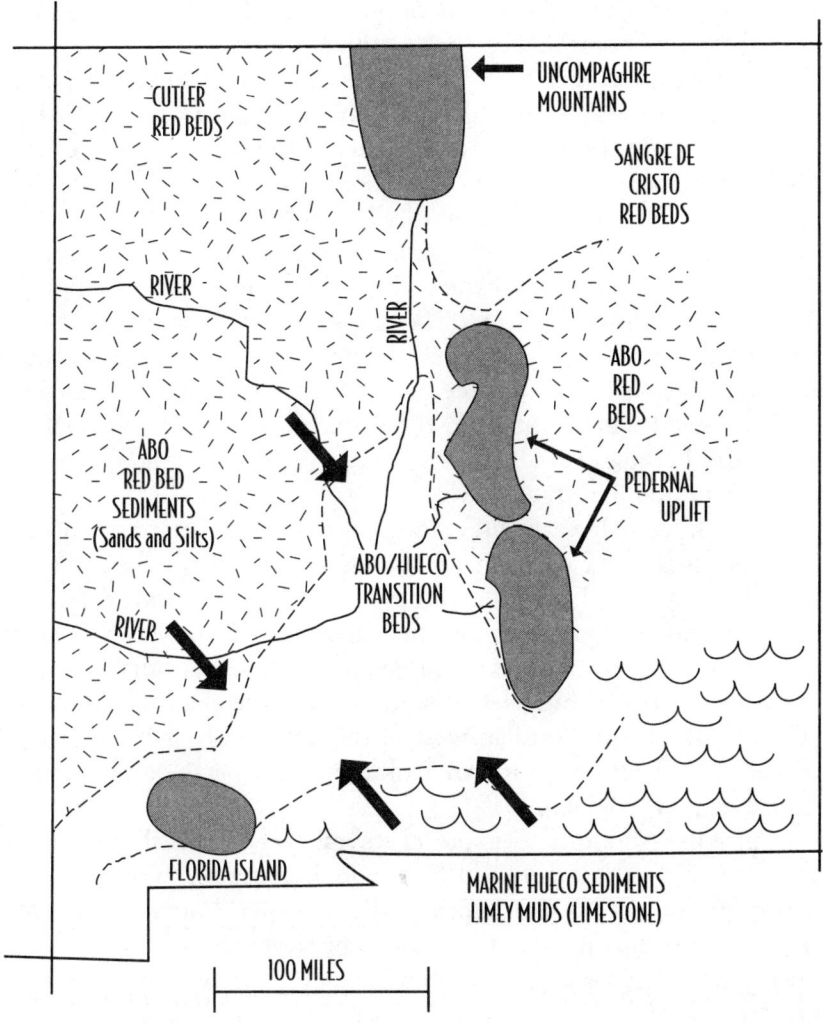

*Paleographic features of New Mexico during the Early Permian. Terrestrial sediments, particularly the Abo red beds to the northwest, traded depositional cycles with the marine (saltwater-lain) Hueco sediments to the south. The battlefield preserving these alternating depositional events are the Abo/Hueco transition beds, or Abo tongue, formed in south-central New Mexico, where a gently fluctuating shoreline made for the preservation of footprints. During the Early Permian, a large island existed to the southwest of the transition beds, and to the east was a large area of uplift. Rivers flowed both west from the Pedernal Mountains and south from mountains in northern New Mexico.* Adapted from Berman and Reisz, "A new species of Trimerorhachis from the Lower Permian of New Mexico," Bulletin of the Carnegie Museum of Natural History, vol. 49, 1980.

would appear if no rifting had occurred. Today, they reside more than forty-five hundred feet below the surface.

The Robledos, with nearly all the younger sediments eroded away, stand alone as the western edge of the basin or bowl with Las Cruces nestled snugly in their shadow. Currently, at the surface, the middle of the bowl is filled with approximately three-million-year-old or younger Quaternary sediments which are locally rich in mammal fossils.

Today, in southern New Mexico, Paleozoic sediments, comprised entirely of Pennsylvanian through Early Permian strata, are approximately fifteen hundred feet thick along the upturned edge of the basin. They record a migrating shoreline, known as the Abo/Hueco tongue, which is between three hundred and five hundred feet thick in the Robledos area. Between the eastern and western edge of the basin, the Permian is overlain by Quaternary strata which are up to fifteen hundred feet thick.

Our knowledge of life along the eastern margins of the Permian inland sea is much more complete than our understanding of life along the western edge. Most information about the ecology and environment of the eastern flank comes from the northwest portion of Texas and southwest Oklahoma, in areas extensively worked by paleontologists for more than one hundred years. Work on the Permian west of the Texas border has primarily centered in Arizona, southern Colorado, and parts of central and northern New Mexico.

Since the Abo formation preserves miles of ancient shoreline that was often only a few hundred feet wide, looking for fabulously rich concentrations of fossil footprints along a one-thousand-plus-mile ancient strand line is a daunting task. The shoreline is preserved only in very small geological sections and not every section has footprints preserved in it.

Abundance or scarcity of tracks, or any fossils for that matter, is based upon two factors: population size and preservation conditions. There may be only scattered footprints along a coastal environment because the area was very sparsely populated. Or the footprint record is poor because environmental conditions were unfavorable for preservation. So even though there were over a dozen coal mines in the same area of Alabama that could theoretically yield trackways, fossil trackways were evidently narrowly concentrated in Mine 11. Could I find my own narrow concentration of tracks? Could I find my own equivalent of Coal Mine 11? I knew that if there was a major trackway locality to be found along the western edge of the seaway, all of the prior work made it obvious that it would be in the Robledos. But even in the Robledos, where would one start?

At the time I had to be realistic and assume that no big trackways lie exposed in situ on a canyon floor, waiting for me to stumble over them. The motherlode had to be well hidden within layers that had remained buried for tens of millions of years, layers that have since been molded into the twisted and folded strata that now make up the Robledos.

In fact, it stood to reason that the motherlode could only exist if it had remained buried. The problem is that these red beds, unlike the massive limey mud that some well-known dinosaur tracks are preserved in, are very poor champions against the elements of nature. They weaken and break apart very easily.

Hours and hours of exploring, poking, and digging turned into weeks. In five weeks I had more material than I had ever had before, but it was similar in quality and variety to the material all former collectors had found. It seemed that my search was just as haphazard as theirs.

The red beds seemed to stretch for miles, stacked ten or fifty feet high in some places. Some of the largest outcrops appeared to be nothing more than jumbled piles of rock or, at best, badly slumping layers broken and weathered into indistinguishable units. Yet other outcrops seemed cemented into impenetrable layers with no toe-hold from which to get a sample. I could spend months just on the debris. And if I did find a track bed, there could be dozens, if not hundreds, of feet of rock cemented over it which would need to be removed if one was to do it right. Did I have the time and the patience for such an undertaking?

Knowledge of the great age of the area reinforced visual observation of unforgiving erosion and weathering and the abundant evidence of tectonic activity. Anyone who hiked the Robledos could attest to the violence that nature had wrought there.

This "shake and bake" geology—sediments that have experienced tectonic displacement and volcanic activity—certainly didn't reinforce the idea that any tranquilly deposited sediments still remained after 280 million years. I began to understand why the Robledo treasures remained so secure and elusive. Also, I began to doubt that there even was a trackway motherlode. In five weeks I had succeeded in reinforcing a fifty-year-old bias.

At home I sat in my rocking chair and ruminated over the rocks of the Robledos. I found a few prints here and there but nothing of the quality of the Torres specimen. I found numerous good marine fossil sites, but anybody could find marine fossils. I had hundreds of specimens and so did about everybody else. I wanted terrestrial fossils.

In all my poking around, I still hadn't found a footprint worthy of my efforts, one that would support my suspicions about a hidden motherlode. It seemed to me that finding a significant footprint in the Robledos was like finding an errant Indian arrowhead. And I had never found one of those either.

Every time I came home I told myself, "That's enough. No more." It was a hassle driving over bad roads, walking through rocky arroyos, fighting the sun and wind, slapping at biting black flies, and digging through rocks and debris. I always came home tired and discouraged. Every evening my mind was made up. "No more. It's a waste of time."

Yet the next morning I began to worry that perhaps I didn't dig deep enough. Or perhaps I should have dug three feet over, or five feet higher. What if I was digging in a blank spot in a hillside packed full of tracks? Maybe there was an outcrop just over the hill where tracks were visible. I could not bear the thought that I might have just missed the mark. These thoughts were much more difficult to endure than the actual work of hunting tracks in the mountains.

Coupled with my great fear of narrowly missing the mark was the exhilaration I anticipated if I did find it. My dreams, though quite different from my experiences in the field, were too powerful to ignore. I dreamed of long trackways in perfect condition, revealed on layer after layer, from all sorts of animals. I dreamed of walking through a canyon and seeing trackways marching across the floor into a mountain. I dreamed of seeing tracks all over a hillside, the debris field from a trackway treasure that made up the mountain. I dreamed of finding the most spectacular tracks ever found.

In one recurring dream, I saw a broad span of mud flat, covered by long and clear trackways, that made up the floor of the Mesilla Valley Mall. Hundreds of people walked over the floor again and again as they did their shopping. It appeared that only I could see the tracks, and my efforts to show them to the shoppers were entirely ignored. Little did I know that this dream would be disturbingly accurate in the months to come.

My exposure to what others had found gave me an excellent way to gauge my finds against specimens collected in earlier years. I had to ask myself, what would I need to find in order for me to say that there was a discovery. After some thought, I decided that I would need to find three things. First, I had to find a trackway with several large prints, prints as large as the single print I found with Ron

Ratkevitch. Second, I had to find the source beds, beds containing consecutive layers of tracks that were big enough and wide enough to peel back. And third, I had to find trackways inside the mountain that were still in perfect condition. If it was good enough for Charles Gilmore, it was good enough for me.

The recollections of a very select group of local hikers, quarrymen, and fossil hunters allowed me to concentrate on various outcrops within the range. No one was secretive about where tracks could be found, although some thought that they were the only ones who knew of this or that outcrop or hillside.

I often hiked over the peaks of the mountains to get a larger perspective, since many of the red beds are obscured with overburden, and only reveal themselves from a distance in low light. I found several outcrops this way. I chose to begin work in any red bed outcrop I could find, but the deeper in the Robledos, the better. I sifted through layer upon layer of sediment at nine different sites for several weeks.

## Eureka! The Footprint Motherlode Is Found

During the early morning hours of June 6, 1987, after an hour of chipping and prying, I pulled a four-foot-long slab of mudstone about eight inches thick out of a hillside. Clearly visible on the top of the slab were what appeared to be several tracks of a very large animal. Even though the individual tracks were damaged from the action of water seepage, the claws were clearly discernible.

What I did next I can't explain, except to say that I knew that there was something fantastic inside the rock so I tried to split the entire slab in two. Anybody else would have been thrilled with the prints on the top of the slab. But I wasn't. I did something that others would probably have considered foolhardy.

I used the chisel end of my rock hammer on the parting plane that separated two slightly different halves of the rock slab, and I hit the hammer end of it with another hammer. I gingerly moved all along the plane in this fashion, rolling the rock on its end so that it was weakened along the plane of cleavage. Then, nervously, I made that one crucial hit, and the slab split open like the pages of a book.

I knew then that my search had come to an end. There inside were five perfectly preserved footprints, each about seven inches long. Transformed in front of me like magic, this large single slab was now in two pieces, preserving both a mold and a cast of a prehistoric

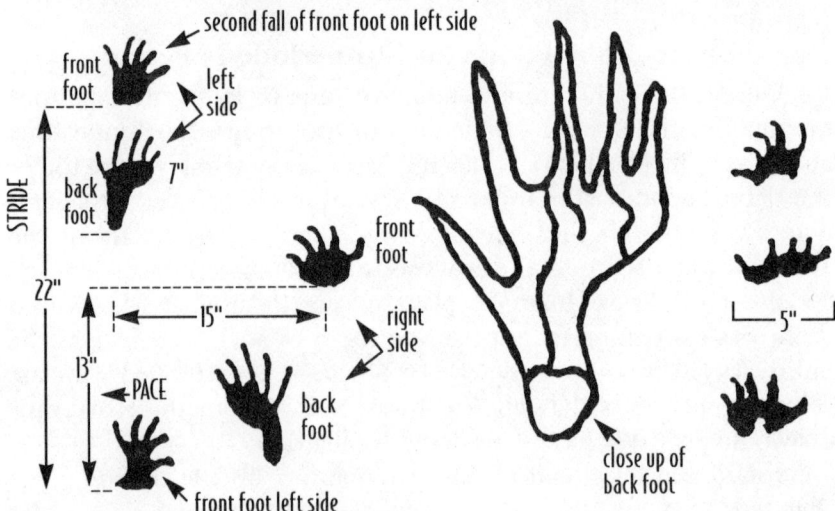

The *"discovery" slabs found on June 6th, 1987, at the AF 2 excavation. The slab on the left is the imprint surface, and the slab on the right is the natural cast made when a fresh layer of mud washed over the trackway. The lines across much of the slabs' surfaces are desiccation cracks which formed when the mud began to dry in the sun. For the first time, trackway systematics could be performed on the slabs, since all four of the reptile's feet were preserved as footprints, as well as an all-important second step of one of the feet. Stride and pace could be mathematically deduced from the tracks, which would then give an approximate guess as to how large the track maker was. This animal was approximately seven feet long.* Photo by Thom Votaw.

reptile's trail. I knew immediately it was the first discovery of consecutive prints that large ever found in the Robledos.

I always ran into a variety of reptiles as I combed the mountains on my hunt. Everything from horned toads to rattlesnakes. In fact, on one occasion my quest for tracks was almost prematurely ended by the sudden strike of one of New Mexico's more venomous inhabitants. He missed.

I saw my share of alligator lizards, collared lizards, spiny lizards, and leopard lizards. We are blessed in New Mexico with a wonderful bounty of lizards, including a few varieties of skinks. The biggest reptile I had ever seen (outside of snakes) was only about thirteen inches long. I was now looking at the tracks of a reptile that had to have been at least eight feet long.

I had once been bitten by a foot-long collared lizard, and it is widely known that this lizard delivers the strongest bite around, mainly because its head is significantly larger than that of any other lizard that lives in the area. The head of the creature I had just found had to have been nearly a foot long, maybe more. It was clear that there were no such giants roaming the desert now. Today, the nearest alligators are found in the swamps of Texas and other Gulf States, where it is always wet and humid.

Whatever animal had made the tracks, its kind had been dead for a very long time. The fact that such a large animal had once lived here suggested to me that there must have been a boatload of smaller animals that provided a stable food source, or perhaps it attacked and ate its own kind. Was I staring at the tracks of the top predator of the Early Permian?

The prints were amazing because they were so perfect. They looked like they were made right after yesterday's rainstorm. How could these tracks be over a quarter of a billion years old? There had to be some kind of mistake, but the context of this trackway dispelled all doubts.

I was at the base of a three-hundred-foot mountain. There were three hundred feet of lithified sediment deposited above me. It was as if this giant reptile had followed the Pied Piper into a hidden door right in front of my eyes. The only evidence that this animal walked into the mountain were its footprints on the slab lying at my feet.

Sometime after the reptile tramped his way across the mud, hundreds if not thousands of feet of sediment were deposited over the trail. For millennia the trail was buried, and then for more millennia the deposited material was subject to erosion. All that remained of this burial shroud were the last three hundred feet of strata above my head.

I could only stand in awe with the thought that this once tranquil shoreline had been transformed into a jagged mountain canyon. Without the footprint sequences, I could almost convince myself that this transformation from mud flat to mountain was the result of a single cataclysm, perhaps the onrush of primeval seas that swept over the land, forever changing the shape of the region. But in the Robledos, alternating layers of first marine, and then terrestrial, and then marine sediments all over again are preserved. The evidence of fossil footprints in each alternating strata argues against the notion of catastrophe and indicates relatively calm conditions at the time the tracks were made and preserved.

The footprints Charles Gilmore excavated from the Grand Canyon are an even better case-in-point example. The thought of a single catastrophe depositing the thousands of feet of layered sediment may seem credible until one considers the Coconino footprint layers smack dab in the middle of the canyon. The footprints from the Coconino sandstone are located more than a thousand feet below the canyon rim. Like in the Robledos, these fossil footprints indicate an array of foraging animals and insects scurrying about their daily routines. Footprint evidence does not support an origin of cataclysmic catastrophe.

Still, I couldn't conceive of a more thrilling experience than to uncover the footprints of an animal that no other human had ever seen. On the spot where I was now standing, 280 million years ago, this giant reptile had slithered past.

At the time I knew very little about trackway research, but it was obvious to me that this was something that didn't belong in someone's personal collection. This was big, very big. For the first time, my experience matched my dream.

Now came the test. Was this slab part of a discernible layer that I could follow along the base of the mountain, or was it a broken piece of shoreline long since ripped from its ancient moorings? There was only one way to find out.

I began to dig laterally at the same height that I found the footprint slab. I moved both north and south of the slab, and each shovel of debris confirmed what I had wished for. The layer was still there, at least twenty-five feet of it. It was still intact. It seemed that it just had been waiting for discovery for millions of years. Right there in front of me was the door to the tomb.

I removed enough overburden to follow the edge of the layer for about forty feet. At first I decided not to pull any more slabs out, although the desire to do so was as intense as any desire I had ever experienced before. I shoveled debris aside for a few minutes to continue to expose the edge of the layer, and then I went back to look at my newly found tracks. I couldn't believe my eyes. I ran my fingers along the grooves made by four-inch claws and my mind raced in a mental time machine back millions of years to a world no human ever knew.

After about an hour of shoveling and daydreaming, I had a very discouraging thought. Although I could see on the mountainside the layer where the track slab came from for forty feet, I was afraid that there might not be any more tracks in that freshly exposed layer. If I stopped right now, I could walk away with the mystery unsolved, thereby preserving my dreams of layers and layers of crisscrossing trackways. Those dreams would never be challenged by the facts. Though this one slab reinforced my dreams, the next one could shatter them.

If I dug up a few more slabs, I might prove what everybody had thought all along: there are no thoroughfares of trackways to be found. I experienced a mixture of doubt and fear that this next slab would prove that the accumulated history of track collecting in the Robledos was right and tremendous excitement that this traditional bias was wrong.

I pulled out the next slab just to the right of the previous one. I placed it on its edge and looked for the plane that matched the splitting horizon on the other slab. It was there. Then I took out my two hammers and worked across the plane as I did before. When the horizon was separated along the entire edge of the slab, it was time to pop it open with a strong hit.

I knew that this could be one of the most crucial slabs I would ever split. It seemed like everything I believed and dreamed about rested on this one blow. I indulged in the customary "Please God, I'll be a good boy for the rest of my life" prayer and any others I could think of. I hit the hammer. It popped open as before. I held both slabs, which were now separated about an inch from each other.

I was afraid to open it fully, so I peeked inside. I saw some elevated relief on one slab and corresponding depressions on the other. I opened it all the way. There they were: four more beautiful tracks of the same animal. I now had a seven-foot trackway with nine consecutive footprints. I hooted and howled for a long time, and it still seemed that I was overflowing with pent-up emotion.

I knew that if I wanted to, I could embark on a journey beyond anything I had ever known before. At that moment my outlook changed from a curiosity seeker to a research scientist. There was no turning back now. The door to a lost world had been discovered, and its secrets, etched on the finest of earth's tablets, would soon be read.

It was really a miracle that these footprints were found at all. Not only were these layers covered with seemingly endless debris, but the tracks themselves were secretly hidden *inside* those layers, locked tight by Nature's key, forever safe until someone invented the metal chisel-hammer. The Egyptian pyramid builders would have been proud of the levels of security the earth had employed to safeguard these pre-historic treasures. Indeed, finding these tracks was like finding a needle in a haystack. Now what was I going to do with the "needle"?

The "needle" I had just found weighed about 125 pounds apiece, and I was nearly a half mile from my car. I knew that I had to take those footprint slabs out as soon as possible for fear that rain might destroy them or that they might be stolen.

I drove home like a crazy man. I was so excited that I almost impaled my car on a big rock on the side of the road. I was lucky to maneuver around it at the insane speed I was going. When I got home, I ran into the house. "You are not going to believe it. You are not going to believe it. I've done it. I've found it. The biggest dog-gone tracks you ever saw. I can't believe it!"

Of course, the kids ran to the car to see the tracks. They came back hopping mad and thought I was playing a trick on them.

"Dad, you liar," my eight-year-old son Justin said. "There're no tracks in the car."

I explained that I had left them at the bottom of the arroyo and now had to figure out a way to bring them out. I rushed to my neighbors' house. John Swenson was retired and often came over to spend time with my dog. We often talked long into the cool of the evening. John knew what I had been doing day after day in the desert, so my crazed excitement did not come as a total shock to him.

John brought out a duffel bag that he had cut down the side and sewed back up with a zipper. If we could somehow slide the rock into the bag, we reasoned we could leave the zipper open for excess rock. We threw it in the car and set out again for the Robledos.

After we had made the twenty-minute walk up the arroyo to the site, the two slabs seemed even bigger than I remembered. We maneuvered the slightly bigger slab into the duffel bag. With bungee cords we strapped the duffel bag to my dad's trusty Korean War army pack. Until today it had always had ample room for my finds. Then I sat down and wiggled into the pack straps. It was now all up to me. I was sitting on the ground with a 125-pound rock on my back.

*Hauling trackways out of the Robledos is no easy task. Vehicles can only come within one-half mile of the AF 2 excavation, so all specimens need to be packed out.* Photos by Pearl MacDonald.

I couldn't stand up. John and I were both laughing. It was a disaster waiting to happen.

It was clearly time for Plan B. We built a three-foot rock platform up which we dragged the slab. Once the pack was again loaded, I had the advantage of slipping into the straps in a standing position. All I needed to do after that was walk. I pushed off the landing with a grunt.

In a strange way, supporting this great weight on my back felt good. It was as if a big iron was working out hidden wrinkles along my spine. The first hundred yards were not too bad, but I was using muscles I had never used before to balance as I walked over and around boulders, rock slides, gravel, and uneven limestone layers that formed much of the arroyo bottom. Steps up and steps down were very difficult, because there were a few seconds during which I was carrying and balancing the rock with only one leg.

It didn't take many of these steps to take their toll. The first to go were my legs. Every step strained them even more; I could feel the strength in them melting away. I desperately looked for another landing to rest the rock on after walking maybe three hundred yards.

I did this six times before I reached my car. After every stop I was just a little bit weaker than the stop before, until by the time I got close to the car, I thought that I might collapse. But I made it. The rock slipped nicely off my back and into the trunk. Now all I had to do was walk back to the site and take out the other one.

When I got home I took off my boots and collapsed on the couch. Later, when I took off my T-shirt, I received quite a surprise. The web straps of the duffel bag, only 1½ inches wide with no padding, weren't designed to carry 125 pounds of clothing, let alone a rock, so they left long, angry marks all across my shoulders from my collar bone to the middle of my back. I looked like I had been whipped. There were three black, blue, and red streaks over each shoulder.

I had not felt a thing when I carried them out. But I certainly felt it the next morning. My back was fine, but the intense pain that throbbed through my feet and my shoulders burned like fire. My legs had almost locked in place and only very slowly and painfully responded to my commands to walk. But I could not stay away. I ate breakfast and had my coffee and raced back to the Robledos.

Back at the discovery site, I soon isolated the layer containing the giant tracks. The task was then a matter of following the layer, connecting my two vertical trenches that were about forty feet apart in a careful and systematic way north and south, to take out the trackway. I had no idea how long it would take me to remove it.

Fortunately, good sense replaced my emotions. How could I get this trackway out without ruining possible track-bearing layers above it? Although it might mean years of work, I had to start at the top of the trackway sediments. I had no idea where the top layer was.

I went upslope until I hit limestone. My red bed sequence rested right under it. I located the contact between the marine sediments and the terrestrial sediments. This was my top layer. It was also the youngest of the terrestrial sediments at that spot. There was nothing preserved in this layer, which seemed to be several feet thick. It was so brittle that I called it "crumbcake." I would encounter more crumbcake layers as I excavated lower and lower down the hillside.

I soon began devoting all my energies to this particular hillside, dubbed AF 2, for Abo formation 2. I traced trackways to the upper-most layer and began to work my way down. The top layer turned out to be twelve feet higher than the discovery layer. These layers had to be peeled off in succession before the big trackway could be removed.

Starting at the top proved to be my most important decision for the future of the trackways and for the protection of the deposit itself, for in the months to come I would find nine more important track-way layers and dozens of sublayers, containing the tracks and trails of as many as fifty separate species of vertebrate and invertebrate animals as well as eight different species of plants.

After sixteen months of work, I would finally be able to get the target trackway out. It would end up being twenty five feet long before the trail would turn abruptly into the mountain. More big trackways would be found on this layer: a twelve-foot trackway just to the north of the discovery trackway, and a spectacular twenty eight-foot trackway that I would find moving south to north on the other side of the discovery slabs.

Of course, I didn't know all this as I stared at my newly uncov-ered trail. But my fervent imagination guided me month after month as I worked to free these imprisoned fossils.

As I looked to my right, I saw that there could be another two hundred running feet of unexcavated tracks just waiting to be exposed. I had just scratched the surface. In short order, I became hopelessly obsessed with my work. The thrill of discovery, reenacted every day, drove me on. My experience was now united with the unbridled energy of my imagination. I was no longer after footprints. I was after my dreams about footprints.

# Chapter Four

## Changing the Diagnosis from "Interesting Curiosities" to "Discovery of the Decade"

The animals that made the tracks I was uncovering left their footprints in the mud tens of millions of years before dinosaurs dominated the earth. I wasn't sure what animals made the tracks, but judging from the anatomy of the foot as revealed through the footprint traces, they were obviously not much like either dinosaurs or the reptiles that are now indigenous to the area. I was fascinated at the prospects, whether dinosaur or not. My fascination, as well as the public's, with dinosaurs is understandable. Dinosaurs are usually the first prehistoric life a child encounters. How many preschool children have impressed grandpa and grandma with their command of dinosaur "linguistics" by rattling off the names of four or five dinosaurs? In fact, many children know much more about dinosaurs than their parents do.

I'll never forget overhearing a father educating his preschool-age son about dinosaurs at the Smithsonian's Natural History Museum. When the parent got to the massive skull at the entrance to the hall, he said, "Look, that's the skull of *Triceratops rex*." The child burst into laughter and said, "No, Daddy, that's just *Triceratops*. Only *Tyrannosaurus* wrecks [*sic*]."

These animals are so large and unique in shape that a great mystique has evolved around them. The Carnegie Museum's *Tyrannosaurus*, one of the largest in the world, is fearsome enough in its bony, deathly stance. But imagine it alive, bearing down on its quarry, snorting and chomping as it gets closer, its legs pounding up and down like pistons, before it finally snaps up its prey with its six-inch teeth.

I, too, learned quite a lot about dinosaurs in much the same fashion. Growing up near Chicago, my family often took me to the Field Museum of Natural History, and, of course, the big attraction was

Dinosaur Hall. I read and studied every book on the subject that I could get my hands on. My favorite coloring books were those with dinosaurs. My favorite movies were those with dinosaurs, including such dubious classics as *Valley of the Gwangi*, which featured a good-sized *Allosaurus*, *The Lost World*, or *When Dinosaurs Ruled the Earth*.

Each movie seemed to explore the discovery of something fantastic, usually scientists discovering live dinosaurs in some hidden valley, or on some lost island, or at the center of the earth, or on some unknown planet. The movies suggested that all of these discoveries were stumbled upon quite by accident. I decided early that I wanted to do the same thing.

If these "B" movies were not enough (and they weren't) I still had my comic books. I was weaned on the dinosaur issues of DC Comics. I especially loved the exciting dinosaur encounters found in the 1960s comic series *Star Spangled War Stories*, where America's military might could be seen battling toe to toe with the prehistoric world's mightiest denizens.

I also couldn't wait for the next issue of Dell Comics 1950s series *Turok: Son of Stone*, which took me far into the past to watch Turok and his faithful band fight an endless array of dinosaurs. Fighting a *Tyrannosaurus* with an armor-plated tank was one thing, but Turok had to fight with sticks and stones!

Such infatuation with these fantastic stories was not without its price. I became convinced at a very tender age that not only did dinosaurs and man live together, but they might still exist somewhere on earth today. At school I would often gaze at world atlas maps and note the vast green-shaded equatorial regions that stood for rain forest and jungle. "Just about anything could be living in there!"

As I grew up, my childlike impressions slowly gave way to the scientific information on dinosaurs that had accumulated by the late 1960s. Dinosaurs were seen then as gray and drab. No colorful patterns were "painted" by nature on their tough skin, no herds roamed the plains, and above all, no dinosaur was as intelligent as the mammals that followed them. Dinosaurs were sluggish and, above all, cold blooded. Few scientists portrayed them with any kind of social structure except for reproduction; otherwise their lives were characterized by eating, hunting or escaping, and dying. Consequently, to us kids, the only really interesting dinosaurs were the ones animated in Hollywood movies or in the comics.

Seeing only the skeletal remains of dinosaurs, regardless of stance, is still a view of death. It is difficult for us to picture them as living, breathing animals. The very fact that so many of them lived for such a long time suggests that these creatures were very active and lived vibrant, successful lives. We know that many dinosaurs were gregarious—their preserved footprints show us that—and that some cared for their young, as crocodiles do. For those that lived in herds or flocks, there may have been hierarchical social structures as intricate as those of birds.

The information we have comes mostly from the exhumation of skeletal remains, but also from the traces that these animals left behind when they were alive. When a paleontologist finds a skeleton, usually only a part of the animal is recovered. Great amplification is needed to get a clear picture of the animal in question. Even if a fully articulated skeleton is found—a rarity—there is still an important difference between the reconstruction of the fossil skeleton and the reconstruction of its external appearance.

Even a casual look through the reconstructions of prehistoric skeletons in the natural history museums of the United States will show that many "solutions" to the re-creation of these extinct animals are possible, and perhaps no one has the "right" one. In fact, the appearance of prehistoric beasts cannot be reconstructed on the basis of skeletal evidence alone. The hump on a camel, the trunk of an elephant, the color of the skin, the abundance or paucity of hair, scales, and feathers, the size and appearance of the ears, the presence of shrouds, hoods, or frills, and other important visual distinctions are mostly or totally lost to paleontologists. Therefore, paleontologists require a thorough knowledge of the biology of present-day animals, especially those that may resemble the extinct creatures under study, in order to make intelligent reconstructions.

That's why paleontologists also use footprints, skin impressions, and evidence of nests and of nest colonies. They have even found eggs containing embryos. In short, paleontologists have found a bit of just about everything these animals did that left a trace on the earth. These traces preserve a little of the daily activities and encounters of animals living out their lives and corroborate locomotion studies conducted primarily by studying skeletal remains.

After John Swenson and I hauled out the "discovery slab," I immediately called Thom Votaw with the news. "You have got to get over here right away," I said with a laugh. "You're not going to believe it. You're going to flip out." And he did.

"This is incredible. Absolutely incredible. What do we do now?" Thom asked with a big grin.

But Thom knew, as I did, that this slab was the tip of an iceberg of evidence that would oblige the paleontological world to reevaluate the traditional views about the quality and abundance of footprints from the Robledo Mountains. And, we knew that this was a significant paleontological find in its own right. We even dared to view these tracks in a global context. A paleontologist's life is largely devoted to discovering and comparing. I had discovered. Now it was time to compare. And that's just what Thom and I were doing right in my front yard. These two slabs had to be world class on at least one criterion alone. The tracks were so absolutely perfect, both the molds and the casts, that it was physically impossible for them to have been any better without bringing the live animal home in a cage.

I reminded Thom that I had uncovered seven more feet of trackway and that there were still another twenty or so feet to be dug. Everything needed to be documented, with photographs, videos, and recordings, to prepare a case for the significance of the Robledo trackways. Although I still could not prove the extent of the deposit, I was certainly ready to prove its quality.

I believed the evidence showed that trackways of excellent quality were locally abundant. But if the plant seam was unique to the quarry, it was entirely possible that these small footprint outcrops were unique to the Robledos. My heart sank as I thought of this possibility.

I told Thom that it was time to hunt for someone who could put a stamp of legitimacy on the slabs, someone who could support our view that this new material was immensely significant. But this would not be easy. Although there may be tens of thousands of fossil collectors around the world, trained paleontologists only number around four thousand. Of those, perhaps three hundred are vertebrate paleontologists. Of those, perhaps fifty specialize in the world of the dinosaur. Nearly all the rest work on postdinosaurian mammals. Only about a dozen are trained vertebrate paleontologists whose specialty is Paleozoic faunas. Again, out of this three hundred, there are a mere handful of trackway specialists. And there is only one paleontologist whose primary area of expertise is Paleozoic footprints. I was determined to make it two, though admittedly through the academic "back door."

It is no exaggeration to say that vertebrate paleontologists are on the endangered species list. New Mexico was fortunate to have two, but neither specialized in Paleozoic faunas or fossil tracks. Yet I did not imagine that any specialist in the broad field of earth science could gaze on these two slabs without agreeing that they were sensational specimens. I was soon to learn otherwise.

## First Impressions

I first took the slabs to the university. One scientist was impressed and quite surprised that they came from the Robledos. He suggested that with the addition of these specimens, my personal trackway collection was the "best around." Yet he seriously doubted that they had any scientific significance beyond their aesthetic beauty.

"Did you see the three slabs *we* have out in the hall by the geology labs?" he queried.

"Yes," I said, "and these slabs are a million times better than those!"

"They're better, Jerry," he said cautiously, "but not any more significant. Look, what can you or anyone else do with them? We could never find out what animal made the tracks."

I was convinced that the slabs had to possess scientific value in addition to their beauty. I could not accept the notion that I had found just nice fossils to display in a trophy case. I believed that my slabs were several orders of magnitude better than anything I had seen from the Robledos. They outshone the three slabs in the hall of the Earth Science Department. Though I certainly proved that beautiful tracks could be found in the mountains if one looked long enough, was that it? Did I want these slabs to possess scientific significance so badly that I had deluded myself? Had I lost my objectivity and insisted on their importance purely on subjective ground? For a moment, all my explorations of the last year faded in significance.

In hindsight, I can't fault the faculty member for his comments. He was probably aware of the fossil footprint phenomenon as it was perceived twenty years before. Though fossil footprints had been known to exist in various parts of the world for well over one hundred years, he probably also knew that fossil footprints had always occupied a place on the fringes of paleontology. Of all the areas of research that could be performed within the strict confines of the discipline, trackway research had almost always been the domain of well-meaning amateurs or very specialized or eccentric professionals. Indeed, fossil footprints had remained outside the mainstream for over a century, in reality ever since the first discoveries. Most vertebrate paleontologists were after the much bigger prize—skeletal remains.

Though no subdiscipline within paleontology is well funded, it is easier to get grants to hunt dinosaurs than it is to hunt their footprints. Finding prehistoric skeletons from any time period, especially skeletons that formerly belonged to a once-living dinosaur, helps to pay the rent and justifies the existence of quite a few natural history museums. Footprints were a different matter. For quite some time, there was no universally accepted manual for their study and no worldwide guidelines for classification. Footprints found in Europe had different names from the same footprints found in North America. There was virtually no cross-pollination of findings among researchers. In fact, there were hardly any researchers. There were few up-to-date research papers on fossil trackways and most scientific papers on the subject were at least fifty years old.

But willingness to accept fossil tracks as important paleontological evidence has increased considerably in the past ten years. The Robledo trackways were discovered at about the same time that fossil trackway research was experiencing dramatic new scholarly interest among professional paleontologists.

In 1986, the New Mexico Museum of Natural History hosted the first international symposium devoted entirely to fossil footprints, primarily dinosaurs. Researchers from around the world met to compare notes and devise a plan to make a universal science of fossil trackways. Such a meeting was long overdue. Even so, beyond this select group, most scientists were unaware of the advances made in analyzing footprints and their usefulness in understanding past ecosystems.

But none of this registered. All I saw at that moment, when I was in the scientist's office at NMSU, was that I had come face to face with an obstruction, a conflicting opinion about the value of my slabs. He was voicing almost verbatim the comment geologist Walter Jones wrote sixty years earlier after his study of the Alabama coal trackways: "The tracks of these ancient animals have been of little benefit to the anatomists and morphologists of the United States." When I left his office, I went to my truck and looked at the slabs again. My head cleared.

My goal in searching the mountains was to find the motherlode. This was a big first step. In and of itself that was extremely significant. I saw no reason to lower my expectations. In fact, the conversation had the opposite effect. I decided to pursue my original beliefs, even if they were wrong. Such is science . . .

## Evaluating the Find: The Road to the Smithsonian

Not long after I took my discovery slabs to NMSU, undaunted, (and probably more stubborn than ever), I decided to take the slabs and fifty photographs with me to the University of Virginia (UVA) when it was time to begin my doctoral studies in sociology. The day I arrived I met with the faculty in my department, and that afternoon I called the head of the Department of Geology and Environmental Science, Dr. Richard Mitchell. At a subsequent meeting I showed him the photographs. Though making clear his ignorance of paleontology, specifically fossil footprints, Dr. Mitchell was impressed. He invited me to a meeting of the UVA regents and supporters who were gathering to hear Dr. Noel Boaz, director of the Virginia Museum of Natural History. Boaz was speaking on the need to resurrect the old UVA Brooks Museum, which had been allowed to fall into disrepair over the years.

I was totally out of place. In the audience were some of Virginia's and Culpepper County's most influential socialites. Here I was, carrying my well-used photo album. At the end of Boaz's talk, he fielded a few questions, and when it became obvious that the museum would not be resurrected, at least not then, he sought to leave with some dispatch. Dr. Mitchell, seeing that I lacked the initiative to intercept Boaz as he sought the door, stood in his way and introduced me.

As Mitchell described my fossil find, Boaz was only minimally interested—until Mitchell mentioned the word *footprints*. Boaz's slight smile disappeared and he again tried to find the door. Mitchell pushed me forward and told me to open the photograph album. Sheepishly, I opened it to the first page. Boaz's jaw dropped. He was hooked. "Where were these found?" he asked.

As he leafed through page after page of footprints, Boaz's gaze became more studied. "Look, this is significant," he said, "but I can't really speak to its importance." He gave me the number of Robert Weems, a U.S. Geological Survey scientist who was studying fossil dinosaur footprints near Culpepper, Virginia, forty miles north of Charlottesville. "Tell Rob that you spoke to me and showed me photos of your fossil tracks," Boaz said, "and that I gave you his number. That should get you through."

That evening, I called Weems. Although he was very interested in the find, he expressed ignorance of nondinosaur tracks. "Look, you need to talk to Dr. Clayton Ray, a vertebrate fossil specialist at the Smithsonian Institution," Weems said. "If he can't tell you what you need to know about your trackways, he would certainly know who could. Tell him that you spoke to me and that I gave you his number. That should cut through the ice."

"The Smithsonian Institution!" I thought. I had to stop for a moment and re-evaluate what I was up to. For the first time, I was daunted by the possibilities. I knew that what I had found was important, but as my calls led higher and higher, I felt more and more insignificant. It took me three days to find the courage to call. When I did, I was more nervous than articulate, fumbling through descriptions of what I had found and what I thought it meant. Dr. Ray was very kind, but my search wasn't over. He gave me another name, Hans-Deiter Sues, a research fellow from Harvard University who was studying at the Smithsonian's Paleobiology Department.

"Oh great," I thought. "My trip through the stars has led me to Dr. Seuss." I called right away. Dr. Sues expressed great interest in my find, and we discussed at length how extensive an area I thought the outcrops covered. But I was still not finished making telephone calls. "I think you need to talk to Nicholas Hotton III. He's an expert in Paleozoic paleontology, which sounds like what you need. Hotton would know for sure what you have. I can't really give you an evaluation of significance that would carry the weight of Hotton's."

At this point, the thing that gave me comfort was that nobody had called me a quack, and nobody had dismissed me out of hand. Yet I struggled with some uncertainty, as I pressed on one more time.

I had no idea who Nicholas Hotton III was, but it was obvious that I was climbing the ladder of expertise with each phone call. I made the call, but only after two more days had passed. Hotton answered on the first ring. "Hotton speaking" broke the silence. It was too soon. I had no time to think. I quickly explained why I had called, but after so many explanations, the fire was gone from my voice. I was going through the description because I felt compelled to do so. I mentioned the quality, the wide diversity of tracks, the extremes of size, and the unending quantity of material still in the ground.

"Listen," he said, "do you think you could come up and see me?" I groped for words. "Could you come up tomorrow?" After explaining that I had commitments for teaching and classwork at UVA, he asked if I could come up on Sunday.

Sunday, September 6, was great for me. "Yeah, sure. Can I bring my wife and kids?"

"You betcha," Hotton bellowed. "The more, the merrier. Look, Jerry, can you come to my home? I know it's not the same as going to the Smithsonian, but I really want to take the time to see this stuff, and I'm just so swamped at the office. I want to take a really good look at what you have. I hope you don't mind."

After getting the particulars, I was off-center again. I had one shot. I had to bring everything. I took my album, my maps, and over five hundred pounds of specimens that I had carefully wrapped in plastic foam and placed in World War II ammo boxes. And I took my family.

A great sense of satisfaction filled me as we drove the 115 miles to Hotton's home. Finally, we came to the address I had written down. "This can't be it," I thought. It was so modest. I told the family to wait in the car while I checked to see if I was at the right place. I had just hit the sidewalk when the door to the house opened and a stately old gentleman stepped out.

"Are you Jerry?" he asked.

"Dr. Hotton?" I asked in return, with more puzzlement than curiosity in my voice.

I got my photo album out and opened it right there on the sidewalk. "Holy cats," Hotton exclaimed. "Boy, you've got something here." He flipped page after page, and we both forgot where we were. My family was still in the car, Hotton's door was open, and we were drooling on the sidewalk.

I opened the back of my truck and pulled out my material. My wife wondered if I loved rocks more than I loved her. My kids grew restless. "Jerry," my wife murmured with some displeasure.

"Oh, I'm sorry. This is my wife, Pearl, and my children, Noah, Justin, and Hannah." I went back to my rocks. Hotton broke my self-induced hypnosis with an invitation into his home.

That afternoon was one of the most wonderful experiences I have ever had. We drank coffee with the grounds swimming around the cup. We ate a plate full of well-done English muffins. Hotton grabbed a pen and notebook and went about classifying some of the photos. Off the top of his head he suggested that I might have as many as seventeen different vertebrate taxa represented, as well as newly discovered insect trackways.

"This is very significant," Hotton exclaimed. "It could be as good as the Coconino trackways of the Grand Canyon."

"Is that good?" I asked.

"They're considered to be the best Paleozoic trackways in the world. I should say it's good!" He puffed on his pipe.

"Would you like to keep the photos?" I asked. "I made a duplicate set."

"I thought you would never ask," was his answer.

"What I need from you, Dr. Hotton . . ."

"Nick. Call me Nick."

"Okay, what I need from you, Nick, is a written opinion of the significance of the collection and suggestions for what I could do with the discovery area."

I still had little idea who Nicholas Hotton III was. "Do you think the Smithsonian would be interested in this find?" I asked, as if the Smithsonian was personified in one person. I wasn't far off, I found out later. I had spent a Sunday with him.

"Jerry, look," Hotton said as he puffed on his pipe. "If I'm interested, the Smithsonian's interested. Believe me. Of course, I'm biased toward the Paleozoic," Nick continued, "but what you've found may rival in significance for the Paleozoic the work Jack Horner is doing in Montana in the Mesozoic with baby dinosaurs and nests. Jack's discovery was the highpoint of the 1970s, and yours might be the best of the 1980s, the discovery of the decade." Later, Hotton would tell the press the same thing.

My hunt for a kindred spirit was over. I had made it to the top. As research curator for the Paleobiology Department of the Smithsonian's Natural History Museum, Hotton's opinion wielded great authority in such matters.

When I got home I called Thom in Las Cruces. "Thom, are you sitting down?" I began. "You know that I went to see a Smithsonian paleontologist today. I brought photos and a lot of specimens." I tried to feign disappointment. "Well, I showed them to an expert in the Permian." Without a change in my voice, I said, "He thinks that they could be the best Paleozoic trackways ever found anywhere in the world. What do you think?"

We were so excited we could hardly stand it. We were amazed that discoveries of this magnitude could still be found today in the United States, particularly so close to a major population center. This rich fossil fauna was lying undisturbed so close to the city and university that we were hard pressed to believe that it had remained undiscovered for so long. It was as if there were dozens of people sitting outside the door. More people walked past the door every day. It seemed impossible that no one had checked to see if it was open. Now it was open, and I was ready to rush through it.

# CHAPTER FIVE

## From "Discovery of the Decade" to "Best in the World"

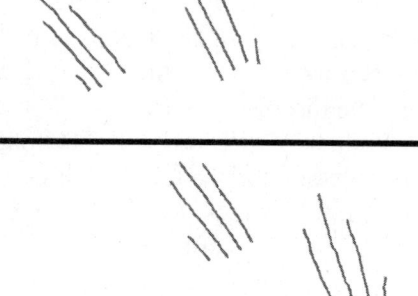

Three apprehensive months after I showed Nick Hotton the material I had collected, his evaluation was complete. There it was one morning in my mailbox, a business envelope on Smithsonian letterhead. I knew immediately what it was. Had he changed his mind about the significance of the discovery? I was so nervous that I hesitated to open it. I was particularly interested in Hotton's comparisons to the Grand Canyon Coconino trackways. After all, most of the Gilmore collection was stored in a line of cabinets right next door to his office.

The opening paragraph said it all:

Dear Jerry:

[I] recall sharply the excitement I felt upon looking at parts of your collection for the first time, for the collection is most impressive. The quality of the material is excellent, and your locality must at least be as rich as any Late Paleozoic footprint locality thus far reported, including the classic ones of the Grand Canyon worked by C. W. Gilmore many years ago. Last, but by no means least, your procedures for collecting and documentation of the material conform to the most up-to-date professional standards.

The material collected so far is highly significant from the point of view of biology, both in the diversity of the preserved biota and in the quality of the trackways, [and] . . . I am confident that most of the Early Permian terrestrial tetrapods with which I am familiar are present. . . . All of these groups are represented by trackways good enough to allow analysis of stride length and gait, which provides access, heretofore lacking, to the locomotor behavior of nearly the whole spectrum of Early Permian terrestrial tetrapods.

A variety of arthropod trackways are also abundant, which I find interesting as evidence of food supply for the smaller and more lizard-like tetrapods, and also because we are finding arthropod body fossils associated with tetrapods in the Early Permian [sediments] of Texas. Plant fossils include the common Early Permian conifer *Walchia*, and at least one other plant I am not paleobotonist enough to identify, but the occurrence of these organisms with well-preserved tetrapod trackways is rather unusual.

Sedimentological evidence indicates that your locality preserves an essentially terrestrial facies. Many of the surfaces upon which the trackways were impressed are marked by raindrops, mud cracks . . . and were subaerial at the time the trackways were made. . . .

In summary, I think the exploitation of your Las Cruces locality will prove of great scientific value. Expressing my personal bias, I've already noted its potential for the study of the locomotor behavior in Permian tetrapods, but I think also its potential for sedimentology and taphonomy are equally great.

. . . I have no doubt that if properly cared for, your material will remain of value to the paleontological community for a long time to come.

I have discussed these matters with Dr. David S. Berman, of the Carnegie Museum of Natural History, Pittsburgh, who has done a lot of work on the vertebrate paleontology of the Abo, and he concurs with me on the importance of continuing work in your locality. In it he finds no conflict with his own activity, and would be interested in hearing more of your plans and progress.

It was all there. He had put it in writing on Smithsonian letterhead. Does paleontology get any more exiting than this? I rushed in to tell my wife the news. I read the letter again as Pearl read it for the first time.

"Oh look, Jerry," Pearl exclaimed. "He complimented you on your methods. See, I told you it would be okay."

"I know, I can't believe it," I replied, hugging her. "I just want to do this whole thing right."

The letter included the names of a panoply of Early Permian animals, only a couple of which I knew. I reached for my books to look up a number of genera, only to find one or two sentences on each. Many of the species were not even listed. It was here that I began to see how lonely this whole project could get. The sections on Permian vertebrates that I was able to find in a number of good books were from a paragraph to a page in length, whereas whole chapters were devoted to dinosaurs. But it didn't matter. I had found Nick Hotton.

Hotton brought David Berman into the picture. Nearly one-half of the experts on Paleozoic vertebrates in the American Southwest were now aware of my discovery. I fell asleep later that night with the letter in my hand.

In a subsequent phone call, Hotton again informed me that he had discussed the discovery with David Berman of the Carnegie Museum. Berman was the only paleontologist working on Early Permian sediments in New Mexico, and he had been doing so for over twenty years. Berman picked up where his mentor, Dr. Peter Vaughn, had left off many years earlier. Hotton wanted to find out if Berman was aware of the area and if not, to inform him of its potential not only for paleontology in general, but for his own research interests. Hotton reported that Berman was anxious to see specimens and photographs at my earliest convenience. A trip to the Carnegie was now on the schedule.

I sent a copy of the Smithsonian evaluation to Thom, who began working in Las Cruces to gather additional support. He made contact with former astronaut Frank Borman, who lived in the area. Borman was a member of the board of directors of the National Geographic Society. Thom and I hoped that perhaps he would be interested in a discovery of this magnitude here in his own hometown.

Borman agreed to report the significance of the discovery to the National Geographic Society. This led to a meeting with National Geographic in Washington, D.C. Present at the meeting, in addition to me, were Nick Hotton, Thomas Canby, science editor for *National Geographic*, and William Allen, illustrations editor.

We met at the Cosmos Club, one of Washington's finest restaurants on the mall. While we wined and dined, Hotton explained the significance of the discovery and how it should be of interest to the National Geographic Society. They agreed to keep close tabs on the discovery for a possible report in an upcoming issue of the magazine and encouraged us to apply for a research grant from the society.

As we got up to leave the club, I reached for my briefcase, while the others reached for theirs. Everybody got his but me. Somehow, my briefcase had been stolen. Everything that had been in it was nicely placed on the shelf, but the briefcase itself was gone. We joked about why someone would steal mine rather than those of *National Geographic* or Smithsonian personnel. I couldn't help but wonder if the thief had examined the contents and subsequently left them because he turned out to be someone else who was not interested in tracks.

## The Paranoia of Secrecy

During my first semester at the University of Virginia, I was filled with apprehension. I was two thousand miles away from the Robledo Mountains, and though I had told only a handful of people in New Mexico of the discovery, I was extremely concerned for the safety of the site and the fossils. My reconnaissance work had exposed several track-bearing layers in place, and I was worried that they might be too visible and thus in danger of being weathered, exploited, or vandalized.

To safeguard the locality and the fossils, and to document further discoveries, Thom and I had gone to a couple of track-bearing localities in the Robledos, including the place I had found the big tracks, and taken videos of the way the hillsides looked before an excavation took place. With video camera rolling, I did some preliminary work at two different sites, one near the quarry and another farther up the canyon. In short order, I uncovered another big track on a slab near the surface. There was no question that the hillside was packed full of tracks and trackways, stacked one on another for an undetermined height.

Other than the two small test holes I had just recently enlarged, the only evidence of excavation work was the edge of the discovery layer I had exposed for about forty feet. Though no tracks were visible there, I was terrified that someone else might pull out a slab from this newly exposed layer, as I had, and find pay dirt. At least the videotape would show us if anyone had worked the area since the discovery.

My nights in Virginia were nerve racking. I had visions of collectors roaming the Robledos searching for tracks. I frequently called Thom for reports on any activity in the area. Thom visited the hillsides several times throughout the year and confirmed that there was no sign of activity, that the area was still virtually untouched. It would stay that way for another year and a half.

But I had another worry. A reporter from the *Las Cruces Sun News* had heard a rumor that I had made a significant discovery in the Las Cruces area, and like a pesky fly in my face, he was determined to break the story to the public, whether I was present or not. This was the last thing I wanted. The reporter called me constantly—at home, at my office in the Sociology Department, even in the computer lab. But I would not budge.

The significance of the material made it essential that we report the occurrence to the Bureau of Land Management, on whose land the first tracks had been found. We had to inform the federal government of the discovery as soon as possible. I could perform no additional work without its approval.

What I wanted to do was significantly different from what everyone else had been doing in the area for years. I proposed to ask the government for permission to systematically excavate tracks from the Robledo red beds, something no one had ever done before.

The Robledos had always been a fossil lover's paradise, and every organization, from the Girl Scouts and gem societies to kindergarten classes, took collecting trips into the Robledos seven days a week. The BLM knew that. All the collecting was harmless. Armed with rock picks and backpacks, sometimes thirty or more people at one time could be seen hunting for invertebrate fossils. It would do me little good to go to the BLM and cry wolf until I was certain that I had found the flock.

The BLM had never been informed of the occurrence of fossils in the terrestrial sediments of the Robledos. It was operating under the assumption that no fossils of significance could be found in the area. I had to change that opinion dramatically, but had no idea how they would view my discovery in the face of these traditional views. Would they agree with our opinions, that the deposit was important, or would they side with locals who thought it was not?

We had to convince the BLM, the only agency that could issue an excavation permit, that the door to the Paleozoic world in the Robledos was unlocked, but we had to do it right in front of everybody else who believed that the door was locked. There I was, in the middle of a hopeless double-bind. Somebody was going to look foolish either way it went.

I felt I had to give the BLM all the evidence I could muster. Thom made the first overtures. Armed with information gathered from our talks together, as well as with the Smithsonian evaluation, he began the process of securing a permit, but not without plenty of worries.

For one thing, once a permit is filed, the information enters public domain, where it can be accessed by anyone. In the permit is information on exactly where the work is to be done, complete with maps and diagrams, and the specific material that the excavation is designed to uncover. It also lists who is involved in the work and which institutions will house any specimens collected.

We wondered about the language we should use in the permit application so as not to compromise the safety of the trackways. We thought we might work with the BLM to give the purpose of the excavation as sedimentary research. Our strategy was that, in a sense, trackways are not fossils at all. They are not the remains of vertebrate or invertebrate bodies. They are not bones, skin, or other animal parts that become fossilized. Footprints are sedimentary features or "traces," and though they are direct results of the life activities of an animal, they are not the remains of the animal itself. By listing them as sedimentary features within the body of the permit, we could protect the nature of the material from those few individuals who might harm the site or the material.

Moreoever, we were concerned that once the significance of the fossils was reported to the BLM, collection of the material might be immediately hindered if not curtailed altogether, because the BLM did not have track protection guidelines and would need time to develop them. Such an overreaction could delay or prevent the excavation that was needed to bring to light the incredible paleontological riches of the Robledo Mountains. It had happened before with other discoveries and we were hoping that it would not happen here.

We were also concerned that the New Mexico BLM might be so undermanned that it would not be able to provide adequate security for the discovery area. It was suggested that a mineral claim, rather than a paleontological permit, might be more appropriate.

Problems of federal protection often center around the fact that the BLM mandate to protect national treasures is generally reactive rather than predictive. Consequently, it can only respond professionally once it is informed of an occurrence. It does not usually employ professionals whose sole task is to look for such occurrences.

The BLM is often dependent on others conscientious or honest enough to bring such valuable information to its attention. Significantly, this never happened before. We had no quibble with the way the BLM had opened the Robledos for public use, but we knew that everything was likely to change once we reported the find to the agency.

As we expected, the BLM told us that they had never been informed of trackways or fossil plants within the Robledo Range. They were very aware of the abundance of marine fossils from the area, but our presentation about the significance of non-marine fossils found in the same area caught the agency by surprise. Naturally, they wondered why such an occurrence had not been reported years earlier. They had a hard time understanding why in-state professionals did not see the fossils as significant enough to report while out-of-staters saw them as paleontologically priceless. The BLM staff argued that if such occurrences had been brought to their attention during the process of opening the rock quarry in the late 1960s, they would have chosen an alternate site.

Then came the bad news. Since we were now on the subject of the rock quarry, we had to tell them that a significant fossil plant layer had been obliterated by earth movers in that same quarry. It happened a long time ago, several people knew of its existence, and no one had been in a position to save it. Worse than that, the plant layer appeared to be unique, found only within the confines of the pit.

The context of the discovery was confusing and embarrassing, to say the least. A single four-inch track from the Robledos was on exhibit at the New Mexico Natural History Museum in Albuquerque. One nice plant slab from the now-destroyed layer from the quarry was also on display. The museum evidently had no idea that there was a possibility of *significant* trackway material in the area. The museum generally assumed that those two specimens on display represented the best that could be found in the Robledos. The museum was probably also unaware that several houses and exterior walls in Las Cruces put the museum specimens to shame, with literally dozens of spectacular slabs built into them. This lack of knowledge regarding the footprints left the trackway picture confusing and set the stage for a potential political mess.

After constructive preliminary meetings with BLM officials in December 1987 which included both Thom Votaw and me, the required forms were filed and subsequently approved in the spring of 1988. We fully revealed both the evaluations of the significance of the tracks and our expectations once the work was under way.

The reconnaissance material suggested to us all that it was definitely in everyone's best interest that the deposit be more fully explored. With the enthusiastic support of the BLM and their thanks that the fossils had finally been evaluated and reported to them, the stage was set for the systematic excavation of these long-hidden treasures.

## On to the Carnegie Museum

In February 1988, I went to see Dr. David Berman at the Carnegie Museum. As Dr. Berman and I discussed the potential of the trackway material, Dr. Mary Dawson, head of the Earth Sciences Department at the Carnegie, entered Berman's office.

"Mary, you have to see this," Berman said. "These are some of the . . . no, these *are* the best fossil footprints I have ever seen."

A short time after this meeting, Berman submitted his evaluation of the Robledo trackway assemblage and its potential. He sent one copy to me and one to Nick Hotton at the Smithsonian:

It is my estimation that this is probably one of the most outstanding fossil trackway localities ever discovered for vertebrate and invertebrate animals in terms of quantity, quality, and variety.

The great variety of trackways provides the best opportunity available to obtain a regional census of the animal life during the Early Permian in south-central New Mexico. The great variety of trackways clearly indicates that this sort of information is only very partially realized by the preservation of skeletal remains, particularly in the case of invertebrates. This locality will undoubtedly not only allow a more precise estimation of diversity, but also possibly the relative numbers or abundance of species, both of which are basic information for determining population or trophic structure.

The trackway impressions are extremely well defined and will yield considerable anatomical detail. They also offer the most direct evidence of an animal's gait, stride, and posture and the range of locomotor capabilities. Unique insights into aspects of the social behavior or activities will undoubtedly be obtained by study of the trackways.

. . . As the identification of the vertebrate species that made the trackways progresses, not only will we have a better knowledge of some of their distribution patterns during the Early Permian, but of the possible role [that] physical barriers, such as water, topography, or climate, [had] in influencing faunal distributions or dispersals.

Mr. MacDonald has employed modern professional procedures and standards in the excavation and care of the trackway, despite the very arduous work required under what must be extremely uncomfortable conditions.

In summary, Mr. Jerry Paul MacDonald's discovery will undoubtedly yield very significant scientific returns. This project should, therefore, be given every encouragement to succeed.

A short time later, further comments on the Robledo collection were received from Mary Dawson:

We are most enthusiastic about the progress of your project on the fossil trackway . . . of New Mexico. We have received glowing reports about your discoveries. The information you have gathered is of very high scientific importance. Many of the animals found in the area will come to be known only by their footprints. This discovery will provide the only record to the existence of many new species.

I was beside myself. On the one hand, I still couldn't believe the significance of what I had uncovered. On the other, I knew the responsibility this put on my shoulders. I called Thom from Virginia with the news. We were both overwhelmed with excitement. And Thom is not one usually given to overt displays of emotion.

"Thom, we've got to get a few people together at your end and tell them the news. We've got to get going on this thing right away," I said.

## Sociology or Paleontology: Siamese Twins?

As soon as I could, I invited my Ph.D. advisor at UVA, Jeffrey K. Hadden, to the house and showed him the vast array of footprints I had stacked in my living room. It was the first time he had ever seen fossil footprints. In fact, he didn't know they existed. He asked me what I was doing in the Sociology Department. "If I was sitting on this find," Hadden began, "I would be back in New Mexico excavating it. The Sociology Department will always be here, but you don't have all the time in the world to spend on those footprints."

I think it was obvious to many faculty members that my ever-growing preoccupation with paleontology was affecting my performance in the department. I was almost entirely preoccupied with my track research, which left very little time for anybody else's. I was spending more time writing research reports for museums than writing reports for my classes. This was not fair to the department and it alienated a few faculty members.

When word of the Carnegie evaluation came in, some faculty members felt awkward about the discovery and about my role as a sociologist. At a couple of faculty/student gatherings I was introduced jokingly as a paleontologist masquerading as a sociologist. There was a certain irony in this. Back in Las Cruces I was probably labeled as a sociologist masquerading as a paleontologist. Regardless of the labels, it had become clear that I had to devote myself to one or the other. It was inevitable that I eventually had to talk to the Sociology Department head, Dr. Donald Black.

Black started off by suggesting that I was an academic bigamist. He was quite serious. I was in love with two disciplines, sociology and paleontology. I had to say good-bye to one of them.

"This so-called discovery is a big black box," I remember him saying to me. "You're gambling that you know precisely what's inside. But you don't. You're only guessing. Here you know for sure what to expect. I think you're wasting your time with this. Why don't you give it over to someone with the time and expertise to do it? I mean, that's what those people are trained to do. Or am I missing something here?"

A few moments of silence finally ended with some questions of my own. "Are you saying that sociology is for sociologists and paleontology is for paleontologists? Your own research has never been so provincial. You use archaeological data as well as information from any and every scientific discipline you can find if it's useful to you. Aren't you the one who has said that everything in the entire world can fall under the studied eye of the sociologist? Pure science is for scientists, and that's what I am." It took a while, but he finally smiled.

"Then wait," Dr. Black answered. "It's been in the ground for, as you say, one hundred million to two hundred million years or whatever. What is two more years going to do? They're not going to sink into the ocean or evaporate into thin air, are they?"

"This discovery will not wait," I replied. "I am enough of a sociologist to know that it's likely that there are a few others who have thought along the same lines I have. I've put a lot of effort into this project, and I can't leave it half done. Too many people have left things half done and have lost everything. I know that if I don't work these fossils, no one will."

I think he realized that I would not be dissuaded. He shook his head and smiled and said, "Take good notes. Write everything down—dates, people you have talked to, places, everything. If you really believe you can, then work as a paleontologist, but think as a sociologist. Everything that happens will be useful. Look for valuable sociological information everywhere. In everything. City reactions, community responses, museum involvement. How they work together, how they don't. If you ever plan to do an ethnographic study on your work in paleontology, then you're going to have to be as intellectually alert as you can possibly be."

Black probably wondered what kind of monster he had hesitantly sent out into the world, but I had heard what I needed. There was no turning back now. The merger made perfect sense to me. The science of studying the footprints of prehistoric animals is called paleoichnology. The science of studying the collective activities of humans, their "social footprints," is called sociology. Human activity often leaves very clear social footprints. With training, those prints can be found and subsequently analyzed. If you're really good at it, you can see the social "trackways" of others down specific organizational paths and predict future behavior.

I saw the connection between physical and social footprints right away. If anything, sociology trained me to have another perspective. A sociologist worth his or her salt never takes anything for granted. Sociologists are also trained to try and avoid value judgments. We write down in great detail the mechanics of the social system or phenomenon that we have set out to study. I was convinced that the merger of the two disciplines would strengthen my pursuit of the project. No one else was quite so sure.

Although Jeff Hadden had already encouraged me to take a leave of absence to pursue the discovery, and Dr. Black had begrudgingly agreed, I needed advice from Nicholas Hotton as well. In early 1988, I made another trip to the Smithsonian. In some respects, I was hoping to hear from Nick that I was out of my element. I was thinking that he would give me a pat on the back for bringing these fossils to the attention of the paleontological community and then tell me it was time to move aside and let the big boys take over. He might even suggest that I could ruin the site if I started to excavate.

I was determined to follow his recommendations, whatever they were. My family and I met Hotton at his museum office. I brought some new specimens for him to look at, and we spent time looking at the earlier material. The family took a tour of the "bone room" and then went out to the museum. Nick and I sat down for a chat.

I confessed academic bigamy.

"Oh, brother," he said with a chuckle. "I think we can all confess to that." Hotton was educated at the University of Chicago before teaching anatomy at the University of Kansas. He joined the staff at the Smithsonian's Natural History Museum in 1959, where he has stayed ever since.

I explained in some detail my present situation at UVA. When I went back to school in the fall of 1982, I tried to get my degrees as fast as I could. I got my bachelor's degree in three years and continued my brisk pace into graduate school, getting my master's degree in a year and a half. I worked so hard because I felt that I had to make up for a decade of inactivity. I never stopped for air. I jumped right into the doctoral program at UVA in the fall of 1987, four years after starting college as a freshman.

Now, I confessed that I was working on my doctorate without the dedication that had characterized my previous academic endeavors. My heart was somewhere else—out in the remote mountains of New Mexico. My mind? My mind refused to respond to rigorous academics. I couldn't read a book. I couldn't think. And I definitely couldn't relax.

Being one who valued the credibility and seasoning of academics, Nick could not disregard the importance of pursuing my Ph.D., but he asked me what I really wanted to do. I was honest.

"I do want to get my Ph.D.," I began. "I love sociology. But I really want the chance to work the fossil site. I feel a real calling to do so. I do not believe that at this point I can concentrate on my studies when a whole new world lies just beyond the horizon. I have to go back. No matter what it takes, I have to go back."

"I was afraid you would say that," Nick chuckled.

I felt that I could get a lot done when I was motivated. I told Hotton that my zeal was now centered squarely on the excavation of those fossil tracks. I knew that if I didn't bring those fossils to the attention of the scientific community, nobody would. I was willing to work in the desert sun for as long as it took to adequately explore the magnitude of what was laying there just below the surface. "Do you believe that I can do it, Nick?" I asked.

Without hesitation, he said, yes. "You've already been doing it. You've done more than anyone else. After all, you're here, aren't you?"

Hotton offered his full support. He would counsel and advise me, supervise my work, offer to be in charge of the specimens collected, and pursue funding for the excavation. I was tremendously excited. A prehistoric mystery was about to unravel. I had found a door to the Paleozoic, and I was about to walk through it to another world. I was no longer in a double bind. I would finally be able to devote all of my energies to the uncovering of this prehistoric community. I could now study everything I could get my hands on that related to these mysterious animals and the rock tomb that encased them.

In the next few months, the locality itself slowly began to speak to me, whispering secrets held hostage for countless millennia. I began to view the layers as pages of a book, and I developed the ability to read the trackway slabs and layers. With my mind's eye I began to understand the dynamics of my 280-million-year-old community.

Worlds did collide. The worlds of past and present, of amateur and professional, of faculty and student, of participant and observer. The unbridled energy spun from my obsessions with *finding* the motherlode were now transferred to *understanding* the motherlode. To do this, I had to learn a new language. The earth itself would be my teacher.

# CHAPTER SIX

## The Robledo Mountains: Window to the Past

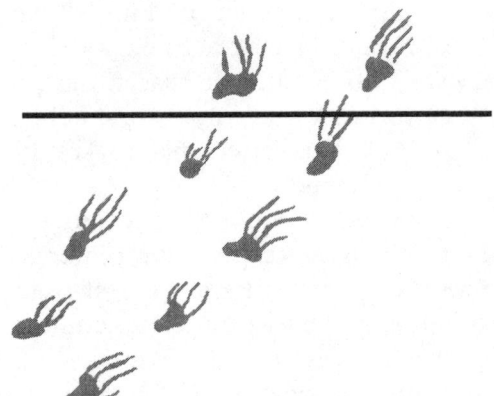

I didn't know exactly what was inside the ancient doorway I had found, but I anticipated that there would be layer upon layer of sensational material. With such an exciting beginning, I now viewed the prior collection history of the Robledo Range as an insignificant chapter in the paleontological history of the area. I fully expected that the unexcavated layers would be just as spectacular as my reconnaissance material suggested.

Hotton was stretching his expectations just a bit to accommodate me. He was a seasoned paleontologist with decades of experience in the field. He knew Paleontological Field Rule 5 all too well: Sometimes the first fossils found become the last fossils found. Years later he would tell me that he wanted to caution me just a bit about my expectations, but felt that such a reminder might quench my enthusiasm.

What fueled my own expectations was in part my background in sociology—specifically, that all life shares the same basic needs and dwells together in some kind of community. Whether human, lower vertebrate, or insect, or some exotic panoply of animals that haven't existed for 280 million years, all life needs an ample food supply, access to water, shelter and/or a home territory, freedom to rest, and socialization. Socialization can run the gamut from simple association of pairs strictly for purposes of reproduction, to more intricate collective behaviors, not all of them sexual, within species. The more members of a species that congregate and the longer the association, the more complex the interactions within the group. This assumption was the basis of my quest for an Early Permian community. But what kind of community would I find?

Strictly speaking, ecological communities have little in common with social communities. Social communities consist of a single species and are characteristic of gregarious organisms in which levels are defined by agonistic (competitive) behavior among cospecifics, like the human species. Ecological communities, on the other hand, consist of numerous species that live in such a limited area that they are all effected by the same physical conditions. Levels are distinguished trophically, defined more or less by who eats whom.

Perhaps a prehistoric *colony* is a better term for what I was searching. A colony can mean several things, most of which are appropriate in this context. A colony can be a transplanted group from one state to another that is still subject to the laws of the parent state. This is a perfect description of the emerging amphibian population I had recently uncovered. A colony can also be defined as an isolated population, free from the influences of surrounding groups. This would certainly apply if evolution was free to adapt and specialize within an isolated population, such as within the barriers surrounding Australia or the now arid deserts of China, but was highly unlikely within the confines of the once extensive Robledos shoreline.

At any rate, in the Early Permian there is no evidence of collective cospecific behaviors beyond the minimal required for reproduction. Still, my hope was to find a limited area frequented by a wide variety of animal life, and in the process, determine whether the animals of the Early Permian, at least in this little corner of the world, were gregarious or not. And were they expansive or isolative? Forward moving or mired in the present? This community (or colony) could be the result of a variety of factors, some organic and some inorganic, such as abundant food supply, availability of water, or simple topographical features that constrained travel routes. Emphasizing food supply, I had come to view this hypothetical community as a cafeteria, an Early Permian restaurant; yet, it was quite a restaurant since the patrons were engaged in eating each other!

Prior sedimentological research indicated a shore or near-shore environment presumably suitable for inhabitants of terrestrial (and semi-aquatic) lowland ecosystems. Perhaps one of these shoreline remnants, now seen as an isolated red bed outcrop within this marine/non-marine transitional zone, may preserve an inlet, lagoon, or creek that might be the perfect setting for the hypothetical restaurant. If for no other reason, this concept helped to focus my search on a potential paleontological goal—the sampling of an Early Permian ecosystem, where the maximum number of species came together.

I imagined myself as an archaeologist who had found the outline of a lost city. Somewhere under the earth would be a bakery, a library, perhaps a school, almost certainly a temple of some sort, as well as a cemetery and, with luck, treasure. But then again, the archaeologist might be unlucky and excavate a big empty space, like a parking lot or a basketball court.

Prior research suggested that under this expanse of Robledo territory would be the remnants of a variety of coastal environments, ranging from fully deltaic habitats to supratidal and tidal settings, lagoonal deposits, ponds, streams and rivers, and the kinds of vegetation that thrived in this varied shoreline habitat. But I was after a big hypothetical prize, a prehistoric restaurant, complete with a menu.

## Earth's Encyclopedias

The initial discovery encouraged us to hope that I had uncovered what some like to call a "window into the past," a paleoecological deposit that would preserve information on a large slice of life as it existed 280 million years ago.

Technically speaking, paleontologists call such a find a "lagerstatt," a German word which means "place of deposit," but in miner's jargon it has come to signify "motherlode." In paleontology, a lagerstatt signifies a fossil deposit which is extraordinary in the quality of preservation, the diversity of organisms represented, and the abundance of material, or all three. As things turned out, the Robledo trackways qualify as a lagerstatt in all of the above criteria.

One could argue that any good trackway assemblage is a lagerstatt because it shows what a variety of animals were doing at a given moment in the past. From this, scientists can determine who was associated with whom when they were alive and thus infer something of the dynamics of the food pyramid. One can see the actual substrate that the animals walked on, what plants grew when these activities took place, and perhaps even the proximity to water at the time. This is in contrast to a body fossil lagerstatt, which shows little more than what the organisms looked like and how they happened to be preserved.

Many famous lagerstätte, or windows to the past, are notable for the preservation of fossils like insects, plants, eggs, and other small and subtle clues into the lost worlds they represent. Small and subtle can be as beautiful in the world of fossils as it is in the world of the living. The famous dinosaur nest sites in Montana discovered by Jack Horner (now at the Museum of the Rockies) is an example of a window into the Late Cretaceous. It has taught us volumes that would have never been learned simply by the discovery and excavation of another large dinosaur skeleton.

Lagerstätte as windows or entryways is an idea that appeals to me. When I think of a paleontological window, I like to think of what is revealed to the one peering through it. The object is to see what's on the other side. The bigger the window, the better the view. I see such a window as a crawl space into a gigantic reference library, for humans are not the only ones that write books. The earth does, too. The layers of rock that make up our planet are like the pages of a huge encyclopedia, and much of earth's history is recorded in the rocks somewhere on earth. With such an entryway opened into earth's private library on the Paleozoic, I couldn't help but climb through. Once inside, we can interpret and reconstruct the past by uncovering and studying those pages.

But earth's books are written in a variety of languages. Time, for example, is written in radioactivity, and position is written in magnetism. Radioactive elements occur in component minerals of many igneous rocks and some sedimentary rocks. These elements break down at a constant rate, and when the breakdown product remains with the parent element, the ratio between the two provides an estimate of the actual time elapsed since the rock was formed. Many kinds of rocks contain magnetic minerals, which tend to become oriented to the earth's magnetic field as the rocks are being emplaced (igneous) or deposited (sedimentary). By studying this orientation, scientists can determine how and where the rocks lay at the time they were being formed, and from that they can infer the position of the land masses on which the rocks lay. In some cases, they can even tell when the rocks were formed from the magnetic properties of their minerals.

Most of earth's books are written in the language of sedimentary rocks and the fossils they contain. Sedimentary rocks are formed by the destruction of other rocks and redeposition of the derived materials. These processes can be chemical, by the solution and precipitation of lime or salt; mechanical, by the breaking-up of silicates to form pebbles, sand, or silt; or both, by the destruction of silicates to form mud or clay. Because the primary agency of all of these processes is water, deposition of sedimentary rocks entails transport of the contained sediments, and because water supports life, deposition of sediments often traps the remains of living things as fossils.

Sedimentary deposits can accumulate in the ocean (marine), in rivers and along their banks during floods (fluvial), or in lakes and ponds (lacustrine or paludal). They can vary in thickness from just a few thin layers to thousands of layers stacked one on top of another for thousands of feet. Contained fossils, both body and trace, commonly provide the clearest indication of the circumstances of deposition. The quality of the preservation of such body or trace fossils may vary considerably depending on a multiplicity of factors, including how quickly the fossils were buried and how much damage and deterioration they sustained prior to final burial.

Sedimentary deposits can also accumulate on dry land through the agency of wind (aeolian), though this is much less common than transportation and deposition by water.

Trace fossils such as footprints can only be recorded on sedimentary rocks that are as fine and impressionable as potter's clay, or in the case of large tracks, as coarse as pebble concrete. Obviously, the finer the substrate, the finer the imprint, especially of small animals, and particularly of invertebrates. Very large animals generally leave imprints too deep to hold their shape in fine-grained mud, especially if it is very wet. So coarse-grained sands will generally preserve sizable imprints better. Most settings producing body fossils are low-energy, sub-aqueous deposits—such as deep water marine environments, sheltered lagoons, river bends, and oxbow lakes. Track-bearing deposits of significant size are still poorly defined and understood because they have not been studied until very recently.

Ancient climates are also written in the language of sedimentary rocks through chemical processes, because many sedimentary processes are climate related. Deposition of lime most commonly takes place in the sea at warm temperatures, while deposition of salt takes place near shore under hot, arid conditions. The colder the climate, the slower the chemical processes, so that mechanical processes predominate in mountains and polar areas. Utilizing these sources of information, earth scientists reconstruct ancient climates from the distribution of limestones, salt beds, red clastic sediments, and coal deposits. Fossil tree rings also demonstrate seasonal climates, most commonly wet-dry seasonality, and the relative thickness of succeeding rings can be useful in determining the prevalence of drought conditions.

Additionally, certain fossil species occur only in specific layers of rock, from which it is deduced that they are restricted to limited time periods. In other words, the life expectancy of any species is limited; there is a time in which they come into being and a later time when they become extinct. A distinctive species of a relatively short but clearly defined time span, which is abundant over a broad area, has all the characteristics necessary for an index fossil. Being distinctive, it is easily recognized; being short-lived, it marks a limited time interval; and by being abundant it permits recognition of that time interval wherever it is found. Such fossils are called index fossils because they work in the same way as an index in a book. Index fossils provide an index to the history of the earth in much the same way as a chronology of kings provides an index to the history of a political entity.

Finally, present physical evidence can be read by specialists to determine a broad range of past terrestrial events and conditions, including glacial activity, volcanic eruptions, ocean levels, drainage patterns, shorelines, climates and environments, directions of prevailing winds, locations of oil and gas deposits, and water tables. It can also imply such astronomical phenomenon as changes in the length of earth's day, past speeds of the earth's rotation, and distance changes to the earth's moon. Earth scientists can also calculate rates of continental drift, reconstruct bombardment events by meteors and comets, estimate how much debris existed in past atmospheres, identify past magnetic field reversals, wobbles in the earth's rotation, and locate previous positions of the earth's magnetic poles.

All of this information and more can be found within earth's global encyclopedia. In many cases, the entries are very specific and cover a whole range of earth processes. But the problem is with the languages. The challenge is to train detectives who can decode these ancient languages.

Earth scientists often view these encyclopedias as published editions within certain time frames, compendiums covering specific periods and events in earth history such as extinctions and radiations, or "explosions" of life. As scientists study the history of life on earth, certain evolutionary themes and episodes begin to emerge, and the impact of these episodes on the history of earth is studied. Modern paleontology has been able to identify with considerable reliability the boundaries that define the emergence and decline of these evolutionary themes or episodes.

Sedimentary layers are in general like the pages of a book lying upside down on the floor. In a book, page one is the oldest because it is the first one written, and the author has numbered each new page in sequence. In a cross-section of the earth's book, the bottom sedimentary layers, like the first pages of a book, are the oldest, having been laid down first, and successively higher layers are progressively younger. Earth's most recently completed page is found on top of all the others and is representative of the soil you use in your gar-

sand you walk over at the beach, and the rock you sit on to fish along the river. The similarity of both writing methods is in the use of sequence and continuity.

Because earth scientists live on top of the youngest layer, they have to start translating at the top of the sequence and work backward to the beginning. The first steps in their translation are the identification of rock types encountered in the section under study, and if there are any fossils found in the sedimentary layers, which would then lead to the recognition of long-term or large-scale changes within the series. Such major changes are those of local environments from sea to coastline to mountains and back as determined by the study of rock types, and the origins and extinctions of life forms as determined by the study of fossils. It is evidence of major changes, more than individual layers, that make up the pages and chapters of earth's geological book.

It must be emphasized that changes in the physical environment are two-way changes, while those wrought in living things by evolution and extinction are strictly one way. Mountains are heaved up by tectonic forces in one cycle, only to be worn down to near sea level by erosion in the next, and coast lines commonly founder into shallow seas while the bottoms of shallow seas are heaved up into land surfaces. This happens over and over again. But evolving groups of organisms, once extinct, never come back, and those which replace them, though related, are different in anatomical detail. This contrast is all important in recognizing temporal sequence. The conditions produced in rocks by mountain building are the same whether the mountain building took place three hundred million or three million years ago. And without fossils one cannot tell which was earlier and which later, or in some cases whether or not they were contemporaneous. But if fossils are present in the rocks affected by mountain building, the older fossils will be different from the younger. By referring to the backlog of knowledge of the fossil record generally, it is easy to tell which event was the earlier and which the later.

In contrast to evidence of large-scale change, individual layers commonly accumulate in large numbers without showing any evidence of change, as illustrated by the Robledo deposits of trackways. These red beds, at least fifteen feet thick at AF 2, are made up of hundreds if not thousands of individual layers, many a small fraction of an inch thick, and many of those covered by a dazzling variety of trackways. But at this writing there is no discernable difference between the trackways at the bottom of the sequence and those at the top. In other words, no change, but over what interval of time? It has been suggested that perhaps each minute layer in the Robledos red beds represents an ebb tide, which, at two a day, would give a minimal estimate of not more than ten to twenty years for the whole red bed sequence. At the opposite extreme, each layer may represent conditions of flooding from the landward side, perhaps seasonal (one or two a year), or five-, ten-, or hundred-year floods. The more likely sedimentation agent may be that the layers represent eustatic processes (global changes in sea level), a slow and methodical increase in height that continued unabated for multiple thousands of years. These assumptions allow a maximum estimate of from a few thousand to perhaps a hundred thousand years for the duration of the conditions that permitted preservation of the trackways. But even one hundred thousand years is but a drop in the proverbial bucket of the fifteen million or so years of the Early Permian, and it is hardly surprising that there is no visible change in the trackway faunas from bottom to top.

This is not to suggest that fossil trackways do not preserve evidence of important evolutionary progression or that tracks from different geological eras do not in some cases chronicle the evolutionary process. In many respects, scientists believe they do.

Around the globe, trackways appear to document in exciting detail the emergence of life on land. In Devonian sediments 370 to 380 million years old, it has been claimed that certain footprints represent the trails of lobe-finned fish, the ancestors of amphibians. A possible scenario explaining such tracks is that these animals were caught in a near-fatal dry spell and the tracks were made when desperate fish ventured from one shrinking water hole to another.

In younger sediments, trackways of fully developed amphibians are preserved. Scientists believe that these creatures developed directly from lobe-finned fish. Such amphibian trackways are fairly common in sediments of Carboniferous age. By Late Permian times, however, amphibian trackways became rare, and by contrast, reptile tracks became more plentiful. A clear change in the composition of terrestrial vertebrates was taking place—a change documented by the abundance of terrestrial footprints in Late Paleozoic rocks and the appearance first of semi-erect, and then fully erect forms. Simply put, during the Permian some reptiles became fully adapted to life on land.

The Robledos trackways fit into this evolutionary progression. Following right on the heels of the Carboniferous, not long after the earth, so-to-speak, took its first steps onto land, the Robledos evidence reveals approximately equal numbers of reptiles and amphibians, and it is clear that any top predatory niches amphibians enjoyed prior to the Early Permian were later filled by reptiles, specifically by pelycosaurs.

The Robledos tracks fit nicely between the footprint evidence from the Carboniferous (showing abundant amphibians), and that from the reptile-rich Late Permian, by documenting the dramatic takeover of the continental margins by reptiles.

Back to our analogy, in a library, we have devised a way to separate recorded data thematically. In like manner, earth scientists have found a way to separate earth history thematically. Earth scientists use evidence of change, of varying scales, to subdivide the "books" of the earth, just as authors subdivide their books into chapters and librarians their holdings into volumes and categories. Useful evidence for sub-dividing the earth's layering range from local volcanic ash-falls or basalt-flows, through regional phenomena such as glacial tills, to global indication of mass extinction of organisms. Because the biosphere has been essentially continuous around the globe for at least the last three billion years, fossil evidence of origin and extinction is commonly useful at a variety of levels—local, regional, or global.

Sedimentary rock can be viewed as the paper the history of life on earth is written on. The more of this paper we find intact, in consecutive order, the more meaningful the preserved information becomes. Paleontology has reached a consensus on the global boundaries of the emergence and decline of organisms, boundaries which, like birthdays and anniversaries in our own lives, mark the changing of eras.

In rare instances, physical evidence may suggest a single event that affected the surface of the whole earth. For example, if we were to sprinkle all of the earth with some rare metal such as iridium at one given moment in time, and then continue to allow the earth to erode and deposit, deposit and erode, for sixty-five million years, such an element layer would be called a time-parallel surface. Such worldwide boundaries are also called time lines or event horizons. Such boundaries would separate the sediments laid down sixty-five million years ago and before from those that were laid down after the metal was deposited.

Just such an iridium rich layer marking the sixty-five-million-year-old Cretaceous-Tertiary (K/T) boundary has been found. The iridium layer does not occur everywhere, for in many places it has been eroded away, but despite its thinness, it is found in land and sea deposits in all of the earth's hemispheres, and always in the same relationship to other rocks. In terrestrial rocks that contain fossils of both the youngest dinosaurs and those of their oldest mammalian successors, the iridium layer lies between the two. Likewise in marine rocks, the iridium layer falls above beds in which fossils are dominated by those of the youngest sea-going contemporaries of dinosaurs, and below beds dominated by the fossil faunas that succeeded them.

Iridium is extremely scarce in rocks of the earth's crust, but much more common in meteors and other interplanetary structures to which we have access. The distribution of the single thin layer in which iridium is concentrated in the earth's outer crust has led to the idea that it was deposited in a geologically instantaneous event, consequent to the collision of an asteroid or comet with the earth.

The relationships of the iridium layer with other rocks indicates that this event coincided with the extinction of dinosaurs and many of their invertebrate and vertebrate contemporaries in the sea. Irrespective of the causal relationships among these phenomena, however, the distinctiveness and global distribution of the iridium makes it a time-marker, or "time-parallel boundary," like no other.

Earth history is presently divided into unique time periods. Each period builds on the one just before, in a kind of progressive collage of both geologic and biologic (evolutionary) events. Each period represents a period of earth history that overlaps with no other and so has a unique geologic and biologic history. The Permian is only one of thirteen such periods, each one possessing a unique geologic history.

In addition to these large blocks of time, (on the order of tens of millions of years) there are even larger, more complex divisions of earth history called eras (hundreds of millions of years), and even larger divisions are called eons. There are three eons and four eras, and each era is composed of a number of periods. Periods run together sequentially, and share certain common and very broad biological and geological themes. Each era also had its distinct flora and geology.

We might look at earth's outer layers like this. There are four wings in the library of earth history. Each represents one of the four eras that encompass the history of life on earth. Within each wing are many bookcases and shelves. These are the boundaries that separate the periods and epochs within each era. The periods and epochs represent evolutionary themes that are different enough from each other to warrant a separate bookcase or shelf within this vast library. On each of the shelves are sets of encyclopedias. These are themselves sorted by volumes based on the alphabet. Within the volumes are chapters, or pages, that represent specific layers or zones within the larger periods and epochs. In every way, the information gets more detailed as one moves from the bookcase to the shelf, from the shelf to the set, from the set to the volume, from the volume to the page.

Just as we might do in the local library, earth scientists pull out of the earth volumes on terrestrial life, marine life, plant life, earth movements, sea levels, climate, and everything in between. Each specific era (bookcase) contains a sequence of periods (bookshelves) that when strung together, are distinctive enough to warrant a separate category.

Geologists have established a convention which divides earth history according to the major changes that it records. The largest subdivisions are the Phanerozoic, Proterozoic, and Archaean, or Archeozoic eon. The Phanerozoic encompasses the time from the present back about six hundred million years to the first appearance of multicellular animals with hard shells. The beginning of the Phanerozoic was once called the "beginning of the fossil record," but we now know that the Proterozoic and Archeozoic eons also have a fossil record. Fossils of a few multicellular organisms are found in rocks about eight hundred million years old, and a variety of simple-celled animals date back to more than 3,500 million (3 billion 500 million) years ago. Today, such fossils have been found in both South Africa and western Australia. These fossils occur as microscopic organisms—bacteria and algae that are often only recognizable if they are found strung together in clumps or growing in mounds known as stromatolites.

The Proterozoic and Archeozoic contain tantalizing hints of early diversification of living things, and indeed of the origin of life, but their record is only a teaser compared with the sequence of events shown by the Phanerozoic record. The Archeozoic (meaning very ancient life) is also known as the Precambrian. This era encompasses everything from the formation of the earth up through the beginning of life, until the appearance of large multicellular or "obvious" life forms. This pre-fossil and primitive fossil era is not only the longest, but it also sets the stage for the emergence and development of more complex and advanced life.

It is, therefore, the Phanerozoic on which we must concentrate, even though it represents but a fraction of the time of life on earth. The Phanerozoic eon is subdivided into three eras, the Cenozoic or Tertiary, from the present to 65 million years ago; the Mesozoic, from 65 to 250 million years ago; and the Paleozoic, from 250 to 600 million years ago. The Cenozoic era, our own, is dominated by mammals and flowering plants and, lately, by us. The Mesozoic era was dominated by advanced reptiles in the sea, and also saw early on the origin of mammals and later that of birds. The Paleozoic era was marked by successive early diversifications of multicellular invertebrates, and in succession the origin of fish, amphibians, and primitive reptiles.

Each era of the Phanerozoic is further subdivided into periods, thirteen in all, most of them ranging from thirty million to seventy-five million years in duration. We needn't list them all, but will concentrate on a few periods represented by lagerstätte that gives us a clear window into the life of the time.

The first of these is the Cambrian, named for Cambria, a Roman name for Wales, a major locality for rocks of that age. The beginning of the Cambrian is the beginning of the Phanerozoic, when the abrupt appearance of a variety of hard-shelled multicellular animals indicates a vibrant "explosion" in diversity.

The Cambrian is characterized by a multitude of sea-dwelling invertebrates (animals without a backbone), of which the most famous are trilobites. Trilobites were arthropods, with segmented bodies, jointed legs, and durable shield-shaped heads. Their fossils show that they could roll up into a tight ball, presumably when threatened, and I like to think of them as looking like overgrown aquatic pillbugs.

The Cambrian period is known to some as the age of Trilobites, but it also featured brachiopods, nautiloids (distant relatives of octopus, squids, and the chambered nautilus), crinoids (sea lilies), clams, snails, and other marine invertebrates with hard external skeletons. These organisms seem to appear as if out of nowhere, and the layers preserving them are said to chronicle an explosion of life.

Nowhere is this explosion of diversity so evident as in the world-famous Burgess shale deposit in British Columbia. Found in 1909 by Dr. Charles D. Walcott, former secretary of the Smithsonian Institution, the Burgess shale preserves layer upon layer of life forms, some so unlike living forms as to boggle the imagination. Many of these organisms were initially classified into known higher categories, but recent investigations by paleontologists have caused them to be reclassified, making the Burgess shale the record of abundant life forms found nowhere else on earth.

The Burgess shale is a classic lagerstatt. Fossils here are unique because the remains are of soft-bodied animals—animals that are not normally preserved because they lack the general fossil requisite of hard parts. They were preserved because an undersea landslide buried the animals quickly and protected them from decay.

The next lagerstatt that we look at is the Rhynie chert, of Late Silurian/Early Devonian age at Aberdeenshire, Scotland. The Rhynie

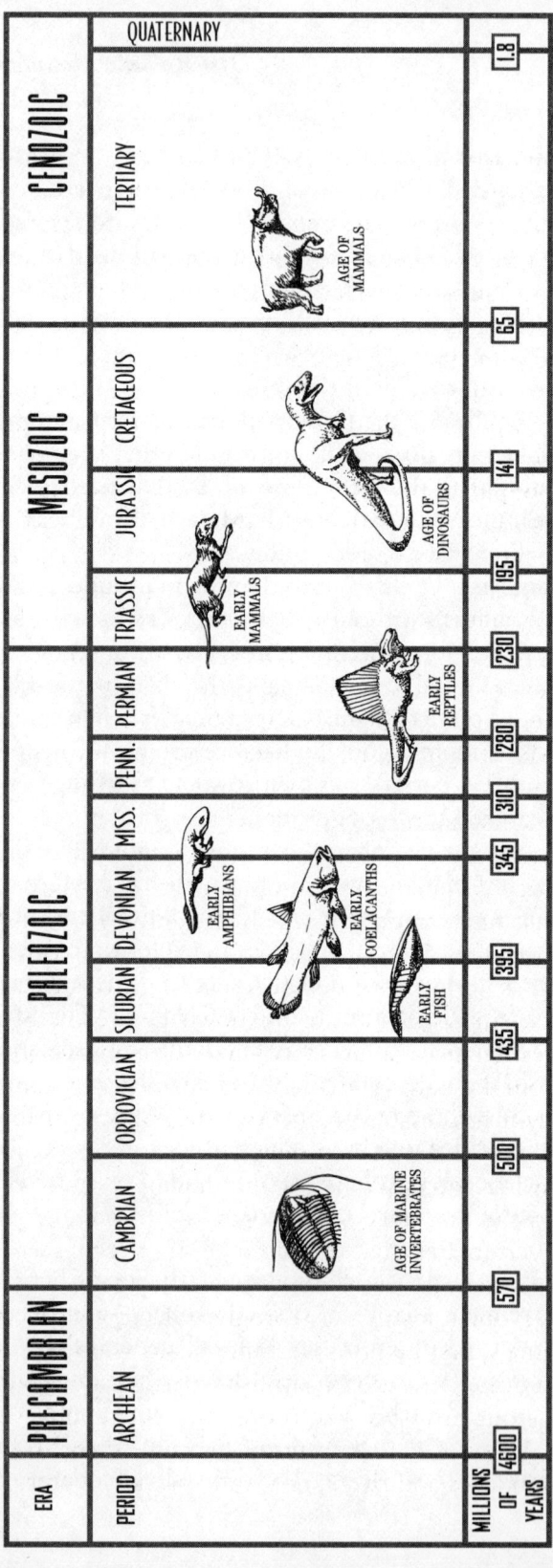

chert preserves in a petrified peat deposit—the three-dimensional remains of a thriving community complete with early land plants and terrestrial invertebrates, and most importantly, found intact in the place where they both lived and died. The fossils are exquisite in quality and abundance and the fauna and flora found here occur nowhere else on earth as a lagerstatt. The first land plants, though small, were upright, and some had distinct structures for transport of water while others did not. Representatives of simple organisms include extensive algal mats comprised of filamentous blue-green algae. Unfortunately, it is at present impossible to deduce how characteristic the Rhynie chert plant population was in relation to other wetland areas in the Lower Devonian.

As a petrified swamp, the Rhynie chert animal fauna consists mainly of microarthropods. Many of these invertebrates occur between plant stems and inside the sporangia. Included in the fauna are springtails (a wingless hopping insect still living today), mites, the first recorded spiders, and other arachnids. The insects ate leaves and leaf litter, and even plant sap, as well as other microorganisms. In other deposits of the same age, trace fossils of herbivorous myriapods (millipedes) and predatory arachnids provide additional evidence of the emergence of animals onto the land.

The Rhynie chert, coupled with other finds of the same age, indicate that three dominant terrestrial invertebrate groups emerged at this particular time: arachnids, which, in addition to spiders, include scorpions and mites; insects, which include flightless forms; and myriapods, such as herbivorous millipedes and carnivorous centipedes.

Terrestrial invertebrates are unknown before the Silurian. The earliest terrestrial invertebrates recognized are some poorly preserved millipeds from the Early Silurian. These millipedes undoubtedly were not the only invertebrates present on land, but the millipedes were preferentially fossilized mainly due to their calcified skin layers and their burrowing habits. We know that millipedes were not alone at this time, as the first trace fossils found are of burrows, tracks, and trails of invertebrates that are difficult to assign specifically, but appear to represent fauna dominated by arthropods.

Later Devonian fossils show progressively greater occupation of land by animals, first by primitive amphibians whose teeth and limb structure indicate derivation from fish—particularly the lobe-finned fish whose stout fins were like proto-legs, eventually evolving into true limbs. Many of these organisms probably came to land via the fresh water of lakes and rivers, or via the brackish water of estuaries.

Primitive plants radiated landward from the coastal wetlands as horsetails, lycopods, seed ferns, and later as conifers.

When we think about the invasion of land we must remember that plants, as primary producers (photosynthesizers), must have led the way, followed by such primary consumers (vegetation eaters) as myriapods. The presence of predatory arachnids in these early terrestrial faunas implies the presence of protozoan and metazoan prey, which so far have not been identified as fossils. Insects presumably followed suit both as primary consumers and predators, and such a terrestrial fauna, once established, provided the incentive for the emergence of predatory amphibians as the first vertebrates to come out on land.

Events in the history of life on earth that have direct bearing on the Robledo discovery occur during the Carboniferous period, within the Paleozoic era. Here we witness the emergence of truly terrestrialized forms of life. The invasion of the land began via plants and invertebrate animals, followed by fish and amphibians. All came to land via fresh water from lakes, rivers, and estuaries.

The emergence of life onto the land was well underway during the last period of the Paleozoic era, the Permian. Beginning 280 million years ago, the Permian is one of the shorter periods of geologic history, lasting only about forty million years. The Permian represents a cross-section of earth history that possesses unique biological and geologic characteristics that set it apart from other geological periods. It provides us with a picture of a major transition.

Whereas the preceding Carboniferous period preserves a record mostly of swampy wetlands along the continental fringes, the Permian shows us the beginnings of colonization of continental interiors by organisms with improved means of reproduction. These were plants that reproduced by means of seeds, and reptiles that reproduced by means of eggs enclosed in membranes and shells.

These changes have been ascribed to increasing aridity on a global scale at the close of the Carboniferous period, in which the drying out of these vast coal-swamp habitats disrupted the entire ecological balance. Coal-swamp forests dominated by lycopods became extinct as wetland environments in North America and Europe shrank into oblivion, and associated vertebrate faunas consisting mainly of amphibians also declined. As wetlands dried out, plants and animals better suited to arid conditions appeared.

The evidence for the decline of sea-margin wetlands in the transition from Carboniferous to Permian is perfectly clear; however, the inference that this change was due to increasing global aridity is not. To start with, we must remember that the ancient supercontinent of Pangaea was undergoing its final assembly at just this time. The end of the Carboniferous wetlands of North America and Europe coincides with the closure of the pre-Atlantic Ocean, which by itself would have been sufficient to do in the wetlands without the help of global climatic change. Furthermore, coal-swamps survived elsewhere. On the east coast of Pangaea, in what is now China, there was no closure of the sea, and there the coal-swamps persisted with little change until after the end of the Permian.

The moral of the story is that until proven otherwise, everything we look at in the fossil record is local. We can't draw global conclusions about such matters as climate until we can see that the phenomena we observe in North America and Europe are observable at the same time on the other side of the globe. In the above case they are not, so we must conclude that the end of the North American and European wetlands were due primarily to local causes, namely the closure of the pre-Atlantic Ocean.

Pangaea itself, however, is another matter. We know this because all present-day continental masses fit together like the pieces of a puzzle. But they don't just fit in terms of shape. They also fit together compositionally, preserving the same kinds of rocks along adjoining edges, and biologically, with fossil beds connecting landmasses long since separated. The picture the puzzle makes when the pieces are put back together makes sense on a global scale, but the picture is very old and its clarity is obscured in some places. Nevertheless, the scenes that remain depict a world much different from the one that exists today.

Imagine how difficult it is to reproduce a puzzle without having any idea of what it looks like beforehand. Many of the pictures from the past are unfamiliar to present-day puzzle solvers. We do know with some certainty that across North America, Europe, parts of Asia, and Australia, shallow seas supported a great variety of life. The information gathered by studying the kinds of sediment deposited today in shallow marine environments aids us in identifying similar ancient sediments and the physical environments in which they accumulated. Just as we know that certain animals depend on certain kinds of physical conditions today, we find the fossils of comparable animals in comparable sediments from long ago.

We also know that on land 280 million years ago, various modern orders of insects were already in existence. We know this because we have found fossil insects that are closely similar to those of today.

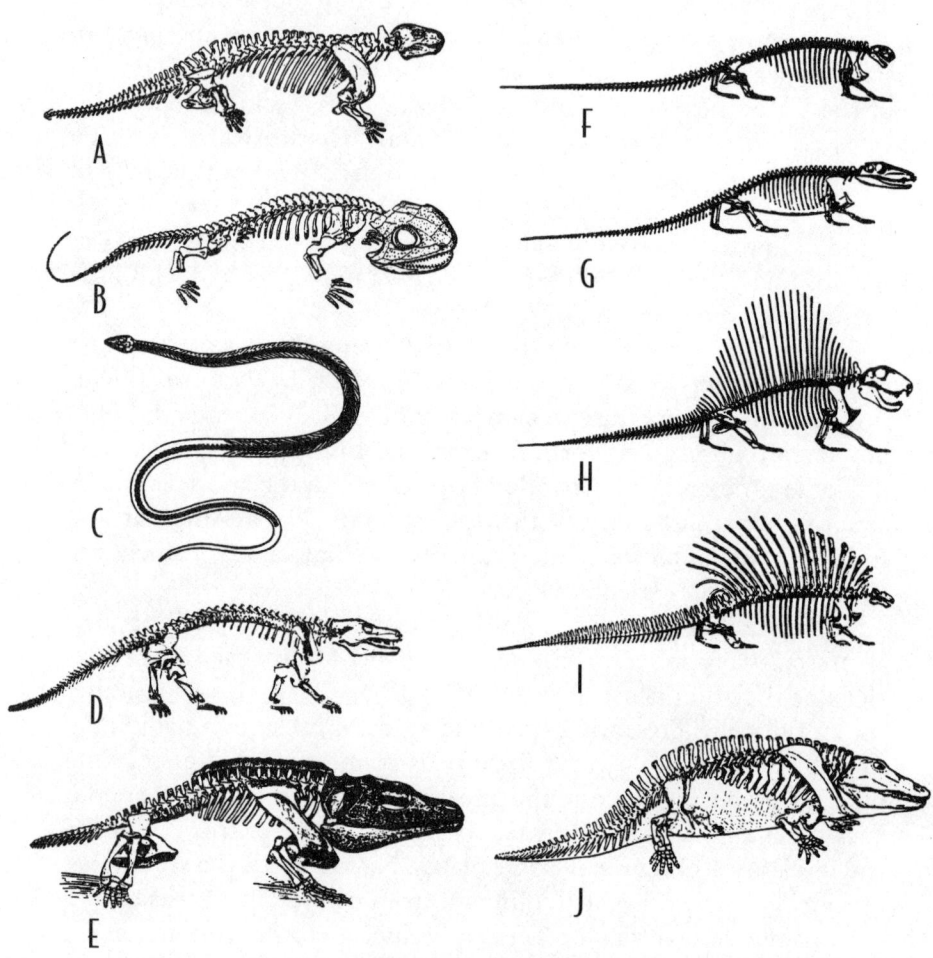

## EARLY PERMIAN VERTEBRATES
### (Not to scale)

A. Diadectes
B. Branchiosaurus,
    a microsaur amphibian
C. Ophiderpeton
D. Seymouria
E. Cacops

F. Casea
G. Varanosaurus
H. Dimetrodon
I. Edaphosaurus
J. Eryops

After Romer, *Vertebrate Paleontology*, Univeristy of Chicago Press, 1966.

The earlier members of some groups were of prodigious proportions. Carboniferous dragonflies had wing spans approaching two feet, and some Silurian scorpions were forty inches long. Some Devonian centipedes and millipede-like animals had a girth the size of a man's arm. Most insects, however, were as those of today. The cockroach, for example, was not much bigger 280 million years ago than it is today.

In the terrestrial environments of the Permian, particularly along the margins of the shallow seas, semitropical forests emerged and continued to flourish for long periods. Many of the plants found in these sediments are similar around the world, suggesting globally comparable ecological conditions.

Where the Permian is preserved, it is characterized by a number of spectacular terrestrial vertebrates that are only known from this time. It includes survivors of the golden age of amphibians, which dominated the coastal swamps of Europe and North America in the Carboniferous. Some of these creatures were well adapted for life on land. *Eryops* (ear'ee-ops), for example, possessed a short "wheelbase," short tail, and short, but very stout, limbs. The head of *Eryops* was enormous. Nearly one-half the length of the body, it gave *Eryops* a distinctly frog-like appearance, but what a frog! Adults were six feet long from head to tail, with rows of long, conical teeth outlining its jaws. *Cacops* (cake'ops) was built like *Eryops* but was less than half its size, and is distinguished by a row of boney plates along its back. These plates are traditionally interpreted as armor, but, as they are tightly articulated with the vertebrae and occur nowhere else on the body, it is more likely that they helped to maintain the integrity of the vertebral column against the pull of gravity. *Platyhistrix* (plat-e-hiss'tricks) was another amphibian about the size of *Cacops*, but its backbone was reinforced by tall neural spines instead of bony plates.

An especially interesting animal of the Lower Permian is *Diadectes* (die-a-deck'tees), a lumbering seven- to eight-foot behemoth that probably weighed close to three hundred pounds. *Diadectes* so combines features characteristic of reptiles as well as amphibians that its formal classification is still a matter of controversy. Unlike most of its contemporaries, *Diadectes* was probably a plant eater.

A wide variety of Early Permian amphibians were persistently aquatic; that is, they spent their adult life as well as their larval life in water. In one form, *Diplocaulus* (dip-low-call'us), the head was large and very flat, with the back corners drawn out into long projections that looked like horns. Many others, such as *Ophiderpeton*

## VARIOUS MICROSAURS

*The mud flats of southern New Mexico were well populated with small-sized amphibians, especially common were salamanders. Most of these animals left both foot and tail or belly drag.* From *The Order Microsauria,* by Robert Carroll, the American Philosophical Society, 1978.

(o´-fid-er´pet´-on) were long and slender, converging to the snake-like forms of later reptiles.

Amphibians continued to enjoy success during the Early Permian in spite of depending on water in which to lay their eggs, but reptiles, which originated the trick of laying shelled eggs on land in the Late Carboniferous, were catching up with time. The most conspicuous of these were the pelycosaurs (pell´ick-o-sawrs), primitive mammal-like reptiles which included the largest land animals of the Early Permian, of which one of the most common was the large sail-backed predator *Dimetrodon* (die-meat´ro´-don). In *Dimetrodon,* the neural spines were up to a yard long, and stood up along the animals back like a row of long sticks. The spines often show healed fractures but in complete skeletons are never displaced, which indicates that something must have been attached to them in life that kept them from falling out of line when broken. That something was no doubt a flexible and relatively thin and well-vascularized membrane, which would have served as a heat exchanger. By turning the surface of the membrane broadside to the rays of the early morning sun, *Dimetrodon* could warm up faster than potential competition and prey, an undoubted advantage in foraging. It must be remembered, however, that *Dimetrodon* lived in the tropics, and such a large animal would be at risk of overheating later in the day. In these circumstances all *Dimetrodon* had to do was to turn so that the membrane was parallel to the sun's rays, whereupon it would serve as a radiator, dumping excess heat to the surrounding air.

As the Permian wore on, reptiles continued to overtake the amphibians in numbers and diversity, probably because they were ready to go as land animals from the time they hatched. *Dimetrodon* and the other reptiles could colonize a much broader range of terrestrial habitats than their amphibian rivals, and as a result reptiles became the dominant terrestrial form for nearly two hundred million years. Mammal-like reptiles were especially successful, producing in the Late Permian herbivores as well as predators that ranged from the size of a chipmunk to that of a small rhino. Unrelated lines of reptiles were also successful at this time, but most of them were small and relatively rare. One of these were the diapsids (die-ap´sids), which didn't amount to much in the Permian, but in the succeeding Triassic period gave rise to lizards, crocodiles, and dinosaurs.

The end of the Permian marks the close of the Paleozoic era with the most significant extinction event in the history of life on earth. Earth scientists have estimated that upwards of 96 percent of earth life may have become extinct at this time. Many of the amphibians were wiped out at the end of the Permian, but a few survived even as reptiles continued to take over dominant roles in the Triassic.

The Mesozoic era begins with the Triassic period. Dinosaurs first appeared in the Late Triassic as their diapsid ancestors overtook the mammal-like reptiles in the Early and Middle Triassic. Dinosaurs flourished in the Jurassic and attained enormous size and great variety. They reached peak diversity and abundance during the subsequent Cretaceous period.

The Mesozoic era closes at the end of the Cretaceous in another massive extinction. Although the causes of this extinction event are hotly debated, there is no question that dinosaurs and a variety of other animals declined so rapidly as to mark a biological boundary between the Mesozoic and the next and last major era, the Cenozoic.

## Restoring Earth's Library

We face problems as we attempt to use earth's extensive library. First, the record is preserved by burial, where it is subject to damage from the tectonic forces that produce earthquakes and volcanos. Even if it escapes this kind of damage, we can't read what we can't see. When earth does open her library to us, she does it by means of erosion, mostly by rain and running water, by the pounding of sea on shore, and occasionally by wind. This is not a gentle process, and it destroys even as it exposes the record to our gaze.

Once exposed, these pages have been left out in the elements. Even though these volumes are written on stone, the indelicate processes of the librarian have obscured the clarity of some texts and obliterated others completely. Some volumes are inaccessible, and some have been left unprotected for millions of years. Of the latter, there is simply nothing left.

As we go farther back in time, finding and reading these ancient encyclopedias becomes more challenging; most are restricted to a few scattered fragments in very poor condition. Conversely, the closer we are to the present, the more complete the encyclopedias are. For the older ones scientists must make inferences based on what sparse information remains, often having to connect vast segments of time with theoretical threads based on limited physical evidence.

If there is ancient evidence that applies to climatic change, for example, scientists can make inferences about a variety of related phenomena based on relationships that are observable today. In this way, additional chapters and volumes within a specific encyclopedia set covering a definite period in earth history can be reliably added. Often scientists borrow from the present to interpret the past. This approach has been formalized as the theory of uniformitarianism. Simply stated, this theory means that the present is the key to the past.

In addition to theoretical links within volumes, scientists also create theoretical assumptions that link one encyclopedia set with another. Again, such links are based on how much physical evidence is preserved within each time period and on how that information can be related to other time periods.

In this manner, information that may not be preserved from one time period but is recorded in another can be used to fill in the gaps. Of course, the validity of such inferences depends on how similar such periods are, how close they are in time to each other, and how much current geological and ecological phenomena has been observed to bear on the past.

Because of this, some of the most interesting periods in the history of life on earth have to be interpreted on the basis of scanty evidence. Concerning dinosaurs, for example, scientists grapple with ideas related to their temperature regulation, whether they were warm or cold blooded, and in many cases the same evidence is used to support divergent hypotheses. Other contradictory theories relate to gradual or catastrophic extinction. Scientists use every scrap of evidence they can get in their quest to reconstruct the past.

As scientists analyze the representative evidence from specific time periods within earth history, and as these analyses are criticized by other scientists, a consensus may emerge that produces a minimum of contradiction. In this regard, reasonable portraits emerge which explain the environment, the ecology, the animals, and the geology that scientists believe were representative of specific time periods. Skeletal discoveries, sediment studies, index fossils, radiometric dating, and other fragmentary evidence, including footprints, contribute to this portrait. Finding a "missing encyclopedia" or a lagerstatt is always a paleontological bonanza.

Once I was aware of the possible "encyclopedia" uncovered in the Robledos, I could not contain my excitement. It certainly appeared that I had found a well-preserved first edition, published 280 million years ago, that gave us not just a peek but a long, studied gaze into the early history of life on land. This discovery had the potential to add significantly to our current knowledge of this important interval in earth history, at least in North America.

All the pages within this encyclopedia written in stone seemed to be intact within the confines of the Robledo Mountains. But how many pages were there, and how long had it taken for the earth to write them down? Conservative estimates of the length of this unbroken interval of time vary from as little as ten thousand years to as much as one hundred thousand years.

Now, this may be a lot of human years, but in relation to the age of the earth itself, or within the context of the Permian period which began 280 million years ago and lasted for nearly fifty million years, an uninterrupted ten-thousand-year sequence may seem insignificant and of little or no scientific value. So what's the big deal?

The big deal is that the pages preserved in the Robledos have legible "writing" on them. Every page is literally covered with stories and pictures. To find an unbroken written record of the dynamic life histories of such an important ancestral community as it existed 280 million years ago, stacked inch on top of inch for ten thousand uninterrupted years, is of great importance to science.

Let's look at it this way. The history of man since he learned to record his experiences on tablets is assumed to have begun about five thousand years ago. I am going to be generous and say we have a written record of man for ten thousand unbroken years. Lets assume that at the end of this ten-thousand-year period man becomes extinct. Two hundred eighty million years later, the new dominant species uncovers a library. Its contents are virtually destroyed by the elements except for an encyclopedia set that describes earth history as it was from 8000 BC to AD 2000. How important would that discovery be to them?

So if the paleobiological record preserved at the numerous Robledo track sites is significantly complete for those ten thousand years, it would indeed be like finding a 280-million-year-old encyclopedia with virtually all of the volumes present and every page intact. In this context, bigger time intervals may not be better.

Most sites that preserve longer records of history are frustratingly incomplete. Though representing periods of time ten to one hundred, or even one thousand times more extensive, the "encyclopedia" these sites yield always has numerous missing volumes and often whole chapters and pages missing at crucial points in the record. As a result, historical continuity is often broken. Probably the best exposed "encyclopedia" is found within the layers of the Grand Canyon. Yet even here key volumes are missing. Geologists call such missing volumes or missing encyclopedia sets unconformities. In the Robledos, however, at least with some of the red beds (fortunately those sections with the most abundant tracks), the layers are as perfect and orderly as layered rock could ever be.

An initial reading of the newly uncovered Robledo encyclopedia clearly suggested that a wide range of basic needs common to the whole spectrum of Early Permian terrestrial life must have been met at this one locality. Layer after layer tells the same story: for some reason a very large population of terrestrial vertebrates known to have existed at the time were drawn to the area, month after month, year after year, millennium after millennium. What I had found was more than a restaurant. It was a resort, and a popular one at that.

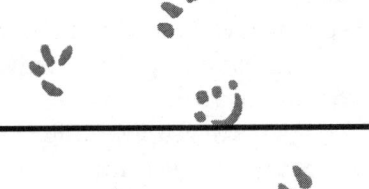

# Chapter Seven

## Presenting the Paleozoic
## Window to the World

I could hardly wait to get back to the deserts of New Mexico. I felt claustrophobic in Virginia, like I was living in the middle of Sherwood Forest. I never saw the sun rise, and I never saw the sun set. It was visible from 9:30 AM until 6:00 PM. The rest of the time, it was obscured by trees. Worst of all, there was no earth to be seen anywhere. If the ground wasn't covered with grass, it was covered with leaves and plant debris. I needed earth. Brown, scoured, desolate earth.

We were living in married student housing, only half a block from UVA's basketball stadium. Yet in the eight months we lived there, we saw a black bear, a fox, an opossum, and deer right in our backyard. The only thing remotely familiar to me was an occasional eastern diamondback rattlesnake.

I barely remember the two-thousand-mile drive back to Las Cruces, but I do remember the fun we had in Biloxi, Mississippi. I stood on the beach watching sandpipers picking off water bugs that were helplessly exposed during low tide. This recreational observation would acquire greater significance later as I began to uncover a 280-million-year-old shoreline. We left Charlottesville on June 2, 1988, and arrived in Las Cruces on June 6. Home at last.

After we had unpacked (*before* we had unpacked my wife insists) I raced back to the Robledos to see the fossils I had missed so much during the last year. I couldn't help but wonder if a year away would give me a better perspective on what I had found. Would my discovery hold up to further scrutiny?

The Paleozoic tomb was just as I had left it—undisturbed, waiting to be entered. But I just had to pull out one more slab from the discovery layer. It had been a year since I had felt the excitement of discovery, and I needed to be primed like an old pump. I had pulled two slabs out the preceding summer, the discovery slab and the adjacent slab to the right. These revealed a trackway seven feet long with nine consecutive prints. "Okay, we know what's to the right. Let's go to the left of the discovery slab."

I wanted to see if the discovery trackway was still running perfectly parallel to the mountainside. If it was, there was nothing preventing me from getting a two-hundred-foot trackway. But if the track maker changed direction, I'd lose the trail. If he turned at a right angle away from the mountainside, the remaining trackway would be lost forever because water had long since scoured away those layers when it was digging the arroyo that led to the site. If he turned at a right angle into the mountain, I could not follow him because I would literally have to move a mountain to do so. But God had been kind.

The slab to the left, when split, picked up the reptile's trail again. Here were five more footprints, making fourteen consecutive tracks. He was still moving parallel to the mountainside. I began to see how remarkably lucky I had been. I climbed up the slope until I reached the top trackway layer. Then I only had to dig down through ten to twelve feet of solid rock before reaching the discovery layer. How hard could that be? During this time rumors continued to float around about a big discovery in the desert. In time, those rumors became counterproductive to the project. We wanted to make certain that the press received the correct information, instead of the tall stories circulating around town. Rumors spread that I had found a long-lost gold mine, the entrance to a giant cave, and even that I had single-handedly unearthed Montezuma's treasure.

Rumor control aside, the discovery itself was clearly so exceptional that we needed to hold a press conference to inform the scientific community as well as the public. I had wanted to delay such an announcement until the experts were comfortable with their conclusions. As a result, from the time I informed Nick Hotton of the discovery until our first press conference, eleven anxious months passed.

While I was slaving out in the desert, Thom was setting up meetings with local officials to inform them of the discovery. Further conversations with the Smithsonian and the Carnegie museums made it clear that we had to announce the discovery.

Dave Berman had been in touch with Dr. Don Wolberg, a paleontologist with the New Mexico Bureau of Mines and Mineral

Resources, when Berman's annual field season in New Mexico commenced. He informed Wolberg of the discovery and then requested that I talk to Wolberg as well, since the Robledos were within New Mexico Tech's turf.

After a letter and a phone call, Wolberg came down for a visit to the site. He was pleased with my desire to work the red beds. In 1963, Frank Kottlowski, director of the New Mexico Bureau of Mines located at New Mexico Tech, had done pioneering work in the area and had published the most notable scientific reference to the Robledo tracks. My work would attempt to ascertain the productivity and significance of the Robledo red beds by building on Kottlowski's observations and the reports of amateurs and geologists that came later. (Years later, one of my greatest joys came when I received a letter from Dr. Kottlowski praising my work. He agreed that the fossil trackways I had found were "immensely significant" and he invited me to contribute a section on the Robledo trackways to "The Geology of the Robledo Mountains," a report that had taken him and others a number of years to complete.)

As Dr. Wolberg was serving as New Mexico's state paleontologist, it was considered appropriate to inform him of the discovery and to seek New Mexico Tech's blessing. He contacted all of the museums interested in the excavation, which included the Carnegie Museum, the Los Angeles County Natural History Museum, and the Smithsonian Institution. New Mexico Tech helped forge a consortium with these museums that would oversee the work, evaluate the material, and provide technical and financial support for the endeavor.

The BLM also approved of the involvement of New Mexico Tech and subsequently decided to refer to Dr. Wolberg as their in-state paleontologist for the excavation. All of the institutions involved, including New Mexico Tech, agreed with my desire to keep the excavated material in New Mexico. All the bases were covered. We were ready for excavation to begin.

## "Are You Sure These Are Real?"

As the press conference neared, it was clear that Thom and I were not getting through to New Mexico State University. The early commitments we had received from the university started to slip away. We considered the situation serious enough that we felt we needed someone who could act as the project's liaison to NMSU.

Thom found a man he thought could help us. Thom had met Gene Elliot through Gene's wife Peggy, who was a member of the board of directors for the Las Cruces Natural History Museum, of which Thom was director. Thom was taken by Gene's sincerity and broad political experience. Thom and I took to Gene immediately. He was a little off-beat in just the right spots—just like Thom and me. He was also intensely creative and full of adventure. He *had* to agree to help us. He was a kindred spirit. We considered Gene's numerous contacts with NMSU invaluable to the project. He was a graduate of the university and had been president of the alumni association. He also had experience with virtually every local institution we needed to work with.

On July 14, 1988, Thom arranged a meeting with Gene Elliot and NMSU's vice president for research. At the request of the university, Thom and I had diligently prepared a needs list for the excavation in preparation for the meeting. Thom, Gene, and I had high hopes for the meeting. Unfortunately, things did not go well from the beginning.

I brought photographs of some of the best tracks, the same photographs that had thrilled scientists at the Smithsonian and Carnegie museums. We also brought the Smithsonian and Carnegie evaluations, but our expectations suffered a first-round knockdown when the first words out of the vice president's mouth as we showed him the photographs were, "Oh, I'm greatly disappointed. I thought that they would be big tracks from dinosaurs. These are so . . . small."

The meeting proceeded from bad to worse. We handed the photographs to the vice president for him to view at his leisure. He paused when he came to a photograph of a siltstone slab preserving dozens of small amphibian tracks. He raised his head, leaned back, and looked me straight in the eye: "Are you sure these are real?" Gene said I looked like someone who had just heard that his mother was a space alien. "You know," the vice president continued, "I could get a nice smooth slab of marble, or even sandstone, and I could chisel out tracks that would look just like that." Our jaws dropped. My heart sank. We were not going to get anywhere today.

"With all due respect, sir," I responded, "I'm not that old." Later, Gene and I tried to guess how old someone would have to be to chisel out tens of thousands of footprints in rock by hand. Even Methuselah wasn't old enough. Years later, we found out that even religious beliefs may have played a role in the cool reception that some gave to the discovery. Apparently, the cosmology of some people included a seven-thousand-year-old earth. Consequently, there was no room for clear evidence disputing that point, which in this case was 280-million-year-old tracks.

None of us wanted to mire the project in politicking and maneuvering, for we had a lot of constructive work ahead. But with only two weeks left until the press conference, we had one last opportunity to gather additional support. All of us agreed that we needed heavier guns this time. We had to go all the way to the president of the university, James Halligan. Maybe the administration was having trouble supporting the project because they thought it was a fly-by-night affair. Or maybe they just didn't have the experience to evaluate paleontological evidence. If some really did think the tracks were forged, perhaps if they met two honest-to-goodness paleontologists who had seen the material with their own eyes, we could cut through the university's skepticism.

Thom called Don Wolberg at New Mexico Tech. I called David Berman at the Carnegie Museum, who was about to commence his field work in New Mexico. We explained the situation and asked if they would be willing to meet with the president of the university. Both agreed and Gene then called the president's office and arranged a meeting the first week of August 1988. Berman drove down to New Mexico Tech the night before and was planning to drive to Las Cruces with Don the morning of the meeting.

Three hours before the meeting, Gene received a call from the president's secretary informing us that the meeting was canceled. No reason was given. Thom, Gene's wife Peggy, and I were in Gene's office when the secretary called. We were all silent for what seemed like an eternity. Then Thom remembered that Berman and Wolberg might already be on their way to Las Cruces. We called Don's office at Tech and found that they hadn't left yet. We told them not to bother. Strike two, from NMSU. We had little choice but to devote ourselves to preparing for the upcoming press conference on our own.

## The Discovery Site Is Visited: Will It Hold Up?

The press conference was tentatively scheduled for the last week of August 1988, nearly one and a half years after the footprints were first discovered. Nick Hotton arrived two days early to visit the site and preview the trackway slabs that had already been excavated. He couldn't wait to go to the site. We left his hotel at 6:00 AM so that the early morning sun would provide the best low-angle light for viewing the trackway layers.

As we traveled the twelve miles to the Robledos, Nick made a remarkable observation. "I just can't get over how much the Robledos look like the Karroo region where I've worked in South Africa," he said. "It's as if I'm back there again."

Early Permian vertebrate fossils are not represented in South Africa, but Late Permian vertebrates are well represented, with specimens at least as good as any other locality on earth. Hotton worked the South Africa Permian sediments extensively, and he also worked the Early Permian sediments of North America in west Texas. Both areas gave Hotton a good glimpse of the entire Permian period, all fifty million years of it.

When South Africa and the American Southwest drifted apart during the end of the Paleozoic, both continents underwent dramatic geographic and geologic change over a period of a quarter of a billion years, only to end up looking similar.

"It's quite remarkable," Nick said again. "They're so similar it's scary."

We arrived at the site a half hour later. The main site is fairly remote and the arroyo extremely uneven. I was concerned that Nick might have trouble negotiating the terrain. Five minutes into the hike, it was obvious he was perfectly at home in the field. I asked him if he would like to try his hand at splitting a slab or two. He took to the suggestion immediately and looked around until he located a small slab the size of a dinner plate, about four inches thick.

"No, Nick. Come on now. Find something bigger," I said with a frown. "There's not going to be anything in that little rock. Try this bigger one."

"Jerry, this one is fine. Let me do my job," he said with a chuckle.

"Oh man, you're so stubborn," I said, shaking my head. He was like a dog that had just found his own bone. He wouldn't take mine. Nick found the horizon line and hit it once. It split perfectly. Inside was a perfect six-inch reptile track.

"Lucky dog," I sneered.

I whipped out my camera and took a picture of Nick with his newfound track. Later, I joked with him that I was as certain as I could be that the slab I had tried to give him had footprints in it. He told me he suspected as much. That's why he went looking for something else. I still wonder how Nick would have reacted if that small slab had not had tracks in it.

Gene, Thom, and I had been preparing for the press conference for several weeks. The first thing was to secure an invitation list. Gene and Peggy were particularly valuable in this regard. With great enthusiasm, they wrote and called scores of newspapers, magazines, and science journals about the upcoming conference. They also sent the media a press kit that included both Berman's and Hotton's evaluations on the significance of the site as well as a letter of commitment from the Natural History Museum of Los Angeles County. Also included was a statement of support from New Mexico Tech.

We anticipated a lot of mistakes when the press published the findings announced at the conference, so we left nothing to chance. We wrote up a press release and included some background material. We explained what fossil trackways are, and that these trackways were made by animals that existed before the dinosaurs. We included a time scale so that they would understand just where these footprints fit into the overall portrait of life on earth. We also explained what kind of information fossil trackways preserve. If the press stuck to these facts, we were confident that the discovery would be correctly reported.

Dave Berman was to arrive the morning of the press conference, which was to be held at the Las Cruces Hilton at 10:30 AM on August 22. It was reassuring that two of North America's foremost experts on the Paleozoic were to testify on the Robledo discovery. Even though I had found and excavated the material, I knew that my opinion would be less than convincing to the journalists and reporters had I not had the support of experts.

None of us had heard from Dave for several days. Since he was doing field work in central New Mexico, we were worried he might be stranded somewhere or unable to come for some other reason. This made Nick Hotton uncomfortable, since for a time it looked like the burden of convincing the public of the trackways' significance was to fall on his shoulders alone. By 10:15, only two reporters had showed up, and it looked as if we had failed to generate much interest. Fifteen minutes later, everything had changed.

All three news networks were there, and reporters from more than a dozen newspapers covering the southwestern United States were present. In all, over forty media people showed up, quite a turnout for a small town in the middle of the New Mexican desert.

Five minutes before the start of the conference, Dave Berman walked in. "What's wrong?" Dave asked, as he saw our anxiety. "I'm not late, am I? I thought it started at 10:30?" Our fears were unnecessary. Dr. Berman was just being punctual.

The room was full of trackway specimens, hidden under a heavy cloth, to be unveiled at the end of our presentation. There was great excitement in the room, and it was obvious that the press was very curious about the forthcoming announcement.

Gene Elliott was the host. He introduced us, then it was up to me. Though I had a prepared speech, following it proved difficult. I was too excited to be nervous and too terrified to be coherent. I was scared to death:

> We have called this press conference to announce another important discovery in the long and rich paleontological history of New Mexico. The discovery took place over a year and a half ago, but I wanted to make certain that what I had found was indeed significant. During this year and a half I have talked to a half-dozen scientists who are knowledgeable in evaluating the discovery. With all of the evaluations now complete and in agreement as to the discovery's significance, with the proper permits and forms filed, with a good representative sample of the specimens previously excavated, and with recognized experts in the field relating to this discovery present, it is now appropriate to officially announce it.
>
> Five miles from Las Cruces, New Mexico's second-largest city, an incredible array of fossil footprints have been discovered that are over 280 million years old. These footprints are among the oldest in the world and document in exciting detail the dramatic emergence of life from the primitive prehistoric seas to the land. The quality of the footprints is excellent, as if they were made yesterday. Such perfect preservation provides scientists the best opportunity yet for understanding what is probably the most important and exciting time in the history of life on earth.

I spent five minutes briefly describing the kinds of tracks that I had found and gave a description of their geographical surroundings. Someone asked if the material could be unveiled so that the press could get an idea of what we were talking about. I complied. This was a mistake, for as soon as the trackways were exposed, the press rushed forward with cameras clicking, right in the middle of the press conference.

I tried to bring the group back to order, but it was no use. I turned the podium over to Dr. Hotton, and he began to speak. People then slowly worked their way back to their seats. Nick scratched his head, and then took off. I had no idea what he was going to say:

> The specimens excavated so far are tremendously diversified. Nearly the whole spectrum of Lower Permian animals are represented. My fieldwork in Texas and other places has led to the excavation of creatures like *Dimetrodon* and *Edaphosaurus,* among others, that are represented with trackways from this deposit. But there are many other animals that will come to be known only from this site.

Already Jerry has collected a tremendous amount of information about the invertebrates, insects, and other creatures without a backbone, about which, for this time period, we know virtually nothing. Because of this, the research potential of the material from this site is absolutely glorious. It's very exciting. The material is just as good as, if not better than the trackways found in the Grand Canyon, which are considered to be the best in the world from that time.

Another point I would like to discuss is simply this: the material that paleontologists such as myself and Dave Berman of the Carnegie Museum collect—bones—represent the dead animal. This may sound like a silly point, but what paleontologists generally find in the rocks is not evidence of how an animal lived but where it died, and we may not even know that for sure. But to see these footprints in these hardened layers, and to be standing on that spot, you know that 270, 280 million years ago something else was standing on that spot, and you are right there.

Footprints tell us a lot about how an animal lived and as such are an extremely important part of what I consider the fun part of vertebrate paleontology, in any case the most productive part, which is trying to restore these animals and figure out how they worked, because they are quite different from anything we know of at the present time. . . . There are so many differences that we need every scrap of information we can get to try to put them back together. Because of this, the exploitation of the MacDonald trackway deposits will prove to be of great scientific value to the scientific community for a long time to come.

Nick then turned the podium over to Dave Berman. During Nick's talk, I know I was as excited as the press was. It was like I was hearing about the discovery for the first time. I was happy. If this was a waste of time, it was sure a wonderful waste. Dave Berman reached the podium and began his presentation:

I first learned of the trackway deposit when Nick Hotton called me in late 1987 with the news. Since then, Jerry has brought to the Carnegie Museum samples of the material, as well as quite a number of photographs of the trackways. I am prepared to say that this is a very impressive and very significant collection. I believe that in terms of quality, quantity, and variety of Lower Permian trackways this is the greatest deposit of its kind found anywhere in the world. It surpasses anything that I have seen reported.

Deposits like this give researchers a greater sense of authority as to how many and what kinds of animals lived together at the same time and in the same region. I have been chasing vertebrate fossil skeletons from the Permian period through much of northern and central New Mexico and the surrounding areas now for nearly a quarter century, and

*After two months of exposing the layered sediments of AF 2 in the summer of 1988, the author (left) discusses excavation plans with Nicholas Hotton of the Smithsonian Institution (center) and David Berman of the Carnegie Museum of Natural History (right).* Photo by Pearl MacDonald.

I dare say the skeletons that we've found probably represent two or three different types of animals; it's often too difficult to tell exactly. But in any case, it is surely far short of the great variety of animals represented by these trackways that Jerry has found. Many of these animals will probably never be identified, and undoubtedly Jerry has uncovered the tracks of many new species as well.

This trackway discovery will allow researchers to work out the locomotor behaviors of these little-known animals—whether they were sprawlers or semierect in their gait. Their stride and length and posture can all be calculated now and this information will prove to be quite helpful in reconstructing the past.

Additionally, these various trackways represent, in part, a portion of the daily wanderings of these animals and so they should provide us with a great deal of information and clues as to these animals' behaviors. The trackways of dinosaurs, for instance, have in some cases shown that dinosaurs were gregarious. Certainly with this discovery, conclusions like this are possible, since so many long trackways have been excavated so far. . . . This information, coupled with the trackway records of chance encounters with other types of animals, should provide us, once the deposit is fully excavated, with a great wealth of information about the life history of these animals.

I believe that it is crucial that I emphasize the importance of this deposit and urge that it be fully explored, that the specimens be carefully and thoroughly documented, and that eventually these collections end up in reputable and well-recognized institutions of research. In this way the specimens will be carefully curated, preserved, and made accessible to research scientists. I believe this deposit has the potential of being a very rich source of information to paleontologists, and this will be the case for many years to come.

The burden of proof was off my shoulders. Now the discovery carried the weight of pronouncements from both the Smithsonian and Carnegie museums. Without the Smithsonian and the Carnegie publicly verifying the significance of the discovery, I would not have been believed as readily. We opened the floor for questions and personal interviews and spent another two hours with the press. The conference was a resounding success.

Great attention had now been drawn to the area, partly because of the stamps of approval from Hotton and Berman. The Smithsonian and the Carnegie museums had publicly committed to help in the excavation of the trackways, and though scientists from the Natural History Museum of Los Angeles County could not be present, the director, Dr. Craig Black, sent a statement of commitment. In addition to support from New Mexico Tech, other museums and academic institutions were also laying the groundwork for further systematic research or participation in the area, including the University of Indiana/Purdue, Texas A&M, the University of Arizona, and the University of Colorado at Denver.

In the next few weeks, word of the discovery literally spanned the globe. I was told of reports from London, Paris, Germany, Hong Kong, and Australia. In the next few years, nearly thirty stories on the trackways would appear in U.S. newspapers, a dozen or so even making the front page. UPI picked up the story right after the press conference. The headline was taken from one of Hotton's comments: "Fossil Find Called 'Glorious.'"

Editors from a number of journals and magazines began calling for interviews and stories. *Geotimes* called, as did the British journal, *Nature*. Additionally, there would be major articles in *Smithsonian* magazine and *Science Probe*, and also a report of the discovery in *National Geographic*.

As if to illustrate the difficulty we had educating the public about the discovery, I received a call from *Nature* editor Alan Anderson just after the release of the newspiece in *Nature* and the *London Times*.

"Jerry, I know you're going to be very upset with the *London Times* article, but it's not my fault. I only write the story. It's the editors that give it a title.

"The title is the problem," Alan continued. "I know that the trackways you have found are not from dinosaurs, but the headline reads 'In Dinosaur's Steps.' The news editor told me that if the word *dinosaur* was not in the title, he doubted if very many subscribers would read it."

I told Alan that I wasn't surprised. I have encountered the same kind of attitude in the United States: Prehistoric equals dinosaurs. It seems that for many people, there are no other kinds of animals that can be labeled prehistoric except dinosaurs. The public's understanding of dinosaurs and prehistoric life includes a generous dose of mythology. Evidently, an astounding 65 percent of adults believe that dinosaurs and man coexisted, and the vast majority of children still do also. Continuing attempts by paleontologists to correct these notions frequently fail because of widely circulated misinformation in movies, children's books, posters, and toys.

The handful of vertebrate paleontologists who excavate and study the animals that appeared in the Paleozoic era are the most frustrated. The biggest crock of paleontological mythology occurs primarily with animals from the Permian period, which began a full sixty million years *before* the dinosaurs. These are the animals that made the tracks I discovered in abundance in the Robledos. Yet even locally, despite all of my attempts to correct this misconception, I am still the man who "discovered the dinosaur tracks."

And the mythology is everywhere. One can purchase a toy from a line of plastic animals marketed as "definitely dinosaurs." Included in the selection is the sail-back reptile *Dimetrodon,* and the therapsid reptile *Moschops* (moss chops). Both are from the Permian, both existed abundantly tens of millions of years before the emergence of dinosaurs. And both are definitely *not* dinosaurs. Yet they are marketed as "definitely dinosaurs." You can hardly buy a children's book on dinosaurs that does not include *Dimetrodon. Dimetrodon* is totally recognizable to millions of children and adults, and everybody believes that it is a dinosaur.

The Permian is almost never discussed with reference to terrestrial prehistoric life, and when it is, it is generally misunderstood. Because of this, few people are aware of the incredible assortment of animals that lived during that time, all of which are, in all respects, as interesting and unique as the dinosaurs. The Permian, one of the least understood periods in all of earth history, is one of the most crucial, because during this time, so much that had a bearing on subsequent terrestrial life is thought to have taken place.

I told Alan not to worry. The *London Times* editor was right. Dinosaurs sell. Permian animals don't.

Even the *National Geographic* report contained an error about dinosaurs. When they sent me the draft, I corrected a sentence that said the mammal-like reptiles, of which *Dimetrodon* is the most famous example, "were the forerunners of dinosaurs that would rule the earth millions of years later." Nothing could be farther from the truth. They were in fact forerunners of mammals, not dinosaurs. A small, inconspicuous line of reptiles, diapsids, were the true forerunners of the dinosaurs. The mammal-like reptiles were the forerunners of the modern mammal clan to which our species belongs. But *Dimetrodon* is visually spectacular, so who cares about diapsids? When I later inquired about the sentence, which was printed without the correction, *National Geographic* said this was the only way they could get the word *dinosaur* into the report.

Nick was impressed with the accuracy of the press kit that we distributed at the news conference in Las Cruces, but he told us to brace ourselves for a lot of hooey.

"Jerry," he said with a laugh, "in time you're going to see that the only important thing you get out of an interview with the press is that they spell your name correctly." As if to prove the point, one report misspelled *his* name, not mine.

## An Excavation Plan Is Begun

After the press conference concluded, Dave Berman asked to see the site. After grabbing lunch at Guacamole's, so that Nick and Dave would see the tracks on the patio floor, we headed for the Robledos. My excavation site had modest dimensions. It was about forty feet wide and about eight feet into the mountain. Approximately twenty layers had been exposed along the edge, so that together they looked like stone stairs. There were trackways that could be found on all of these layers, crisscrossing in every direction. Each layer, however, was only exposed for just a few feet into the mountain. But even so, we were all intrigued by the thought of what could be found when these small trails were followed deeper into the hillside.

"Okay, Jerry," Nick began as he found a vacant spot to sit, "we need to get a lot of long trackways, and if there was ever a site to give us that, this appears to be it. Don't you agree, Dave?"

"Definitely," Dave answered. "The abundance of good trackways is just amazing. Even little trackways are very long. We're really going to get a good idea of how many of these animals lived and moved."

"These trackways," Nick continued, "have a great deal of information in them. They are long enough so that we can see different kinds of movements—when the animals stop, when they run, even if they are foraging. I'm not aware of any other Early Permian trackways that could provide us with this kind of information. It looks like we have the trails of every animal previously known only from bones. For the first time we could get information on the locomotor behavior of nearly the whole spectrum of Early Permian terrestrial animals."

"What a job!" Nick exclaimed. "You could spend the rest of your life here!"

As we crawled around on the various layers, subtle differences began to emerge. Several of the layers preserved conifer branches, and a few preserved some invertebrate trails. Some seemed to preserve only small tracks, while others seemed to be peppered with large ones. As we started to synthesize all these observations, we began to talk about what kinds of things I should really watch out for as I commenced the formidable task of excavating the hillsides.

These fossil footprints preserved a record of the activity of numerous animals during a portion of their lives. My excavation could not be approached in the same way as one would approach the excavation of a skeleton. Each layer had to be peeled off in succession, preserved, and read like a book.

There would also be a sharp contrast between the type of information I would be gathering through footprint analysis and the information Nick and Dave would be gathering as they excavated skeletal remains. This brings up Paleontological Field Rule 6: Bone concentrations where a variety of animals are found together in death does not necessarily mean that these animals were together in life. But there are some notable exceptions, however. Many fossil bone beds smack of death and destruction—the mass deaths of scores or even hundreds of animals caught in some kind of local natural disaster at one instant. The rocks in which bone beds like these are found most commonly were laid down in river channels, and the animals were presumably killed and buried while trying to cross a large river during a flood. The model for this interpretation is that of the wildebeests of modern Africa, which stop at nothing during their seasonal migrations. When they come to a flooded river they plunge right in and some fail to make it, because of weakness, illness, or just plain bad luck, and are drowned and buried in the river. The herds are so enormous that those who die in the river, though a minority, are commonly numbered in the thousands. It is significant that the animals that make up most fossil bone beds, whether dinosaur or mammal, are—like wildebeests—large herbivores which presumably underwent seasonal migrations. For the animals that died it was a catastrophe, but it was a local one, not regional and definitely not global. Needless to say, no footprints have ever been found in the high-energy conditions in which these mass death bone beds are preserved.

Additionally, in rare cases the formation and subsequent fossilization of bone beds may be due to volcanic eruption in which mudflows and ashfalls kill and bury thousands of animals in the area. Just such a scenario has been suggested for a massive bone bed of perhaps ten thousand dinosaurs that Jack Horner and his parties found while engaged in continued exploration of dinosaur nesting sites in Montana.

Even the death and subsequent fossilization of the animals found in the Burgess shale owe their origin to a disaster—in this case an undersea landslide, most likely triggered by an earthquake, quickly buried the marine life that thrived just below the fractured sea wall.

Yet all arguments for sudden mass death are not necessarily true. For example, the frozen muck of Siberia contains the remains of hundreds of thousands (some say millions) of mammoths and other Pleistoncene mammals. It has been argued that these animals were all killed at the same time by some sort of cosmic catastrophe that turned the atmosphere upside down and froze them in their tracks. This argument, however, does not conform to the facts, because there is abundant evidence that different animals died at different times of the year. The carcasses are frozen, and some are preserved with hair and stomach contents intact. Where stomach contents are preserved, some consist of springtime foliage, some of autumnal hay, and some of spruce and other conifer buds, the meagre fodder of late winter.

Quite in contrast to a sudden catastrophe, the remains of mammoths appear to have accumulated, a few each year, over thousands of years. The land here is flat with large rivers meandering across it. Over most of the area the ground is permanently frozen, thawing to a depth of a few inches only during the summer. Along the rivers, however, the ground remains unfrozen for several feet year round, making excellent traps for hungry, thirsty, or otherwise incautious large herbivores. Due to the flat topography, the rivers are continually changing their courses, and an animal trapped at one time would be preserved as a frozen carcass as soon as the river changed its course and the ground refroze.

Yet the preservation of footprints occur in a manner almost the opposite of the preservation of bone beds. Bones are representative of death, either solitary or en masse, but higher concentrations of fossil footprints represent life in a more stable environment. Fossil footprints found in a series of alternating strata are like markers saying, at least for the time being, that all is well. And trackways show much more convincingly than bone beds who an animal's real neighbors were.

Foremost in everyone's mind was the need to excavate as much of each layer as possible. In the process, Dave wanted me to record whether the plant fronds were all oriented in the same direction. He also wanted me to notice if complete fronds, or layers of plant debris, were the norm. If the plant fronds were all oriented in the same direction, it might indicate that the layer represents a storm deposit and that the prevailing winds ripped the fronds off the trees and laid them in a preferred direction. We could also get an idea of how these ancient conifers shed. Did they shed the whole frond, or only needles? Did they shed annually, or did they shed at all?

Nick was interested in finding out if there were any footprints preserved on the plant layers. Such an association would be interesting. Tracks on such plant layers might reveal a forest floor community, where the ground was littered with plant debris and humus. This would encourage the proliferation of insects that commonly exist in these kind of habitats today.

As we sat on an exposed layer at the site, we decided that there were two crucial goals. First, I should collect as many different kinds of tracks, regardless of length, as I could, so that we could subsequently determine how much variety of animal life was represented. Second, I should go after the longest trackways possible, so that we could get an idea of how these various animals walked.

With regard to the first goal, studies of as many different taxonomies as could be found in the Robledos would begin to provide subsequent researchers with a reliable regional census of Early Permian animal life from the American Southwest. This would be valuable for comparative work with other Early Permian deposits around the world.

If we could estimate animal diversity in this particular region, we could begin to reconstruct a food pyramid, all the way from the top

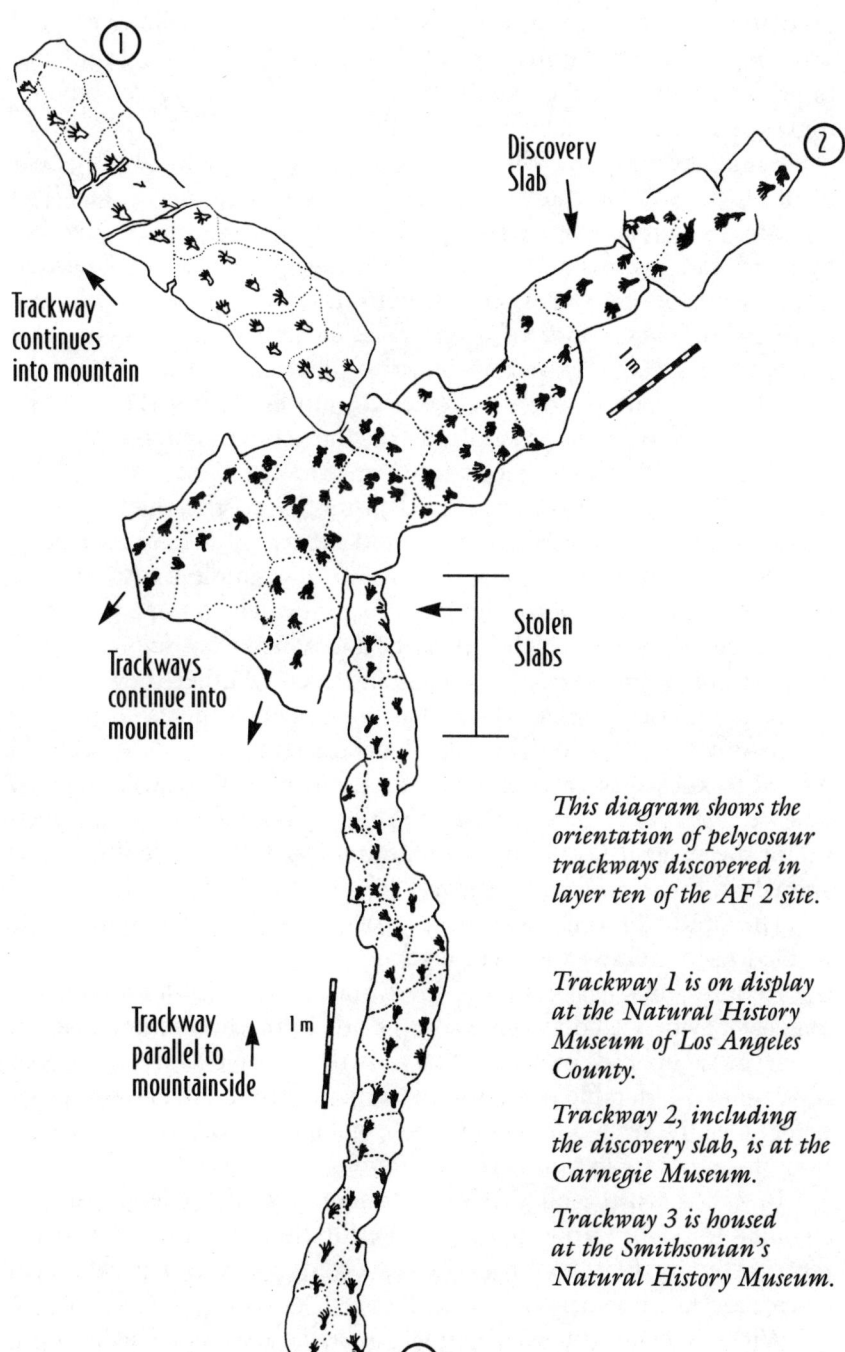

Discovery
Slab

Trackway
continues
into mountain

Trackways
continue into
mountain

Stolen
Slabs

Trackway
parallel to
mountainside

1 m

*This diagram shows the orientation of pelycosaur trackways discovered in layer ten of the AF 2 site.*

*Trackway 1 is on display at the Natural History Museum of Los Angeles County.*

*Trackway 2, including the discovery slab, is at the Carnegie Museum.*

*Trackway 3 is housed at the Smithsonian's Natural History Museum.*

predator to the primary consumers. The numbers of replicative track-ways of one kind of animal would also reveal the relative abundance of particular species. We would also be able to demonstrate convincingly which animals really lived together.

Remember, finding the bones of a variety of animals together in death does not mean that the animals were together in life. The carcasses of animals from a variety of habitats can be jumbled together by rivers and streams and then washed downstream to be deposited in the bends of the river where the current is weak and can no longer carry them. These kinds of mass graves are relatively common, and paleontologists actively seek ancient river deposits like this. They may indeed be the one of the best places to find bone, but they are not necessarily the best places to reconstruct ancient ecosystems.

The variety of life that is represented on extensively exposed track-bearing surfaces offers special insights into the track maker's behavior. All of this information would be crucial in understanding the life habits of these ancient creatures. For example, trackways can provide a quick census of number of species, which were common and which were rare, which were large and which were small, and the proportions of juveniles and adults, and even whether they congregated together or tended to travel as separate individuals.

As more and more of the Robledo trackways are identified and related to known skeletal remains, distribution patterns will begin to emerge. Paleontologists may then be able to refine their understanding of the diversity of Permian communities and the distribution of animals in the American Southwest.

The study of the great variety of animals represented in the Robledo Mountains might also disclose important information about the feeding and social habits of these animals. For the first time, we may have evidence concerning whether these predinosaurian animals congregated in herds or were solitary. Evidence can be gathered which reveals in considerable detail the dynamics of the food chain at a particular locality. We would also begin to get a good idea of the proportion of reptiles to amphibians.

In other words, all of this sedimentological evidence can be assumed to be important in reconstructing the habitat of the animals represented by the trackways. The same evidence can be used to then re-create the track maker.

With regard to our second goal, I needed to get as much length as possible on the trackways, even if some of the layers directly above a long trackway were damaged. Although skeletal reconstruction offers the paleontologist a relatively accurate portrait of an animal, the stance and gait of the creature are still open to speculation and debate. Only by recovering long trackways can we obtain a confident assessment of the locomotor behavior of the animal in question. With so many trackways preserved in the Robledos, the locomotor capabilities of many of these ancient animals could be studied and related to theories concerning the evolution of terrestrial locomotion.

Good trackways allow researchers to determine if an animal was primarily bipedal (two-footed) or quadrupedal (four-footed), if it walked flat-footed (plantigrade) or on its toes (digitigrade), or if it was pigeon-toed or duck-footed. Trackways reveal how the animals' limbs were positioned when it was active. Were the animals sprawlers, with their limbs spread out to the sides, or did they walk in a semierect or erect manner by moving their limbs directly under the body? Narrow trackways, for example, may indicate that an animal's limbs were held directly underneath the body. In fact, based on the shape and length of the toes and the possession of claws, an educated guess can be made as to whether or not the animal in question was a carnivore.

We can also determine which kinds of animals, if any, dragged their tails and which ones held them off the ground. A lack of tail drag may mean that the track maker's body was held well clear of the ground or that it simply had a short, stubby tail. When the length of the limbs of these track makers can be estimated, we can calculate the speed of these animals.

Trackways allow researchers to determine the size relationships of the animal's front and back feet (anatomically, the hand and foot). By analyzing the pattern of the hand- and footprints, paleontologists can not only get an idea of how the animal walked but can also reliably determine its size.

The location of an animal's shoulder joint can be determined by measuring the distance between handprints, and that of the hip joint by measuring the distance between the animal's hind footprints. Then, the distance between shoulder and hip can be easily calculated giving the length of the animal's trunk, excluding its head and tail. The size of the head can be reliably estimated when the proportions of the animal are known. The same can be said for the tail.

The long and the short of it is that paleontologists consider themselves lucky if they can get one-tenth of this data from the discovery of a few bones. Yet from a good trackway, one can reconstruct the general dimensions of a whole skeleton, even if one doesn't put a name on that skeleton.

# Footprint Glossary

## The Making of a Footprint

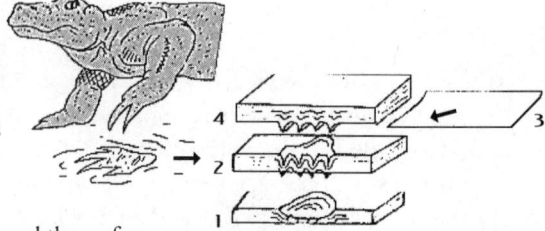

When some of the early animals stepped in mud or sand (layer 2), they made a mold of their feet as underprints or "ghost tracks" (layer 1), which hardened or dried out, forming mud cracks. Sometime during this process, a delaminating film (layer 3) of dust covered the surface, preventing additional sediment from tides or floods (layer 4) from bonding to the trackway surface. The soft sediments slowly lithified (turned to stone) and then millions of years later split along the delaminating layer seperating layers 4 and 2, revealing both a natural cast and a mold of the tracks.

**Footprint:** The imprint left when an animal walks over an impressionable surface such as mud. Footprints preserve the life activities of an animal.

**Trackway:** A trackway is a series of footprints that preserves three or more consecutive prints. Two consecutive prints allow researchers to measure the pace of the animal, three its stride. Scientists can calculate the midline of the animal from the distance between the tracks.

**Pace:** The measured distance between successive alternating footprints, such as left-right, or right-left steps.

**Stride:** A measured distance from successive prints of the *same* foot, such as from front left to front left.

**Trail:** A series of at least five consecutive footprints, which enables researchers to determine a variety of mathematical calculations with great reliability. The longer the trail, the more accurate the calculation of stride and pace become, because researchers can calculate the average of several stride and pace measurements. Additionally, an excellent "perfect" single footprint can be calculated by measuring the mean angles of an animal's digits through several prints of the same foot.

**Trackway deposit:** A locality preserving numerous tracks and trails as part of the geology of the area, which cannot be entirely removed or excavated. A deposit preserving numerous trackways in a variety of sediments is highly prized.

**Trackways** can be reduced to mathematical information that can then be related to other trackways. Each of the following calculations and/or measurements needs to be done to every step:

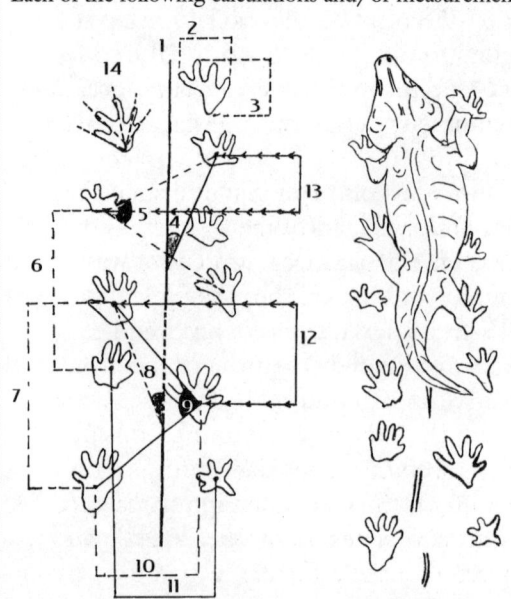

1. Midline of trackway
2. Width of foot
3. Length of foot
4. Rotation of hand from midline
5. Pace angle of hands
6. Stride of hands
7. Stride of feet
8. Rotation of foot from midline
9. Pace angle of feet
10. Distance between feet
11. Distance between hands
12. Pace of feet
13. Pace of hands
14. Digit (toe) divarication

The result provides a good idea of the animal's size, stance, gait, and speed of walk/run.

The animal at left was approximately 1.8 meters (6 ft.) long and weighed 90 kilograms (200 pounds). *Art by Noah MacDonald.*

## The Looting of the Discovery Site

After the press conference there was a powerful ground swell of support from the public in Las Cruces and around the state. Many people were converted to believers when they first saw the fossils. One month after the press conference the biggest political dignitary to date came to view the site. Larry Woodard, state director of the BLM from Santa Fe, wanted to see the site and ascertain how the BLM could help in facilitating the research.

I had just found another big trackway, and I wanted to uncover as much of it as I could for his visit. It started at the base of the mountain. A big reptile had abruptly made a left turn in the direction of the present hillside. It then turned upslope for twenty feet. It's upslope now, but when the animal made the trail the surface was uniform and flat. Then, it turned back to the right, into rock long since destroyed by the course of the arroyo.

Because this trackway proceeded along the edge of the hillside, it was relatively easy to excavate. Water had been seeping into the layers just below the surface for a long time, sufficiently loosening the cement that bound the rock strata together. In less than a week, I had sixteen feet of trackway exposed in place. It was a wonderful sight to behold. The weekend before Larry was to come I worked until I excavated the whole thing, all twenty feet. As was my habit after the close of every day, I placed a heavy canvas tarp over the trackway and went home.

Larry Woodard and other BLM officials arrived the next morning. "You're going to love this, Larry," I said, as we all walked the twenty minutes to the site. "I've worked for two solid weeks getting this ready to view. It's a perfect example of the kind of material this area produces."

Like a magician about to pull back the curtain to reveal an unexplainable wonder, I pulled back the tarp that lay over the trackway. I nearly died. My twenty-foot trackway was now only fourteen feet long. At least six feet of rock that preserved ten of the best tracks had been stolen. I fell to my knees with my hands over my head. I was in a bad dream.

Frantically, I went back to the missing layer over and over again, as if I had seen an illusion the time before. My project had been senselessly violated. I was enraged, devastated. Those tracks were irreplaceable. Of course, Larry and the others were stunned.

The thieves had pried out the slabs with careless abandon, throwing away slabs that did not contain footprints, even though those slabs were necessary for the integrity and completeness of the trackway surface. We had to act fast. We were especially fortunate that I knew exactly when the theft occurred. It was one day old. Special federal agents were called in from Santa Fe to gather evidence and obtain interviews. The thieves had committed a federal felony. The BLM wanted the culprits, but not as badly as we wanted the stolen trackway.

We had another advantage. I was absolutely convinced that there were at least two thieves. Since I had already carried out more than a ton of slabs on my back, I knew it was impossible for one person to do it, unless he made at least two trips. To me, that seemed foolhardy. There was only one way in and one way out. A single thief would have to be out there a minimum of one and one-half hours. I could see by the broken material around the missing tracks, that this was a quick hit. This fact might allow us to play one against the other, by offering possible immunity and a sizable reward for information leading to the arrest of the perpetrator(s). The theft did not look like a black market job. If it was, we knew we would never get the tracks back. The thieves were probably amateurs who lived in the immediate area.

It crossed my mind that, at this very moment, the thieves might be bragging to others about finding my site and how easy it was to plunder after I had done the hard work of excavating the trackway. It was obvious to all of us that I had been watched for some time before the theft. The culprits knew exactly when to strike. If they had told others, there could be potential informants.

We publicized both the theft and a $1,000 reward in the *El Paso Times*, the *Las Cruces Sun News*, and the *Albuquerque Journal*. Less than a day later, an unidentified man went to the Las Cruces BLM office during lunch, when most of the staff was gone, and left the missing track slabs at the doorway of the building. When the surprised secretary asked who he was, he said that he was the attorney for the thieves, and he hoped that the return of the slabs would end the investigation. He left as quickly as possible.

I was called immediately. I was amazed that the tracks had been returned. The BLM informed the newspapers that this was the first time in their history that important archaeological or paleontological specimens were returned without further coercion by the authorities.

This disturbing episode made us realize that added security was needed. The BLM quickly closed the only road through Quarry Canyon that brought vehicles within one-half mile of the excavation. They placed a chain at the narrowest point and gave me a key. Signs were erected, warning people not to remove material from the area, as well as a large sign at the entrance to the quarry, informing the public that flagstone could not be removed without a permit.

These measures were taken immediately, and with the very public "hunt" for the missing trackway, the BLM succeeded in deterring looters. Although there were two cases of minor vandalism at the excavation during the next five years there were no more incidents of looting. However, someone found my tool stash and walked away with about $200 worth of hammers, chisels, pry bars, and levers.

Although a trackway had been stolen, not to mention my tools, I always had a great sense of excitement that energized me daily for the demanding excavation work. Nobody could steal that from me, or at least that's what I thought.

# CHAPTER EIGHT

## Robledo Footprints: "Best in the World" or "Insidious Hoax"

I will never forget the day Gene Elliot told me that some local academics were calling the discovery a hoax. It was the first anniversary of my meeting with Nick Hotton in Washington, D.C., and only one month after the press conference. Since Gene's office was only four blocks from my home, I often stopped by on my way back from the field. Gene, Peggy, and I had a lot of fun when I brought the latest footprints I had found. But this morning was different. Something was wrong. Thom Votaw was in the office.

"The word is out that the discovery is a hoax, a fraud," Thom said sternly. "The rumors are that the material discovered isn't significant, and that you might have chiseled out the tracks yourself."

You know the feeling when your heart sinks to the floor? Flabbergasted, I asked, "But what are they saying about the Smithsonian and the Carnegie? Why would their scientists say we've found some of the best tracks in the world if it's a hoax?"

"From what I am able to gather, I don't think they are aware that Berman and Hotton were actually here at the press conference," Gene said. "The news articles were not clear on that point. They think that we just read a statement from each. They believe that we have deceived those museums and are exploiting their names for our own gain."

I fell back in my chair in a state of shock. Intellectually, we all knew early on that the news of the discovery would come as a surprise to many in the community. Years of experience and awareness of what had been found in the Robledos previously would have a tendency to overrule the reports by relative newcomers to the area of world-class, one-of-a-kind material.

*A pelycosaur trackway marches boldly into the base of a three-hundred-foot mountain at the AF 2 site. It is one of three such trails excavated from discovery layer ten. The trail is on exhibit at the Natural History Museum of Los Angeles County.* Photo by Jerry MacDonald.

One rumor circulated that I had salted the excavation with trackway material from some other trackway site. But how could anybody believe that? The strange thing about this allegation is that it did not deny that I found world-class material, but that I had used it to salt the unproductive Robledo red beds. This was bizarre. If the fossil footprints were indeed world class, why would I go to all the trouble of collecting them from a productive spot only to place them in an unproductive one? Why not just take scientists to the original spot?

The notion that I had carved the tracks was perhaps not quite as absurd. But the concentrations of tracks on some slabs exceeded fifty per square foot. I had brought several slabs with a total count of at least one thousand individual tracks to the press conference. How could I have had the time to carve so many? Who would embark on such a foolish hoax, doomed to failure? Who would be foolish enough to think that such forgeries could pass the inspection of experts like Hotton and Berman?

Gene, Thom, and I had prepared ourselves for the onslaught of criticism, but we expected it to be based on scientific concerns. Indeed, during our initial contacts with Don Wolberg, he cautioned that the "politics of paleontology in New Mexico can be rough." We were advised to get our case in order before making an announcement of our discovery. But hoaxes and frauds? Surely not. This was like the famous Cope and Marsh fossil feud. This was "Bone War" tactics.

## The War Over Bones

Each scientific discipline has its own embarrassing moments, and the Bone Wars or "Fossil Feuds," as they have come to be called, is one of paleontology's "best of the worst." Paleontology can be a very competitive science. In the late 1800s two of America's best paleontologists waged a war over hunting, excavating, promoting, and publishing their fossil finds. It was as much a clash of personalities as it was a war over bones.

The decade was the 1870s, and the age of dinosaur discovery was just now coming into its own. Edward Drinker Cope, a man of modest independent means and with a loose affiliation with the Academy of Natural Sciences in Philadelphia, and Othniel Charles Marsh, well-endowed professor of paleontology at the Peabody Museum at Yale University, were to be the vanguard of a movement that aroused American science to the rich research possibilities inherent in the discovery, excavation, and promotion of dinosaurs. But this movement, as strong as it was to become, was not ushered in with a spirit of harmony and cooperation between Cope and Marsh. Rather, American dinosaur paleontology was the afterbirth of one of the most notorious and acrimonious rivalries in the history of science.

The American frontier had just opened up after the end of the Civil War, and it was not just settlers who were moving en masse to the West. Science was carried west as well. All of the great dinosaur discoveries before 1877 were from the relatively rich deposits of the eastern United States, especially New Jersey.

Cope and Marsh began their relationship as cordial friends. They exchanged letters and even named species after each other. In fact, Cope let Marsh visit one of his sites. If there were any stifled antagonisms toward one another, they were gracefully hidden until 1872, when Marsh, intensely possessive in the field, took issue with a small expedition of Cope's into the Bridger Basin of northern Utah and southwestern Montana. The area was rich in prehistoric mammal bones, and Marsh viewed the Cope expedition as a gross trespass of his turf.

Even Marsh, however, could not lay first claim to the area. The fossils had been worked years earlier by a medical doctor from Fort Bridger. But when he pushed his spade into the dirt in the Bridger Basin, he considered the hundreds of square miles of land surrounding him as his realm. Cope might have done the same had the circumstances been reversed.

By 1877, when Cope and Marsh were fully baptized into their intense hatred of one another, both had received word of dinosaur bone discoveries near Morrison, Colorado. Arthur Lakes, a graduate of Oxford University, was a schoolmaster lured to the American West by the call of the wild. And it did not disappoint him. While roaming the wastelands of Colorado, he found a rich cache of giant bones, recognized their importance, and sent a letter along with a brief diagram of some of the bones to Marsh. It was well known that Marsh would pay for bones. Lakes did not receive a reply. Undaunted, he gathered a few of the more manageable bones, ten boxes worth, wrote up a more elaborate description of them and their surroundings, and sent the reports and specimens to Marsh. Lakes sent a similar collection of specimens to Cope. You can guess the rest. Lakes couldn't have created a better cat fight even if he had carefully planned it.

Marsh was unaware that Cope had also received a package from Lakes, and sent Lakes $100 to continue to work the area for him. While Marsh was refining an agreement of employment with Lakes, Cope had already completed a good draft of a scientific report on the bones sent to him from Lakes. After Marsh and Lakes inked their agreement, Lakes requested that the fossils he had sent Cope be turned over to Marsh. Needless to say, that didn't go over very well. You don't give a man with a sweet tooth a candy bar and then take it away from him and give it to his arch enemy. But there was nothing Cope could do. Marsh won squatter's rights to Morrison, and later to Como Bluff in Wyoming, an even more important site.

But destiny also had a hand in fueling the fierce competition between the two paleontologists for the fossil treasures of the West, for, in an amazing coincidence, another schoolmaster, O. W. Lucas, had found big bones in the same deposits as Morrison, but about one hundred miles to the south, in Garden Park, near Cañon City, Colorado. Lucas sent a report and specimens to Cope alone, proving that though history repeats itself, it sometimes gives a person a second chance. Now, Cope had his own site, but not for long. Marsh soon moved into Garden Park too and the war over bones continued, but the acrimony in American science was more than compensated for by the wealth of new fossils and publications that the two men produced.

Yet the bitter rivalry between Cope and Marsh was not just over dinosaurs. Curiously, one of the first confrontations between the two paleontologists occurred over Early Permian fossils from New Mexico. Marsh had hired a fossil hunter named David Baldwin for the purpose of prospecting for vertebrate fossils. Baldwin had been searching northwestern New Mexico for quite some time. In 1877, the same year Arthur Lakes stirred the bees with his dinosaur discovery in Colorado, Baldwin found vertebrate fossils in the red beds of the Chama valley of New Mexico. Baldwin shipped a considerable amount of bone to Marsh in New Haven. Marsh was disinterested and some of the packages from Baldwin were not even opened. Eventually, Marsh became disinterested in Baldwin as well. Soon, Baldwin was hired as a fossil prospector by Cope.

In the spring of 1878, both Cope and Marsh attended a paleontological conference in Philadelphia. At the meeting, Cope announced the discovery of vertebrate fossils of Permian age which had been found in the red beds of west Texas. Marsh suddenly remembered Baldwin's shipments of a year earlier. As legend would have it, Marsh left the meeting, rushed back to New Haven, and broke open the crates. The fossils were indeed similar to the ones described by Cope in Philadelphia. Marsh quickly wrote a four-page description of the bones and published it in the *American Journal of Science*, which he controlled. Although Marsh beat Cope in the race to be the first to describe in print Permian vertebrates from North America, the article was a disaster. In his haste, Marsh combined bones from a pelycosaur and an amphibian into a single genus, and otherwise inadequately described the lot. Cope was stunned by what he considered to be an unethical coup on Marsh's part of his discovery, and rumor has it that Cope pre-dated his own research on the Texas material to beat Marsh.

Further scientific compromises resulted from this bitter rivalry. Too often, many of the reports were rushed into print to beat the other to the punch, and sometimes skeleton reconstruction was inaccurate because slow and contemplative research could spell the difference between winning and losing. Both men's scientific objectivity was all too often tainted by disdain for the other, and to the present day it is nearly impossible to study the careers and the discoveries of either man without having to sift through this sea of mutual contempt.

Each man kept current on the activities, both good and bad, of the other, and sprang nice little barbs of information anytime the other was perceived to be gaining in prestige. Their characters were often maligned with accusations of incompetence, plagiarism, laziness, poor research methods, and exaggerated findings. Each man often diminished the research of their rival, sight (or site) unseen, and dismissed their foe's discoveries with a promotion of their own.

Each man felt frustrated by the other's discoveries, and the professionalism of one seemed in jeopardy every time a new discovery was announced by the other. It is clear that each felt himself the better pale-ontologist, and each soon developed irrational expectations. Both men were anxious to get the lion's share of bones from the West and went to various lengths to make sure that all reports of fossils were directed to him alone. If some were found by one rival, the other felt upstaged. Each would sleep better at night if they could best the other.

Eventually, Marsh used his extensive scientific influence to attempt to have the U.S. government confiscate Cope's fossils, argu-ing that the fossils were displaced government property, poorly curated, and unavailable to more "objective" scientific eyes—the biggest eyes, of course, being Marsh's. This was the lowest Marsh ever sank in his campaign against Cope, and it was seen by Cope as the ultimate ruination of his livelihood, as well as a callous dismissal of his work, an affront to his tireless energies in the field, and a theft of his scientific achievements.

This attempt to confiscate Cope's fossils brought the Bone Wars to the front pages of the newspapers. Cope made his own accusa-tions. With depositions from some of Marsh's best field hands, he claimed that Marsh never did a hard day's work in the field, that he plagiarized the field reports of his workers and called them his own, that he ran roughshod over his men with poor pay and an iron hand, and that he never gave his researchers credit for any of the discover-ies they made.

The conflict brewing in New Mexico in 1988 was somewhat reminiscent of the 1877 fiasco. Although the Bone Wars between Cope and Marsh were primarily rooted in personality clashes and pathological competitiveness, the Robledo "War" was surfacing not as the result of personalities but of conflicting assumptions—new ver-sus old perceptions. It was as if Marsh had roamed the Robledos and declared it paleontologically unproductive only to have Cope wander the same range some time later and declare it to be of world-class sig-nificance. In a nutshell, the Robledo fossil discovery was out of its element. It was discovered too late historically to be so rich paleon-tologically. It was a collision of new data against old. It was also a col-lision of old turf against new.

Though many of the allegations against the Robledo footprint dis-covery are reminiscent of the discrediting tactics used during the Bone Wars, there were some new tactics employed in 1988. The allegations that our tracks were somehow falsified, though not as absurd as the "bait and switch" allegation, *was* surprising. There was simply so much material already collected that even the most brilliant forger or artist would be overwhelmed with the sheer magnitude of the forgery or the complexity of the endless varieties. Yet it is true that throughout the history of paleontology, fossil tracks and trackways have been vulnerable to falsification. The most famous example of trackway fraud is the dinosaur and "man track" locality in Glen Rose, Texas.

In Glen Rose, Texas, just south of Forth Worth, there is a very impressive footprint occurrence. The footprints, which are preserved in the Paluxy River bed, were made by a few varieties of dinosaurs that existed 110 million years ago in the Cretaceous period. Some of the most impressive tracks are on display at the American Museum of Natural History (AMNH) in New York. Many of the trackways were exposed and excavated fifty-five years ago by Roland T. Bird, a field assistant to Barnum Brown, a famous paleontologist with the AMNH.

Bird found out about the Paluxy River site by accident. He noticed a couple of large slabs with fossil dinosaur footprints on them in a trader's shop near Gallup, New Mexico. Inquiring further, he found out that the footprints came from Glen Rose, Texas. Included among the dinosaur footprints were two more slabs preserving curious prints that looked uncannily like human tracks, but the prints were over fifteen inches long. Bird was extremely interested in the dinosaur tracks, which, after inspection, he believed to be genuine, but he concluded that the two humanlike tracks were carvings, not real tracks.

Bird was told that there were a lot more man tracks to be found in the Paluxy River bed and that these tracks were interspersed with dinosaur footprints in situ. Bird was shown additional man tracks by Jack Hill, owner of the Gallup shop. "They were fine specimens," Bird wrote a year later. "Too fine. I had every reason to suspect that the entire lot had been fashioned by some stone artist."

Though intensely skeptical of the stories of human tracks at the locality, Bird still felt compelled to investigate. In 1938, he arrived at Glen Rose and was taken to the area where the trackways were found. Bird was very impressed. He immediately determined to explore the area more thoroughly. He particularly wanted to expose a layer that appeared to have tracks of both two-footed and four-footed dinosaurs. Even though theropod (two-footed carnivorous dinosaurs) tracks are by far the most common dinosaur tracks to be found, no one had yet found the tracks of a brontosaur (a type of large four-footed dinosaur). Bird felt he was on the verge of finally finding one. (In fact, on the way from Gallup to Texas, Bird visited the Purgatoire brontosaur tracksite in Colorado, which was technically the first discovery of sauropod tracks.) What Bird found in Glen Rose was indeed remarkable.

As he worked, Bird was frequently informed about the man track phenomenon. Yet he never observed the phenomenon in the field. He was shown tracks that were explained to him as man tracks, but he was not convinced. He sought advice from local residents, and though he was taken to several spots, he was never satisfied with the man track interpretations. His steadfastness in his interpretations riled local residents. One man couldn't understand why Bird would completely ignore the man tracks while being so enthusiastic about run-of-the-mill dinosaur tracks.

The rumors and claims of man and dinosaurs together continued, and when Bird published his 1939 report on his findings at the Paluxy site in the American Museum of Natural History's *Natural History* magazine, he wrote that he believed that the "man tracks" were in fact made by some heretofore undiscovered dinosaur. However, a creationist group in Los Angeles was made aware of Bird's article and became interested in the spot. The Society for the Study of Creation, the Deluge, and Related Science appointed a five-man team to investigate the site as possible evidence of creationism and a young earth. In the early 1940s, the team first began to study the area, and the creationists have continued to explore it ever since.

In the 1960s, news of the occurrence reached Stan Taylor, director of Films for Christ. In 1973, Taylor made a film of the site, appropriately entitled *Footprints in Stone*. He presents superficially convincing evidence of human and dinosaur tracks in the same strata. The movie was convincing to the uneducated, creation scientists, and other religious groups, but met with great skepticism in the scientific community.

This polarity of opinion was interpreted by many creationists as unwillingness by the scientific community to investigate the occurrence firsthand, for fear of losing the creationist/evolutionist battle that has raged in this country for nearly a century. Creationists held up the Paluxy trackways as one of their best lines of evidence for creationism. The Paluxy evidence was promoted repeatedly in all of their literature on origins. Books began citing the evidence, and at least one book was produced solely on this occurrence.

*Tracking Those Incredible Dinosaurs and the Men Who Know Them*, written by John Morris, became an indispensible companion volume to *Footprints in Stone*. In fact, it even contains guidelines informing readers how to distinguish dinosaur tracks from man tracks.

Finally, in 1980, the Glen Rose area was investigated by objective researchers. Glen Kuban, a serious student of fossil tracks and trackway preservation techniques, began what was to become an in-depth, five-year study of the human footprint claims. Kuban immediately went to the heart of the matter, the Taylor site, which was touted as the best occurrence of the man track phenomenon. He spent considerable time exposing the layer for the beginning of his study. Kuban confided in me that he had kept an open mind with regard to creationist issues, and he even hoped that perhaps the "man-track" evidence was true, but he concluded that the "human tracks here are elongate, metatarsal (heel) dinosaur tracks, . . . and not human footprints."

Other sites fared even worse when studied. At the Baugh/Mcfall sites, Kuban again found that the markings were the result of dinosaurs and even invertebrate trace patterns, and not human footprints. More disturbing, however, was the fact that Kuban became convinced that "some markings [preserved] evidence of deliberate alteration."

Kuban also investigated the evidence of alleged man tracks and "cat tracks" at one locality. He concluded that "anatomical problems with the prints, knowledge of past carving practices in Glen Rose, and problematic cross-sectional features, [leads] most researchers to reject their authenticity." Kuban concluded that the rejection of these tracks was indeed warranted.

There were also reports of the discovery of a "human tooth" near the man tracks, which creationists used as evidence of "out of order" fossils. However, after Kuban studied the evidence, he noted that "the tooth, found in the Paluxy in 1987, has been conclusively shown to be a fish tooth." He concluded that the dinosaur tracks are indeed real, and scientifically important, especially in terms of how some theropods walked, but that the "claims of human tracks have not withstood close scientific scrutiny, and in recent years have been largely abandoned even by most creationists." As a result of Kuban's research, John Morris subsequently published a leaflet in 1986 that stated in part that "none of the trails at the Taylor site can today be regarded as unquestionably human," although he hedged on the wholesale abandonment of the "man-track" evidence. The film *Footprints in Stone* was withdrawn from circulation.

Kuban's findings have been accepted by both creationists and the scientific community. He presented two papers at the 1986 trackways symposium held at the New Mexico Museum of Natural History and has single-handedly resolved much of the mystery surrounding the Glen Rose trackways.

Kuban's findings confirming the widespread misdiagnosis of the trackways, as well as scattered evidence of fraud, were well publicized. The Robledo trackways discovery occurred a little over a year after Kuban's findings were made public. Undoubtedly, these reports could have made local scientists that much more skeptical of our claims with regard to the Robledo trackways. The possibility of trackway forgery was fresh in many paleontologists' minds, and the timing of the announcement of the Robledo assemblage was not the best in this regard.

Years later, in August 1993, Glen Kuban spent a week with me in the Robledos and in the lab. The Robledo material did not disappoint him. Having just finished an inventory of type specimens in the Connecticut Valley trackway assemblage excavated by Edward Hitchcock in the 1830s to 1860s, Kuban concluded that the Robledo assemblage was richer than any other Paleozoic track site known, and that it compared favorably with the Connecticut Valley assemblage as one of the best in the world, from any age, anywhere. That was saying a lot. Moreover, the Robledo trackways easily passed the test of Kuban's scrutiny for fraud, and he proclaimed them genuine.

## A Cheap Two-bit Chiseler

As the Glen Rose "man tracks" proved, footprints are relatively easy to falsify because they are sedimentary, not organic, features. Chiseling out toes in sandstone or mudstone is much easier than making or falsifying a bone. Fraud from skeletal remains are most often a manipulation of the bones geographic context, not its content, although this has been tried, as the famous Piltdown hoax illustrates.

Though most people would consider a hoax and a fraud the same thing, they are really somewhat different. A hoax usually centers around faked material, for example, chiseled out material, whereas a fraud generally centers around the presentation of such material, for example, the assertion that a set of tracks were real though they had actually come from somewhere else. In this last case, it is possible to present legitimate material fraudulently. In paleontological or archaeological circles, this kind of fraud is rare, but it would be called salting a dig or a quarry. A more common example would be the salting of an area with gold dust or small nuggets to lure unsuspecting investors.

The Robledo trackway discovery was considered by a few to be both a hoax and a fraud: a hoax in the sense that the spectacular trackways that no one else had ever found had to have been chiseled or faked in some way, and a fraud because the new material was now proclaimed among the best fossil footprint material in the world.

The Piltdown man discovery, which occurred about 1910, (the exact discovery date is not known), is anthropology's most notorious example of scientific fraud. The Piltdown evidence was comprised of skull fragments as well as part of the lower jaw and an eyetooth. Piltdown was touted as man's most convincing ancestor for over forty years until 1953 when Joseph Weiner from Oxford, along with Kenneth Oakley and Sir Wilfred Le Gros Clark, published a report that the Piltdown evidence had indeed been faked. The mandible was from a living species of chimpanzee and it had been fraudulently altered. Striae were also detected on some of the molars suggesting that the furrows were artificial. The jaw and teeth were not even from the same animal as the skull fragments. None of the fragments were indigenous to the quarry where the fragments were "found."

Although Cope and Marsh bashed each other relentlessly over methods, demagoguery, squatter's rights, and inaccurate reconstructions, they never accused each other of perpetrating a hoax. It was well known that everything found by either man was genuine.

The Piltdown discovery should be considered both a hoax and a fraud, the former because sections of some of the bones were tampered with, and the latter because a few of the bones were real but were placed at the quarry by stealth. In this case, someone found legitimate fossil evidence, altered some of its features, and placed disparate pieces into a new locality to make it appear that the bones were from the same animal.

Some of the greatest anthropological minds were deceived for forty years by the Piltdown hoax. Evidently, because of this, it seemed to some that it was entirely possible that the Robledo "discovery" had deceived scientists from some of the world's greatest museums. The best way to perpetuate a hoax is to get an honest man to unwittingly promote it. As an amateur paleontologist, I was fair game. But my "honest men" were Dave Berman of the Carnegie Museum and Nick Hotton of the Smithsonian Institution. We thought it was impossible for anyone to believe that those men, and the museums they represented, could support me in my excavation endeavors or promote the material I was uncovering if they had the slightest inkling that the material was faked or fraudulent.

Later on, Gene and I thought back to July 1988. In hindsight, we realized we should have expected we would be accused of perpetrating a hoax. Gene and I remembered how NMSU's vice president for research had suggested to us that our trackways were fraudulent as early as July 14. We did not take the statement seriously then, but we probably should have. Now the allegation was slowly spreading. Someone even called the three regional newspapers to inform them of the "hoax." The editor of one newspaper subsequently chewed out the reporter who covered the press conference for being "bamboozled."

Again, years later, I was told that the idea of a hoax was circulated by one man who interpreted a few preparation scratchings as specimen tampering. On some of the large pelycosaur trackways, the claw impressions, when excavated, are sometimes filled in with sediment that needed to be popped out with dental picks or punches. This was a very rare occurrence, but popping out the matrix is a relatively easy job. As a result, preparation markings would sometimes appear in the claw impressions. Such preparation techniques are sometimes used by other trackway experts and is standard practice in getting bone out of rock. To allege that the removal of matrix from some of the tracks constituted fraud was tantamount to accusing a fossil preparator of fraud for leaving a few scratchings on the bones he was cleaning. Call him a poor preparator if you must, but don't accuse him of fraud.

Fortunately, most of the trackways found in the Robledos preserve both the natural cast (negative relief), where some matrix may be removed, and the natural mold (positive relief), where normally no preparation is needed. Though it would be less difficult to chisel out negative relief footprints, it would be impossible to do so with the natural footprint molds. The allegation of a hoax is decisively put to rest by the preservation and collection of the natural molds.

Kuban said as much after viewing the fossil track evidence from the Robledos. In a letter of evaluation to the Smithsonian and the Bureau of Land Management, Kuban wrote:

> Early suggestions that the tracks Jerry MacDonald has found in the Robleo Mountains might have been carved or even salted into the area are readily dispelled once the sites are visited. Whereas a handful of realistic-looking tracks might be carved by a skilled artist, to suppose that someone could have carved thousands of such tracks, representing dozens of vertebrates and invertebrates, with upper and lower surfaces in perfectly matched relief, is patently absurd.
>
> The idea becomes even more ludicrous when one considers the associated overtracks and undertracks (subtle track relief above and below the original track layer), as well as the repeated excavation of new and extended trackways as overlying beds were removed time and again. Such a carving task would not only represent the most stupendous

sculptural feat in history, but the masterpieces would have had to be buried inside the mountains of Las Cruces to await later discovery.

The salting suggestion is also nonsensical, requiring the excavation and transport of thousands of tracks from an equally fabulous site. Besides, any notion of salting is instantly refuted by the many in situ trackways still at the site.

My experience with dinosaur tracks and the "man track" controversy in Texas points up an interesting irony. For many years the obvious (and legitimate) dinosaur tracks at Glen Rose competed for attention with markings alleged by some enthusiastic observers to be "man tracks." The latter actually consist of indistinct elongate (metatarsal) dinosaur tracks, erosional markings and nondescript depressions that vaguely resemble human footprints, plus a few outright carvings. Yet even though the carved tracks were typically malproportioned and generally artificial looking, some individuals insisted that they were perfect in every way. MacDonald's excavated material, as well as those still in situ, in contrast, are both numerous and natural in appearance, and yet, some observers seriously proposed that they might be carved.

When Nick Hotton returned to the Robledo tracksites with me in the spring of 1990, he gave a lecture at New Mexico State University's Kent Hall Museum explaining these allegations. He used several specimens to show the impossibility of fraud. He also explained that preparation of trackways is certainly appropriate, especially if they are to be exhibited. He categorically stated that the Robledo material was legitimate and that the allegation of a hoax was entirely unfounded. Though members of the press were present at the lecture (who, after Hotton's talk became convinced that the hoax allegations were false), a total of only twenty people were in attendance. None of the project detractors came.

I drove Nick back to his hotel after the lecture. We sat in the car for a good fifteen minutes talking about the rumors.

"Jerry," he said to me, "there's just so much I can do. I've written letters and now I've given a lecture on the legitimacy and importance of the trackways. But if people don't come, I don't know what else to do."

"I just don't know how much longer I can take this," I said. "Is this kind of thing normal?"

"Sometimes it's worse," Nick answered.

"Nick," I said, "the reason I call you at least once a week is just to hear again that the work I am doing is important and that you haven't changed your mind about what I'm trying to do."

"Look," he responded firmly, "I have told you before. Call me any time you need to. I'll say the same thing every time. I can say it as many times as you need to hear it."

"Thanks," I said. "Expect a lot of calls."

## Rumors and More Rumors

Although very few attended that lecture, word did get around. The hoax and fraud allegations ceased almost overnight. Yet rumors continued as collectors and academics compared notes on the quality of their own material. Nobody had material as good as ours. A biology professor who had collected isolated tracks over a period of years categorically stated, "It was impossible for MacDonald to have collected trackways twenty feet long or more. There just are none to be found in the area." Another collector exclaimed, "I've got tracks on my back porch, I don't understand what all the hoopla's about." Others questioned the statement that amphibian tracks had been collected in the area. "Absolutely not," they said. "Amphibians in the desert?" Still others doubted that individual tracks could be eight inches or more in length since no one had ever found tracks that large before in the Robledos.

Questions arose concerning the quality of the tracks as well. Since all the tracks collected prior to the discovery were found as debris, the specimens had all undergone significant weathering and were badly broken up. How could there be such continuity for fifty feet or more, as we claimed, and so perfectly preserved, in such badly eroded beds? The claim that there was a wide assortment of vertebrates represented by tracks was considered nonsense, as most still believed that the track makers could never be identified.

Through the rumor mill, we learned of an incredible plot to discredit the project. The plan in a nutshell was for some to adopt a "wait and see" attitude. This hands-off policy was justified early on as a result of the hoax allegation. As one scientific defector explained it, if scientists joined the work and the discovery was a hoax, it would become a significant embarrassment to those institutions involved. But if the discovery was not a hoax, there would be no way that we could sustain any kind of research endeavor for very long. In six months, it was believed that we would come crawling to in-staters with our proverbial tail between our legs for financial support. When this happened, they believed that they could push us aside and get control of the project.

It was also argued that since we had virtually no in-state support (for some reason everybody chose to ignore the support of New Mexico Tech) scientists from the Smithsonian and the Carnegie would not stand with us at the press conference. It was believed certain that we could never get Smithsonian and Carnegie scientists to fly out here anyway. But even if we did, we would never get support from them to continue the work. "Institutions fund other institutions, not individuals," we were told. Some local scientists even argued that they could not justify participation in a paleontological excavation run by an amateur. Were we really in the midst of a scientific conspiracy? What difference did it make if we were? We agreed that we were going to ignore the rumors and continue with the project. If we were contacted by participating institutions about some concern about our work, then we would deal with it. Until that time, it was back to work for all of us. The honeymoon—if there ever was one—was over. We had entered into a new and much less pleasant phase. I had asked for it when I checked to see if the door to the Robledos was unlocked.

## Switching Hats

Though I expected scrutiny in a matter of such significance, I was inclined to take the allegations personally. This was because the project was essentially a one-man show; I either got all the credit or all the blame. Except for personal support from Gene and Thom, I searched on my own, sought validation of the discovery on my own, funded the search with my own money, and became convinced of the significance of the material in spite of the opinions of local scientists. It was very hard for me to ignore the allegations.

How could I accept this barrage of criticism objectively? As a paleontologist, this phase of the discovery process was the most difficult for me to endure. I knew I needed some kind of healthy perspective quick, or my research would suffer. My wife had the answer. Next to the advice I received on going back to school (the "tractor" versus the "hoe"), it turned out to be the best piece of advice I ever received. "If it hurts as a paleontologist," she suggested, "then take off the paleontologist's hat. Put on your sociologist's hat and look at the controversy as a sociologist would."

There was immediate relief. "Of course," I exclaimed with great relief, "I've been so stupid." What had seemed so horrible to the paleontologist was fascinating to the sociologist. "What data!" I had within my grasp a wealth of novel information that I had been blind to before that moment.

I remembered my conversation with Donald Black at the University of Virginia. If I wanted good data on the process of discovery, both the good and the bad, I was certainly going to get more than my share. After all, I was a sociologist right smack in the middle of a big paleontological controversy. As a paleontologist I was in hell. As a sociologist I was in heaven.

The controversy was fascinating on a number of different fronts, but especially as a sociological study in discovery legitimation. Naturally, much to the chagrin of some parties involved, I had kept every memo, every article, every letter, all the dates of all the meetings, summaries of phone conversations, even videotape. I had a lot of objective, verifiable data.

Most of the controversy surrounding the trackway discovery took the form of rumors and hearsay. The written record took the form of miscellaneous interdepartmental memos circulating here or there seeking clarification based on this rumor or that. But eventually some clear documentation emerged which captured the essence of the allegations against the Robledo discovery.

About seven months after the rumors surfaced, we finally received some solid, objective information. We had a letter. Now the rumors gave way to what we hoped would be more legitimate scientific concerns. Now perhaps we could begin to address doubts with scientific answers. The letter was sent to the Las Cruces BLM office, and we were surprised that it contained all of the issues that previously circulated as rumor, although the allegations of hoax and fraud were omitted.

It was a strange letter. It was as if it had been lost in the mail for six months before being delivered. Most of the claims had long since been dealt with. But there were a few new arguments, and it was helpful for us to finally have written verification of the rumors circulated previously by word of mouth.

But after reading the letter, Gene, Thom, and I were left with the impression that there *was* some big secret meeting held somewhere in the state, in which scientists and administrators (the letter referred to them as the "scientific community") discussed how it seemed that we were systematically destroying fossils as well as reputations.

"Have you ever heard of this guy?" Gene asked.

"I don't have the foggiest idea who he is," I replied. "He's never called me, visited the site, seen the collected specimens or so much as a photograph. His name has never even come up in any previous discussions."

"I thought we had a pretty good idea where all the trouble was coming from, until this," Thom said. "Who in the world is this guy? And who is this 'scientific community' he refers to?"

"It's obvious that it is not anybody already involved in the project," I noted with some relief. "There's a pretty significant scientific community in our corner."

"That narrows it down," Gene huffed. "We can only assume that the scientific community referred to in the letter are people who are not involved."

"Everybody wants to be in the loop," I noted, "but it seems to me that there are better ways to ask to be involved than this."

This was the first time that we or the local BLM office had ever heard that there may be some widespread concern over the excavation. The news was as much of a shock to the BLM as it was to us. Everything up to this point seemed to be going great. The museums and institutions participating in the research were pleased with the progress we had made. For the year and a half since I made the discovery of the big trackways there was not the slightest hint of a problem from anywhere. Those who for one reason or another were not interested in participating in the project never gave us a thought. What had stirred the bees now? What brought about this deluge in the desert?

Although superficially it seemed that the gist of the letter was to discredit my work and question my expertise and technical support, the real point of the letter was in its recommendations. It suggested that because of the evidence of my incompetence, and, by inference, that of the Las Cruces BLM office as well, that authority over the fossils should be transferred from the Las Cruces District, on whose land the discovery was made, to the Albuquerque District.

I first learned of the letter when I came home from a difficult day of excavating. I had a flashing red light on my answering machine. I innocently pushed the play button.

"Hi, Jerry, this is Mike at the BLM. We have a big problem. It appears that some people are trying to close down the trackway project, and they're really going after you, personally. It's an unfortunate thing, but can you come down to the office so that we can have your help in trying to answer this thing. We'd sure appreciate it. Since the Smithsonian and the Carnegie museums are involved in the project, we have asked them to respond as well. So you're not alone."

I drove to the BLM office feeling like a man who had been run over by a steam roller. Tim Salt, the area manager, met me at the door.

"I don't want you to worry about this, Jerry," Tim began. "We have this under control. We don't condone this kind of thing. If you want to, you can read the letter, but I have to warn you, it's pretty severe."

I made a mistake. I read the letter. Forgetting the advice of my wife, I did not read it as a sociologist would have. I did get hurt. The wound still has not healed. I was immersed in a kind of inquisition and was totally unprepared for the politics of paleontology. All of my training and experience as a sociologist did not help.

"He obviously knows who I am," I said. "I don't understand why he just didn't call me up and voice his concerns to me."

"None of us understand it," said Pam Smith, the BLM worker in charge of the sobering task of answering the letter's allegations.

"But, Jerry," Pam continued, "he didn't call any of us in our district office, or anyone else who has seen the sites or been involved with the project. He didn't call any of us."

It was small consolation. Before this, the rumors were from faceless people from institutions that could not be identified, from critics who had not come out in the open. The letter put a face on the opposition. A name on the post. Now we knew.

The letter was charged with sensational rhetoric. It made it appear like my trackway project had the power to destroy the credibility of the science of paleontology and the good name of the unblemished "scientific community."

It said that the project's new research endeavors were causing "incalculable damage to the site," and, further, that the "material is nothing more than worthless souvenirs." The project was "damaging the integrity and credibility of the paleontology program." My work was also an utter failure. "What could be a valid, important, scientific research effort [is] a disappointing failure, so far."

"What on earth do they think the quarry miners were doing to the material?" I exploded to Tim. "If a planned excavation of the material, supervised by the Smithsonian and Carnegie museums, was causing incalculable damage to the tracks, why had the quarry operation continued for twenty years without a single paleontological protest?"

"And I'd like to know why these people who 'knew' about the tracks never informed us of the occurrence and did nothing to save them all those years," Tim added.

I thought back to the Alabama coal mine. The coal miners came across tracks in Mine 11 as they were ripping out the coal. They informed the supervisor. He notified the owner, who in turn notified a geologist. With a cooperative agreement from the owner, the tracks began to be excavated. If the Alabama coal mine discovery was dealt with as the Robledo discovery was, the reports of tracks in the mine would have been ignored in Birmingham, and the Geological Survey, not the mining operation, would have been accused of causing significant damage to the trackway layers.

"They really don't know the extent of what's going on down here," Tim said.

"That's no excuse," I fumed. "Doesn't anybody check anything out before they claim that the scientific sky is falling? I mean, we do have phones here in New Mexico, don't we? How did I become the bad guy in this? Why are they going after me now? The discovery was almost two years ago and the press conference happened six months ago."

I took a copy of the letter to Gene's office. We also called Thom Votaw. They, too, were amazed at the allegation that I was destroying the footprints.

"What about the collectors who were making fireplace walls out of track material? What about the professor who had tracks on his back porch?" Gene asked as he leaned back in his chair. "Now, Jerry, tell me," Gene said sarcastically. "I really want to know. How does your systematic excavation of these track sites cause incalculable damage to the track sites? I mean, they can't be serious. This has got to be a joke."

Then he grinned. "I see that Nick's name is spelled wrong again."

"No way," I said.

"Take a look for yourself. It's right there. 'Not even the eminent Dr. Hotten'—Hotten, with an 'e'."

We joked about how Nick had told us that the only important thing about the press is that they spell your name correctly. It didn't happen to Nick at the press conference, and it didn't happen to him this time. That was the only funny thing we could find in the whole letter, and we all latched on to this tiny ray of humor like apes to bananas.

After I calmed down a little, I gave Nick Hotton a call. He had already been informed of the letter and the allegations by the BLM. In fact, the letter was on his desk when I called. It had been faxed to him minutes before.

"Jerry," he said in a businesslike tone, "first thing is this—I've seen worse. I know that this may be small consolation to you, but it's really not as bad as it could be. I get this kind of bug squat all the time. There's always somebody somewhere ruffling his feathers. I mean, the stories I could tell you . . ."

"I don't want to hear them," I said quickly.

"No, I didn't think you did," Nick said with a chuckle. "How's the BLM taking this?"

"Great, just great. They say they are still behind my work 100 percent."

"That's good," Nick said, "because I would really hate to see this excavation stopped. It's really that important. It's not the end of the world," Nick continued. "You'll get through this. You just keep digging, and it'll all be taken care of. Hang in there, kiddo."

*Nicholas Hotton of the Smithsonian studies a pelycosaur trackway from layer ten of AF 2.* Photo by Jerry MacDonald.

I was about to hang up the phone when Nick said, "Oh, by the way, I noticed that my name was misspelled again."

As I look back on it now, it was kind of funny. I heard the phrase "Jerry, calm down" at least twice a minute. But from a sociological point of view, I found it worrisome that a letter like this could be circulated as truth within the nebulous "scientific community" when there was no attempt to verify any of the information the letter contained. All of these allegations had been answered months ago.

Thinking back to the Alabama coal mine again, I remembered that when word of the tracks reached Arthur Blair's ears in Birmingham, by his own admission, he was skeptical. Yet he made a special trip to see the site for himself before jumping to conclusions. He undoubtedly saved months, if not years, of adversarial encounters. And a skeptical Roland Bird traveled to Glen Rose to investigate the footprint occurrences there solely on the basis of the reports of a shop owner over a thousand miles away. He traveled there even though he knew that half of the specimens at the shop were forgeries.

In 1929, Walter Jones visited the Alabama coal mine, collected specimens along with others, and wrote a report on the occurrence for publication in the Alabama Geological Survey journal even though he noted in his article that the trackways were insignificant. To their credit, Alabama geologists wrote a commendable report on the coal mine tracks, in spite of the trackways' perceived insignificance. This kind of thing did not happen with the Robledo tracks. Apparently, the tracks were considered to be so insignificant that no kind of preliminary report was ever written by the "scientific community." They were virtually ignored, until now.

If the Alabama site, as insignificant as it was, was described thoroughly, why were the Robledo tracks ignored sixty years later? Had science regressed since 1929? Certainly the written opinions of the Smithsonian and the Carnegie concerning the Robledo trackways should have carried more weight than the report of a shop owner in New Mexico about the Glen Rose trackways. Yet no one came to investigate the claims firsthand.

Was it legitimate scientifically for some to brush aside two evaluations noting the great significance of the Robledo deposit by acknowledged experts in the Permian of North America? To dismiss two years of subsequent scientific research as exaggeration? And to condemn two years of hard excavation work an incompetent failure? This festering skepticism promoted adversarial encounters that lasted for years.

Glen Kuban noticed the unusual amount of skepticism generated over the discovery and suggested a possible source:

> Motivation for any carving or salting suggestions must be sought outside the realm of science. Perhaps one factor behind the suggestions of hoax or fraud (I hesitate to say 'sour grapes') is that the ichnological richness of the area was largely unknown to local geologists—many of whom expressed skepticism that anything more than an occasional track could be found in the Robledos. Moreover, it was one highly motivated individual, and not a large team from a major museum, university, or federal agency, who brought the richness of the area to light.
>
> Indeed, perhaps as impressive as the tracks themselves is the stamina and persistence of Jerry MacDonald in locating the major track beds, and then excavating (by hand), and transporting (by foot) hundreds of heavy slabs down treacherous mountain washes—all the while contending with criticisms that his finds were dubious, minor, or even nonexistent.

Although it was almost one hundred years since the Bone Wars had ended, the quirks of human nature that brought them into existence seemed to be alive and well and just waiting to surface.

My training in sociology saved me in a number of ways. I was always entirely open with the Las Cruces BLM office. I often provided verbal reports of my work. I was also appointed a volunteer for the agency and was listed as a guest scientific researcher for the duration of my excavation. I invited BLM officials to the sites, informed them of newly discovered outcrops, and showed them new material. I also made sure that they met personally with the scientists who came to visit the discovery sites, including, on several occasions, Hotton and Berman. On their part, the Las Cruces BLM office very often asked me to lead political and agency dignitaries on tours of the site or the lab, and I never refused them. We had a fine working relationship based on goodwill and frequent communication. Yet, if there had been minimal communication between the project and the BLM, the letter could have had more serious results. I now like to look at the letter as a gift from that great sociologist in the sky.

Presently, I understand that I was really a pawn in a turf battle. The maligning that was done to my character and my professionalism was simply a stepping stone in the bigger battle over turf. What was said about me would have been said about anybody who had done what I had done. The issues were political in nature and were between Albuquerque and Las Cruces, and I was unfortunate enough to be stuck smack-dab in the middle. And more importantly, the author of the letter is now one of the project's supporters.

Still, the rumors and allegations weighed heavily on my mind. But again my wife came to my rescue.

"They want you to stop," she suggested. "They want you to give up, to lose heart. They think one man doesn't have a chance against an army. But you're tougher than that. You just keep doing what you've done all along. Keep working. Let the fossils convince them of the importance of the work. Defend the material. Only you can expose them to the world."

"You're right," I said. "Exposing the fossils is my greatest defense. I'll just have to work harder."

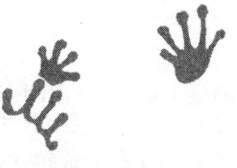

# Chapter Nine

## One Man Against a Mountain: Full-time Excavation Work Begins

The excavation I began during the summer of 1987 is still entirely "human powered." Most of the sites, including the discovery site, AF 2, are very remote, and four-wheel-vehicles can only come within one-half mile of the excavation.

By the summer of 1988, the excavation was proceeding at full throttle. The year 1988 was spent marking out the perimeters of the main excavation, removing the overburden, and investigating other outcrops in the Robledos for tracks and trails. By the end of 1988, I had found fourteen other track-bearing outcrops, and three of them appeared to be even richer than the discovery site. The fourteen trackway outcrops preserved in this small geographic region vary in size from thirty feet to nearly one thousand feet in extent. Some are eight to ten feet thick, and others, like AF 10 and AF 13, are at least fifty feet thick with one hundred track-bearing layers.

The year 1989 was a banner one for me and the project. I expanded the excavation at AF 2 horizontally from forty feet to 120 feet. I worked like a madman, taking my frustrations out on every limestone slab that stood in my way. The limestone slabs contained no fossils and were simply in the way, so I could be as destructive with them as I was careful with the trackway slabs. I swung my sledge-hammer as hard as I could to break the one-thousand-pound limestone slabs into one-hundred-pound pieces. I would then heave them down the mountain to get them out of the way.

I suffered the normal beatings of a seasoned quarryman. Sometimes, while trying to pry apart layers still in place, I missed the chisel and hit my wrist with the hammer. Or my prybar would slip and jam my fingers between two slabs. Sometimes rock chips would fly up into my face and, even though I wore protective glasses, the shards, sharp as glass, would often become imbedded in my face. I occasionally lost control of a rock that I stood on edge and it would crash down onto my foot.

Taking out rock from the site to the truck was usually no easy matter. Sometimes I stumbled to the ground while hauling out one-hundred-pound rocks on my back. Sometimes I got sick from the heat, and all the symptoms of heat stroke, which are too unsavory to mention, accompanied me all the way back to my truck.

In 1989 alone, in my solitary effort to preserve the trackways, I hauled on my back more than twenty tons of trackway material over the one-half-mile walk to my jeep. I often averaged four trips a day with a cumulative weight of over five hundred pounds. The heaviest slab I carried out weighed 175 pounds and preserved eight perfect pelycosaur footprints. It took an hour to get out. I carried out its other half, all 150 pounds of it, the next day. These loaded trips to the jeep must have looked comical to anyone who came across my path. I looked like a big moving rock with a hat and legs.

That year I also carried out the three long trackways from layer ten, which included the discovery trackway that had waited patiently for nearly two years to be reunited with the discovery slab I took out on June 6, 1987. By the end of 1989, I had rearranged more than 120 tons of rock.

The physical toll on my body was great: a torn rotator cuff in my shoulder, nerve damage in my right heel, torn cartilage in my right knee, a large cyst in my right ankle which emerged after a bad sprain, numbness in my right thumb and my left wrist from unprotected hits with a heavy hammer, a thickening of the membranes around my left eye, which keeps it constantly red and sore, and continual bruises on my shoulders and neck from the straps of my backpack. This is to say nothing of smashed fingers, periodic heat stroke, the worst menace of all—swarms of blackflies—and the ongoing menace of scorpions, centipedes, and rattlesnakes.

The work was really not so solitary. The trackways kept me company, and as I said earlier, I learned the fine art of talking out loud to myself. The silence and loneliness was deafening. I brought no radio. I worked alone in the quiet in the middle of the mountains. Often the only sounds were my tools clanging against solid rock. I brought no beer, no pop, no food. Just water and trail mix. I was in heaven. Paleontology and sociology are in large part solitary sciences. I was at home in either world.

*The author undertakes his solitary work at AF 2.* Photo by Pearl MacDonald.

*The AF 2 site in May 1990. It is considered the largest single-handed excavation currently known. Only hand tools are used.* Photo by Jerry MacDonald.

In 1991, when *Smithsonian* writer Doug Stuart came for a week to gather information for an article on the project, he remarked with amazement that I could not give him directions to Las Cruces from the El Paso airport forty miles away, or from his hotel in Las Cruces, but I knew every jeep and animal trail in the Robledos. There were no signs, no artificial rock pile to point the way, no streamer strategically placed on a cactus. Nothing. As far as Doug was concerned, we were in the middle of nowhere.

As I was excavating out in the desert, allegations and rumors continued to fly back and forth, but the thrill of discovery helped create an impenetrable shield. There was nothing more satisfying than forgetting the politics and discovering something new every day, that is if you can call Permian rock new! Every day something remarkable would turn up. Sometimes it would be a new trackway, other times it would be a better example of a trackway that I had already found. In seven years of consistent work in the Robledos, I never had a disappointing day. There was always another treasure from the past.

In a short time the specimens mounted up, until by the end of 1989 I had recovered nearly one thousand trackways. You can probably understand my concern when I learned that some people claimed that I had discovered nothing!

So when is something a discovery? The key sociological question is this: Is general awareness of the existence of "treasure" equal with the specific discovery of "treasure"? The Robledo discovery could be compared, in principle if not in magnitude, to two other scientific discoveries that occurred about seventy years earlier. Both of these earlier finds were field (as opposed to lab) discoveries, and both of them were initially considered improbable. The first was the discovery of the ninth planet, Pluto, in 1930, and the second was the discovery of King Tut's tomb in 1922. The first discovery was considered improbable because an amateur was searching among a troop of professionals, and the other was considered improbable because professionals had supposedly combed the area so thoroughly that it was believed impossible that they all could have missed it.

Both discoveries relied heavily on the work of earlier scientists, both were openly sought, and both were widely believed to exist. The same could be said of the Robledo tracks. They were at least known to exist, yet whether anyone other than myself really believed in the motherlode is open to question.

After observing unexplained gravitational forces tugging on Uranus and Neptune, astronomers began to suspect that perhaps there was a ninth planet circling the sun. Percival Lowell, a man of independent wealth, and one who loved astronomy so much that he built his own observatory, was the key man in the hunt. In 1915, Lowell carried out a computation (similar to the one that had led to the discovery of Neptune) to determine the possible mass and position of this unknown planet. Based on his calculations, Lowell believed that he knew of Planet X's location in the sky, and set out to find it. The discovery of Planet X would have been the capstone in Lowell's controversial career in astronomy, but he died one year after starting his search for the mystery planet.

The existence of Planet X was no secret, and numerous scientists around the world continued to hunt for it after Lowell's death in 1916. Many of these astronomers had better telescopes than the one at Lowell Observatory in Flagstaff, Arizona. Yet, the ninth planet eluded discovery until 1930.

Clyde Tombaugh built a nine-inch telescope out of old farm machinery parts and passed his free time by gazing at the stars and planets. He longed to go to college to study astronomy, but his family was too poor to send him. Undaunted, Tombaugh secured a job as an assistant at Lowell Observatory in 1929. Though Lowell had been dead for fourteen years, the hunt for Planet X was still very much alive. Tombaugh, an untrained and uneducated amateur, jumped into the race with remarkable confidence.

For nearly a year, he photographed three-quarters of all the stars observed through Lowell's telescope, believing that the elusive planet would only be detected by its movements. Each photograph contained between fifty thousand and half a million stars. He thought that if he compared photographs of the same section of sky two nights in a row, he might be able to detect if one of those "stars" moved against a motionless background.

Yet Tombaugh observed just such a movement on February 18, 1930. He observed a "star" in a pair of photographs which was in a slightly different place from one day to the next. To verify the discovery, Tombaugh suppressed news of it for a month while he verified his observations—a necessity ethically, but very dangerous since someone else could announce its discovery before him. On March 13, 1930, Tombaugh announced to an astonished profession that he had found the planet that had eluded the experts for fifteen years. In fact, after Tombaugh's impressive discovery, the University of Kansas gave him a full scholarship and opportunity to receive the accreditation he desired. But Tombaugh was a scientist long before he was a degree-carrying astronomer.

The Valley of the Kings in Egypt was known by Egyptologists to contain Eighteenth Dynasty tombs and artifacts, but the tombs that were found had been looted, and it seemed very unlikely that anyone would find one that was completely intact. In fact, by 1922, all but one of the tombs built during the Eighteenth Dynasty had been found. The likelihood of finding the last tomb was fading. The Valley of the Kings had been so well searched that very few archaeologists continued to work in the area, and those that remained were working previous discoveries. One lone benefactor, Lord Carnarvon, remained to search for the last tomb. In November 1922, Carnavon's field man, Howard Carter, shocked the archaeological world by discovering King Tutankhamen's tomb, right smack in the middle of major excavations of other much larger tombs.

There had been tantalizing clues to the existence and location of Tutankhamen's tomb. Fragmentary references to King Tut had been found by archaeologists for years, all in the Valley of the Kings. Since all other Eighteenth Dynasty pharaohs were buried in the Valley of the Kings, it seemed certain that Tutankhamen's tomb was located there as well. Still, his tomb could not be found, and, in time, everybody gave up, including foremost archaeologist and excavator of the Valley of the Kings Theodore Davis.

Another dampening effect on continued searches for the tomb was the fact that because all of the other tombs had been looted and that Tutankhamen was a minor pharaoh, the prospects of finding significant artifacts inside his tomb were slim. But Lord Carnarvon and his outstanding field man, Howard Carter, were not deferred. Carter looked for the tomb right next to the already excavated tomb of Ramses VI, but his excavation debris began to block tourist access to Ramses's much-visited tomb.

Carter broke off the excavation and moved his search to around the tomb of Tuthmosis III. Work in this locality was poorly rewarded. Carter's workers grew weary, but he did not give up the search. Lord Carnarvon wired him money for one last look around the tomb of Ramses VI. Carter decided to remove the pharaonic workers' huts, where the men who built the pharaoh's tomb had lived. As he cleared the first hut he found the steps of a staircase that had been filled in with stones. It took two days to clear it. The stairs led to a walled-up door bearing the seal of Tutankhamen. The entrance to Tutankhamen's tomb had been buried by the builders of Ramses's tomb.

On November 26, 1922, Carter and his men found a second sealed door, but unable to gain access through it, they broke through an area of the adjoining wall. Entering a room lit only by their torches, Carter and his men were stunned by the sight— Tutanhkamen's tomb at last, perfectly intact. Carter's discovery was the talk of the world.

## A Line in the Sand

The Robledo discovery had certain elements in common with both of these earlier discoveries. Like the discovery of Pluto, it was made by an amateur in a geological area so well studied that the existence of a trackway motherlode was never seriously considered. It was difficult to comprehend the abundance, variety, and quality of the fossils. They were so much above anything found before that the fossils are best analyzed by comparison. What I found in the Robledos is a discovery of contrast. How did the newly discovered specimens compare and the quality of the trackways compare with those found prior to 1987? How great was the variety of tracks as opposed to those previously collected? And how did the continuity of the trackway faunules compare with the broken-up debris that was characteristic of pre-1987 collecting?

Initially, only five specimens from the Robledos were curated, three at NMSU, one at the NMMNH, and one, the Torres slab, at the Las Cruces Natural History Museum. But that was it. Five small slabs don't make a trackway bonanza, but over a thousand slabs, collected in a single year—well, that's quite a different-sized scientific sample.

To the Smithsonian and Carnegie museums, the *new* declaration of significance, based upon a never-before acquired collection, *was* the discovery. Though general awareness of tracks from the Robledos was well-known, specific knowledge was much harder to come by, as my search for the motherlode proved.

As with the discoveries of the planet Pluto and King Tut's tomb, awareness of the existence of objects as big as a planet or as small as a tomb results in no tangible activity until someone decides to hunt for them. Subsequent questions about just where the planet or tomb would be, as well as making plans as to how one goes about finding them, is an important part of the pre-discovery phase and involves a lot of preliminary work.

Prior awareness that the area produced occasional footprints was sufficient enough for me to begin the formulation of both research and excavation plans. I considered the few tracks found prior to 1987 significant enough to initiate a search for the "motherlode." My attachment of significance before 1987 was my "bug in the brain." I began the search, not because of what was known to be, but because of what I imagined *could* be out there. Prior awareness on my part was transformed into specific knowledge on June 6, 1987. It was that event that had to be confirmed by the experts. These experts finally had enough material to base an opinion of significance on the Robledo deposit. All other opinions, including mine before June 6, 1987, were hypothetical.

With hundreds of new specimens to evaluate, Hotton pointed out that the old trackway material just couldn't stand up to the endless array of new material now found in the locality. Awareness gave way to knowledge, knowledge that a motherlode existed in the Robledos. I was holding the proof of it in my hands. What happened in the summer of 1987 was the discovery of a bonanza of tracks and trails, which for the first time gave scientists a wealth of material to base authoritative evaluations of significance.

"The significance of this trackway locality is not exaggerated," Hotton said in this regard. "I suspect that there are at least as many species represented in the Robledos locality as in the Coconino [of the Grand Canyon] . . . The Robledos locality provides a glimpse of the life activities of most, and probably all major taxanomic categories of Lower Permian tetrapods otherwise known only from bones, to say nothing of the life activities of otherwise virtually unknown arthropods. I, therefore, cannot accept the view that ascribing great significance to this locality is erroneous and misleading." Berman agreed. "To date," Berman asserted, "[MacDonald's] collection, with its accompanying data, constitutes an invaluable scientific discovery. In quality, quantity, and diversity it surpasses anything that I have seen reported."

So the essence of the discovery was in the recovery of hundreds upon hundreds of specimens that could be evaluated on three levels: On the quantity of trackways, the quality of the trackways, and the variety of the trackways. The conclusion? On these three points, the Robledo Mountains *are* the home of the best Paleozoic trackway sites in the world. On June 6, 1987, awareness gave way to knowledge.

## God's Saran Wrap

So what was I doing out in the middle of nowhere day after day, for over six years? I was digging up the past. And as I did so, the wonderful panoply of animals that engaged in eating each other at the

Permian restaurant slowly began taking shape. I was also slowly reading the menu by which these animals chose their meals.

It was also on June 6, 1987, that I found out why the Robledos material got so much better once excavation work began. I found a thin film of dust in between the two halves of the discovery slab. I remember pealing it off the tracks with my fingernail. Its thickness was no more than a thirty-second of an inch. At first, I thought it was a nasty inconvenience. I didn't recognize or understand the great importance of that separation layer (some call such a feature a delaminating horizon) for several months.

The separation layer is also called a "clay drape." It results from low energy conditions during breaks in sedimentation. Clay drapes often occur between the episodes of sedimentation that produce the main layers. Track making often takes place during these breaks in sedimentation.

Ron Ratkevitch first mentioned the layer to me years before, but its importance eluded me until I had quite a bit of experience splitting slabs. The layers with the film split relatively easily, those lacking it, with great difficulty. Fifty percent of the material from AF 2 possessed the film, the rest did not.

I have come to view that super-thin film as the most crucial layer from the excavations. I affectionately call it "God's saran wrap," because that tiny layer served to protect the trackway surface from bonding with the overwash mud or sand that came into the area a short time after the tracks were made. This film determines the quality of the Robledo trackway deposit, for without it, six years of work would have taken twelve years, and there may have been too little material too late to have kept me going. My work might have reinforced a fifty-year-old bias about the insignificance of the tracks.

When people found small slabs with tiny tracks, weathered for who knows how long, the "saran wrap" was long gone, easily washed away and dissolved by the first rain after exposure. The impression left when these small slabs were found was that without a thin delaminating layer, splitting the layers in situ would be about the same as trying to separate two layers of concrete poured one on top of the other. Bigfoot could have walked across the first layer of concrete, forever proving its existence, and yet we would never be able to split that horizon for any measurable distance because the concrete layers bonded to one another.

Finally, the false assumption found in literature and popular opinion that these and many other tracks could never be properly identified, either due to poor quality, or to lack of supportive research, was the most significant hindrance to their proper study. It seemed that the prevailing view was that these trackways could easily languish in a museum drawer for another 280 million years before they were finally identified.

The assumption that tracks are not useful has fueled an almost universal neglect of such evidence. In reality tracks are varied and interesting from a paleontological point of view, and much can be learned if we start at the beginning and work systematically at the problem. It is just that few people have done so until now. It is a big Pandora's box waiting to be opened—a lot of work and trouble for those who dare open it.

The main problem is how do we identify ancient track makers when we cannot see the animal that made the tracks in the first place? For decades, this problem hindered research efforts into fossil trackways. But today, false assumptions concerning the identification and analysis of trackways have been overturned by a decade of valuable research in the comparison and compilation of trackway catalogues. These fossil footprint identification catalogues are similar to modern footprint identification guides that one can purchase at the local bookstore. But, unlike modern track guides that boldly state which trackmaker belongs to which tracks, fossil footprint catalogues are primarily ones of comparison. Just like modern catalogues, these fossil trackway descriptions make the identification process much simpler. The best trackway catalogues were compiled by German scientist Hartmut Haubold in 1984 and by Italian scientist Giuseppe Leonardi in 1987.

Scientists in Europe, for example, can look at the Robledo catalogue and say, "Yes, this trackway that I've found in the red beds of France is very similar to those found in the red beds of New Mexico." Conversely, I have been able to match a number of Robledo trackways to trackways described in the aforementioned catalogues. Still other tracks that I have found have no companion trackways listed in any of the fossil trackway catalogues published to date.

Just as with skeletal remains, ichnologists attach scientific names to tracks. But these scientific names are not the same as those given to animals known from skeletal evidence. For example, *Dimetrodon* is the genus name for the animal itself, whereas *Dimetropus* may be the genus name for its fossilized trail. This has sometimes led to confusion over just who or what made certain tracks. Unfortunately, no one can be authoritative as to exactly which animal made which track, and it will remain that way until someone is lucky enough to follow a fossilized trail that preserved the track maker itself at the end of it. This occasionally happens with invertebrate trails, where an insect or arthropod is found squished in the mud at the end of a trail. But with vertebrates, don't hold your breath.

Yet trackway identification has become infinitely more rigorous than it was even fifteen years ago. The new Robledo research material, coupled with recent research results on fossil trackways from around the world, prove that many Robledo trackways can be identified at various levels—such as class, order, family, and genus—and daring souls seem to be able to identify ichnospecies.

The Robledo material seems to be representative of a wide range of taxonomic track categories. The preliminary assessment of track makers appears to include five subclasses of vertebrates, three among the reptiles (anapsids, diapsids, and synapsids) and two among the amphibians (labrynthodonts and lepospondyls) alone, breaking down into perhaps eleven distinct orders. There appear to be numerous families and genera. And then there are the invertebrate trackways, which are somewhat easier to identify since many taxonomic categories still exist today. One can only guess at the number of various arthropods and insects represented. By the fall of 1989 there appeared to be dozens of separate ichnotaxa of both invertebrate and vertebrate animals represented, as well as several plant species.

However, even more exciting than the amazing diversity of animal life was the fact that many of these animals (some estimates suggest perhaps half of the census) are new, undiscovered species. These mysterious trackways have no match found anywhere else within existing catalogues.

In spring 1990, Dave Berman of the Carnegie Museum of Natural History arrived to transport two long reptile trackways back east. One, a twenty-five-foot trackway, preserved the trails of two pelycosaurs moving sub-parallel to each other. Included in this trackway was the discovery slab. This trackway (still my personal favorite) was to be exhibited at the Carnegie Museum in Pittsburgh. The other trackway, a twenty-foot trackway of a single pelycosaur, was bound for the Smithsonian to be used for research purposes by Nick Hotton. The last six feet of this trackway included the slabs that were stolen in October 1988.

When Dave and I visited the site, nearly two years had passed since Dave had first viewed the site. I had twelve layers exposed with fifteen different trackways. In a heartwarming compliment, Dave told me that my work was the largest single-manned, human-powered excavation that he had ever seen or heard about. I felt very proud.

"What you have found is a virtual telephone directory of probably every animal known from bones," Dave remarked, "and a whole range of animals we know nothing about. It just shows how bone discoveries have just scratched the surface for understanding the varieties and numbers of these animals," Dave continued.

Dave and I were battling pesky black flies all morning, so we were preoccupied with insect warfare as we viewed the layers. "I have never seen so many different trackmakers at one site," Dave said. "And I have never heard or read of any site that preserves this many different animals. You could spend several lifetimes here, you know."

"Yes, I know," I said with an exhausted look.

I knew that I had already sacrificed my entire body to this work. I gave everything I had to expose this ancient and unknown community. I just didn't know how much "umph" I had left. Jesus told a parable to his disciples that sums up what I did when I found the motherlode. "The Kingdom of Heaven is like a treasure hidden in a field, and when a man found it, he sold all that he had and bought the field."

Although I couldn't go out and buy the mountain, I "bought" it in every other way. But the treasure I found and preserved was on public land. Access and rights of "ownership" was still a hotly debated topic. Federal, state, and local politics became more and more involved in the project, and more and more competitive. By 1990, it had become apparent that two different camps were working under two different opinions about the Robledo trackways. Something had to breach this deadlock or the big loser was going to be "science" itself.

# Chapter Ten

## Dune Canyon

"It is hard to tell you of the discoveries of the last month without my emotions rushing through the keys," I wrote to Nick Hotton in September 1989. Something big had happened. We had made another discovery, and this one turned the Paleozoic window into a bank of French doors.

About twenty miles northeast of the Robledo red bed sites there was another deposit of tracks and trackways preserved on very thick slabs of yellow rock. The deposits were found completely by accident. We literally stumbled over them.

I was working at one of the Robledo track sites on a Saturday, when I heard the sound of footsteps echoing through the canyon. I was apprehensive about working when hikers went by, because I did not want anybody to know the location of any of the track sites. My visitors turned out to be a young man, his wife, and seven children.

"Are you all out for a hike in the mountains?" I asked rhetorically.

"Not exactly," the young man said. "We're looking for the fossil footprints we read about in *Earth Science*. Do you know where they are?"

Oh, no, I said to myself. "Yeah, they're over in the next canyon," I said to him. "But the locations are secret. I don't think it's a good idea to go out looking for them."

"What are *you* doing here?" the young man asked.

"I'm doing sedimentological research," I answered. "I'm gathering samples of a variety of sedimentary features for analysis." This was my standard response. I had used it on several previous occasions to deflect further questions. "So you read *Earth Science*?" I continued. "That's kind of a specialized journal, isn't it?"

"I'm a geologist of sorts," the young man replied. "I'm a graduate student in the Education Department at NMSU. My undergraduate work was in earth science, but I'm now enrolled in the
Education Department for my master's degree."

Now where have I heard this before? I asked myself. Should I say
something or keep my big mouth shut?

"So you think there are no tracks in this canyon?" the young man
asked. "That's kind of strange because I have been following little
bits and pieces of track debris for the last hour or so and it all leads
right here."

That does it, I thought. I saw myself in this young man. He had
done the very thing I had done to get to this site, which I had labeled
AF 13, and which lay about a mile south of the discovery site (AF 2).
I wasn't sure if I should be honest or evasive. If I told him the truth,
he might tell others, or he might come back to collect "my" footprints when I wasn't here.

"Okay, there are tracks here," I answered. "I'm the guy you've
read about. I have to be very careful, because my first concern is the
safety of the tracks."

"I understand," the young man said.

"I have to hand it to you," I said. You've followed your nose to
a site that no one but me has ever found. Now that you're here, what
are you planning to do? It's illegal for you to collect fossils, you
know."

"Your secret's safe with me," he answered, "but I was wondering
if I could work with you. No pay. Most of my graduate courses are at
night, so most of my days are free."

Where have I heard *that* before? I said to myself. It looked more
and more like the only difference between this guy and me was that
he had kept having kids when I stopped at three. "Your last name
isn't MacDonald, is it?" I asked in amazement.

"No," he answered rather puzzled. "My name is Doug Wood.
I thought *you* were MacDonald?"

"I am," I answered. "It's just that you really remind me of someone. Me!"

Doug Wood became my first trackway excavation assistant. I needed
another me. Doug was a gift from God. He had three months to go
before completing his master's and moving back to Utah, but in the
meantime, his job was simple. He was to look for more trackway sites.

After Doug had worked with me for a little over a month, he
went with some friends to look at a petroglyph site to the north of

the Robledos. As he was scouring the rocks looking for signs, his recently acquired eye for tracks caused him to pause for a moment. There at his feet was a small track. Even more surprising than finding the track was the color of the rock it was on, an orangish yellow slab of mudstone. Doug wasn't immediately sure of what he had found. But as he looked around, he noticed he was standing on a slope loaded with rocks of the same type. It didn't take long to find more tracks. He collected some samples and rushed to my house.

"Jerry, I found a site," he said excitedly.

"Great," I answered. "Where is it?"

"It's not in the Robledos," he answered. "It's in another mountain range."

"You're kidding."

"They're in the Dune Canyon mountains.

"No way, Doug. Those mountains are made up of nothing but volcanic material. They're deader than a doornail in terms of fossils."

I suddenly caught myself. Here was a young man with a box full of tracks who was seeking a response from me, and I was skeptical. Worse, my mind was no longer open. I had taken on the role of the skeptic to whom I first brought *my* tracks a couple of years ago, and I had just answered Doug in the same way I was answered, skeptically.

We went to Doug's pick-up. In the back there were a half-dozen track-bearing slabs. "They sure are tracks," I said. I was determined to avoid the closed-minded attitude that I had just expressed, but any remaining thoughts of skepticism quickly vanished. "This one is fantastic," I said as Doug held up an amphibian trackway. "It's definitely something new. I don't have anything even remotely like it from the Robledos. Let's get a geological map and see what's up."

Doug showed me on the map approximately where he had found the tracks. Sure enough, there was a tiny seam of the Abo formation in a couple of canyons in the north range. "Look at that," I said excitedly. "The shore is there, sure enough. And this is all that remains of it in the entire range. Isn't that interesting?"

We went back out early the next day to take advantage of the low-angle sun. One immediate observation as we approached the Abo from the south was that the Early Permian sediments in the Dune Canyon mountains were actually lower than the surrounding relief, hidden by deposits of young sand and alluvium. As we drove to the access road from the highway, Doug pointed out where the tracks had come from. From the interstate all we could see were sand dunes with the sterile volcanics of the Dune Canyon Range in the background. But that was the secret, for in between the dunes and the mountains was the slightest little sliver of Abo strata, so minute when compared to the relatively abundant Robledo outcrops as to be totally overshadowed and easy to overlook.

The road to the sediments was actually a jeep trail through countless dunes. It betrayed no hint of red bed sediments, but once we crossed the deepest arroyo, the geography changed from sand to rock. The sand dunes disappeared and red bed and limestone layers predominated.

There was no report of trackways from this locality in any of the literature. And no wonder. One would never have guessed there would be any Permian deposits in the area. We were stunned by the sheer size of the "sliver." Finding tracks in this area was a breakthrough for us conceptually, as it expanded our vision beyond a few square miles of earth to a much bigger study area. Later, we were to learn how much bigger the track area really was. From now on it seemed we could take nothing for granted. I began to realize that, for the most part, southern New Mexico had never undergone a comprehensive vertebrate fossil search. Everything was open to investigation.

"Here's where I found the track debris," Doug said.

"How strange the material is here," I commented as we got out of my jeep and walked to a small slope. The trackway debris was concentrated in about an eighty-foot section of hillside. There was a starting point about halfway up the hill, and the tracks continued all the way to the bottom.

We picked up several more slabs, all hand size, nothing bigger. We dug into the hillside for a while to get an idea of the condition of the deeper layers. Would they be structurally sound, or would they be badly broken? After a couple of hours it was clear that the Robledo occurrences remained unique. There appeared to be no intact layers to be excavated at this spot.

"Let's find some more sites," I said. "Where there is one, there have to be others."

Since there was a canyon separating the discovery outcrop, the natural thing to do was to walk cross-canyon to see if the trackway seam picked up again on the other side. It did. Doug walked the opposite hillside and noted that it was about three times as long as the discovery slope. There also appeared to be a better chance of finding the continuation of the layers.

While Doug was looking at this hillside, I was one little arroyo over. It was a tiny drainage, about five hundred feet long, that fed into the main canyon. I approached it from the back side, where the drainage started. Though there was some red material, it was unproductive. As I continued down the drainage, however, I observed some telltale signs of possible trackway layers: raindrop impressions, mudcracks and ripple marks, thin laminate layers about one-half inch or less and relatively uniform in thickness.

About one hundred feet from the opening to the canyon, I hit pay dirt. But these tracks were on yellow-white slabs, not on red ones. And the slabs were not one-half-inch thick, but more like eight inches thick. I was staring at the tracks of something, but what? On five big slabs in the wash were the largest tracks I had ever seen. And they were not like anything I had ever seen before.

Unlike the seven- to eight-inch tracks of pelycosaurs that are common in the Robledos, these tracks were massive, deep, and heavy. They had five fat and blunt toes, and the foot was entirely impressed into the mud. The front feet appeared to be smaller than the more robust back feet, and I had absolutely no idea what kind of animal made them, reptile or otherwise. I was leaning toward some monster-sized amphibian by the non-clawed look of the feet. There appeared to be no imposing five-inch claws like the Robledo pelycosaur tracks had. I did not know it then, but I would meet this animal again, but not here in Dune Canyon. I was about to meet him again back at AF 2, just three layers down.

The five tracks that I found that day were the largest found to date. They were ten inches long and eight to ten inches wide. And this was debris! The layer that yielded the big tracks was extensive on both sides of the arroyo, and Doug had marked off the same layer on the hillside that corresponded to the discovery slope. So we had three segments of the same shoreline that was cut through by two canyons. The seam extended for about three hundred feet, although the vertical exposure was as little as perhaps ten to twelve feet. All of the tracks were found in yellow material. Extensive combing of the red debris was fruitless, even for tracks.

Across the wash to the north, about five hundred feet from the discovery slope, was another gentle slope of yellow mudstone where wonderful tracks, primarily of amphibians, were found. We also discovered very nice invertebrate material there, again as debris. The layers dipped down at exactly the slope of the hillside.

This hillside showed us more trackway debris for another one hundred feet. Down the wash to the west was yet another large outcrop of yellow and red. The exposure extended impressively for one

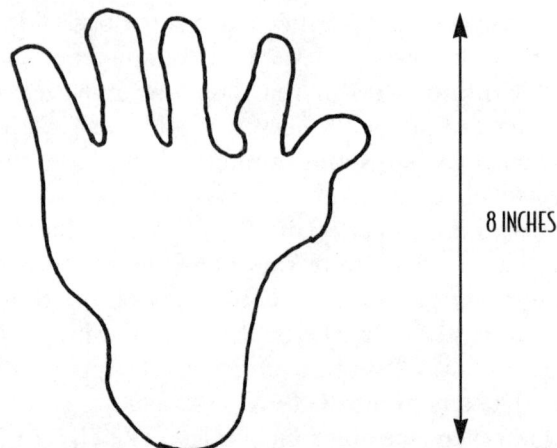

8 INCHES

*The largest footprints discovered to date (spring 1990) were found in Dune Canyon. A total of five prints were found, one of which is illustrated here. Similar tracks would soon be discovered in the Robledos at AF 2 when layer twenty-five was uncovered six months later.*

thousand feet. But the tracks we found there were much more elusive, again demonstrating the erratic nature of footprint preservation. Curiously, no plants were found in any of the initial outcrops Doug and I looked at, but that was about to change.

## A Canyon Full of Footprints: The Discovery of Rippletrack Draw

The arroyo just to the north of the canyon Doug and I had just explored showed promise of preserving tracks. As we left, I spied more yellow layers on the north slope of this new arroyo, which was about one-half mile from the canyon we had just left. We knew it had to be checked out. At this point, I didn't give another thought to continuing the excavation in the Robledos. The scent of discovery was present again, and I couldn't sleep that night. Four AM did not come soon enough.

I planned to walk the entire canyon, whatever its length. The first quarter-mile was disappointingly sterile. Then I found a plant fossil. It was a *Walchia* branch, common in the Robledo assemblage. But again, this frond was found in thick yellow rock—a good sign, but the evidence was much harder to read. It was clear that the signs indicating tracks in this new mountain range were much different from those I recognized from the Robledos.

A short distance from the plant frond were several more plant-filled rocks. But these were different. They were fossilized horsetail reeds (*Cordaites*), the kind of plants one finds in shallow, backwater lagoons or swamps. I saw a lot of living examples of them back in the Wisconsin wetlands when I was a boy.

As I walked up canyon from this point, I looked at what I was walking on. "My God," I said. "I'm literally walking on the shore." A seemingly endless succession of water ripple marks radiated out from beneath my feet, perhaps a hundred or more. And on the ripples were tracks. Amphibian tracks, good-size dissorophids I thought, marching perpendicular to the long axis of the ripple marks. I had to walk on this rippled floor to continue through the canyon.

I looked at both sides of the canyon. The tracks were there, lying on the surface like gold. "Surely it can't get any better than this,"

*Fossil ripple marks from shallow water lapping along the shore were found at Dune Canyon. No ripple marks have been found in the Robledos.* Photo by Jerry MacDonald.

I thought. But it did. As I proceeded up the canyon, I walked over slabs of rock weighing perhaps five hundred pounds each just covered with tracks. They were everywhere—on the slopes and in the arroyo bottom. I had never seen anything like it in my life. My years of Robledo work, as fantastic as they were, did not prepare me for this.

In the Robledos, all the tracks are hidden. Though there was track debris, it was almost entirely piecemeal. Here, this whole section of canyon contained clearly visible footprints. The quality was not perfect, but it was certainly good enough to be of great value to the growing Robledo census. In fact, I had not seen debris this rich even in the AF 2 tailings. The color of the material was grayish green to light yellow. The canyon turned out to be full of tracks for a good quarter of a mile. Then, on the north slope of a small drainage that fed into this canyon, I found a more familiar red outcrop that was full of plants and tracks. In a few minutes of digging, I added four new plants to the census.

I had thought that nothing could tear me away from the Robledos, but suddenly I was not so sure. AF 2 was superior in terms of length, diversity, and quality (and it still is), but the debris was so rich in this canyon that I decided that I would now divide my work between the two mountain ranges. I would explore and sample in the Dune Canyon Range and excavate in the Robledos.

I couldn't contain my excitement. Even my wildest dreams weren't this good. Though nearly all of my expectations had been met in the Robledos, before this day I had never walked through a canyon so full of tracks.

In the canyon that contained the rippled floor was a badly weathered but still visible trackway of a large animal, with tracks about five or six inches long. There were about twenty-five in succession, and I had to walk on them to continue through the canyon. It was reptilian, but again, like nothing I had found in the Robledos. What amazed me most was that no one had discovered this canyon full of tracks previously. Doug and I had found a motherlode right on the surface.

On the topographical and geological maps, I saw another little outcropping of Abo strata, but even smaller in size. As a result, I decided to check the canyon just to the south of the drainage in which I found the big tracks. Again, I couldn't sleep.

As I woke up the next morning at 4:00 AM, I thought of the wealth of tracks that I seen. Now I was afraid that someone else would find them, too. I hoped that the area would remain just as I had found it, at least until Nick Hotton's next trip to New Mexico.

I wanted Nick to experience the excitement for himself. Yet, I knew that this canyon would be vulnerable to looting, much more so than most of the red bed outcrops in the Robledos.

## Making a Poor Man's Map

I drove out to the Dune Canyon mountains, followed the jeep trail to the initial discovery slope, and then took a right turn onto another road. I followed it south to the next canyon. The road crossed the top of a saddle, and the canyon lay just below me. I drove to the opening of the canyon and stopped. Would this canyon be as good as the one I found yesterday?

I walked the length of the canyon, which extended a half-mile before ending at the mouth of the main canyon. It was a big disappointment. There was nothing visible that gave even the slightest hint of trackways below the surface. This was as sterile as the canyon I had found the day before was fertile. Still, I looked carefully at everything, poked around a little with my hammer and pry bar, and then gave up. I went back to the good canyon (I decided to call it Rippletrack Draw) and got ready to make a pace map.

A pace map is a poor man's geological map. It's very easy to make. All you have to do is count the number of steps you take from an initial geological landmark point until you reach something you want to make note of on the map. For example, my pace map of Rippletrack Draw started at the mouth of the drainage and continued up the gradient until I reached its source. You take normal steps, and if you have to make short steps over big rocks or down into depressions, you count those as well.

One hundred ten paces into the draw was a fork. I noted the feature on my map, how many paces it took to get there, and continued to draw a line on the paper that veered to the right drainage of the fork. Every little turn of the drainage was noted on my map.

Another fifty-two paces up the draw, the drainage widened, and for the next one hundred paces I was walking on level limestone pavement. Forty-five paces after the pavement ended, I found my first *Walchia* frond. I noted this on my map and continued making notations until I reached the source, 3,457 paces from the mouth of the drainage. The ripple layer was 2,706 paces from the mouth of the draw. I walked the draw several times, counting my paces each time, and I was always within just a few paces of my first measurements.

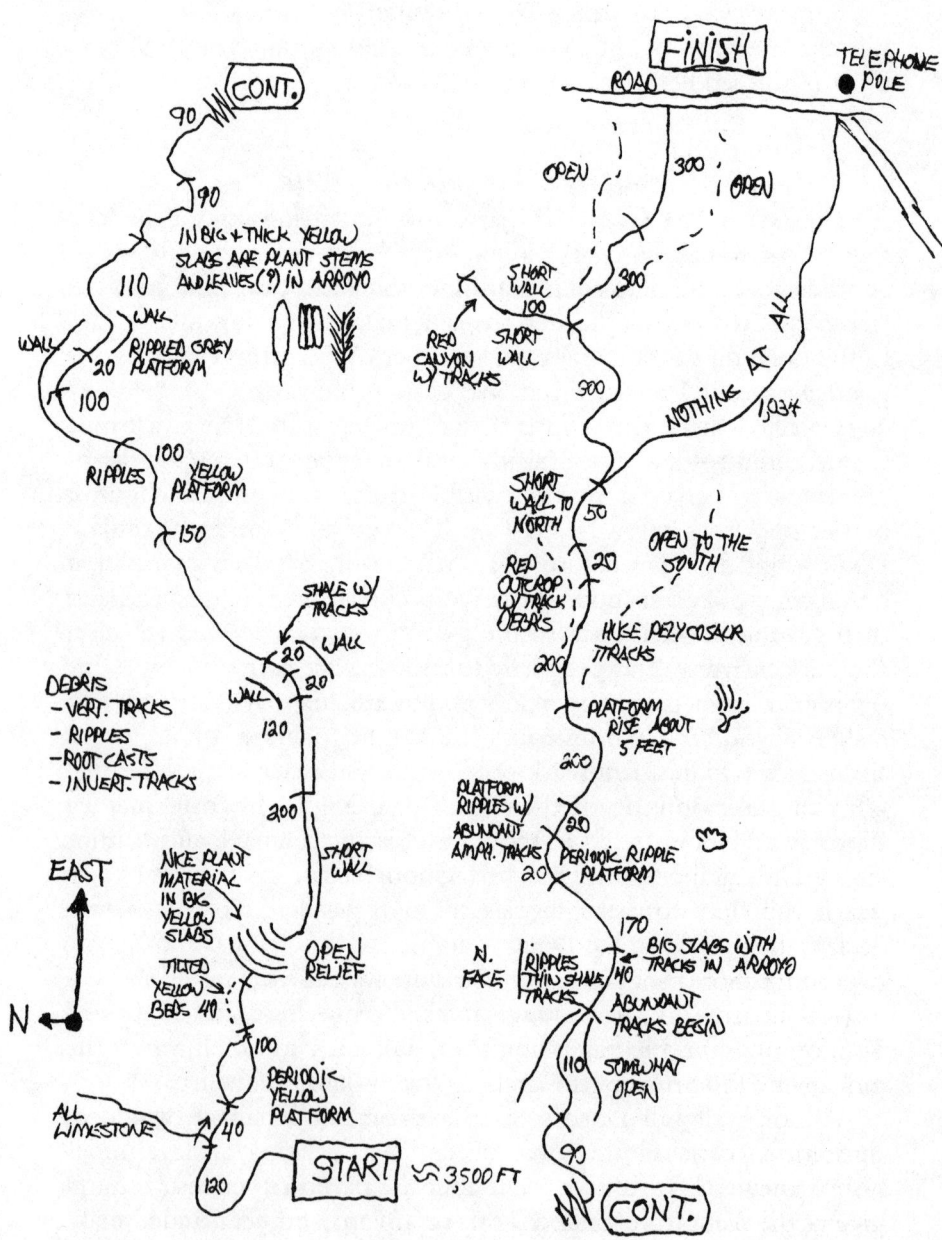

*A poor man's map of Rippletrack Draw in the newly discovered Dune Canyon deposit. The written numbers equal the approximate number of steps from one feature to another.*

After two days of exploring, it was clear that we had another significant trackway deposit on our hands. We were certain that this occurrence had never been reported, and that the area had not been picked over by collectors. After informing the BLM of this new trackway deposit, I called Nick that evening.

The usual "Hotton speaking," greeted my call.

"Hi, Nick," I began. "It's Jerry. Are you sitting down?"

"Okay, what's up?" Nick asked. "You've yet to disappoint me."

"We've found another rich trackway deposit," I began, "and it's not in the Robledos. It's twenty miles away."

"No kidding," Nick said. "Is it still Early Permian?"

"Oh, yes," I answered. "The occurrence could not be more strategically placed than this is. It's a little sliver of Abo on the geological map, but it's neatly tucked away in a pocket of sand."

"How good is it in comparison to the sites I've seen in the Robledos?" Nick asked.

"If the debris is any indication, it's very rich," I answered. "But I think its potential is going to be in its comparative value in relation to the Robledo track beds."

Nick mentioned that he would again visit the trackways at the end of his field season in west Texas, which was going to begin in a few days.

"I'm going to save it for you," I told him, and I hung up. I leaned back in my rocking chair with a smile and a great sense of satisfaction.

Doug and I got together again and planned an exploration strategy. I told Doug about the new plants I had found a few days earlier and stressed how important it was to find more plants, and the plant seam, which had eluded me in my walk through Rippletrack Draw. I went back to the Robledos, and Doug continued to search the Dune Canyon deposit for more productive outcrops and the elusive plant seam.

About ten days later, Doug was again at my front door. "I think I've found what you're looking for," he said. I followed him to his pickup and saw that he had about a dozen slabs.

"Look at these," Doug said, as he dropped the tailgate and lifted up some specimens.

"I knew it," I exulted. "The Dune Canyon deposit is going to give us the plants I've longed for since I heard of the Robledo quarry plant seam. I never had a chance to see it. You're a great field man, Doug," I said, giving him a pat on the back. "I suppose there's no chance of keeping you for a while after you graduate, is there?"

I am convinced that you can give someone all the book and lab training that they can absorb, but there is still something about field paleontology that you just cannot teach. You can teach a hound dog to point and chase and fetch, but you can't teach him to smell. A good field man has a nose for fossils.

What Doug had found were some wonderful fronds that were not *Walchia*. Quite frankly, I was getting sick and tired of finding nothing but *Walchia* month after month. Until now, all the plants I had ever found from the Robledos were *Walchia* fronds except for two other specimens: one solitary seed fern, *Neuropteris*, and a small sprig of some as yet unidentified plant. That was it. I was swimming in *Walchia*. In his truck Doug had four new plants. He also had *Walchia* fronds, but they were carbonized, which to me was a good sign.

"The plant site is only about twenty-five feet long," Doug explained. "And don't get your hopes up too high. The seam doesn't yield specimens very easily. You really have to work it. I might get two good slabs an hour. I also found some petrified wood about half a mile away."

"Are you serious?" I asked.

"Yes, they're not pretty, but there is some scattered material around."

*Walchia is believed to be related to the conifers of today. In Permian times Walchia grew to a height of fifty feet with an eight–inch girth.* Photo by Jerry MacDonald.

*Reconstruction of Walchia.* After Henry Andrews Jr.'s *Ancient Plants and the World They Lived In,* Comstock Publishing, 1947.

"Is it in the Abo or is it associated with the dune material?"

"I think it's related to the Abo," Doug answered.

"Take me there, also," I said.

"What do you want me to do with the plant seam?"

"I want you to keep working it. I can't stress how important a good representative sample of plants from the area is."

Plants have sometimes been a useful way to determine the age of some deposits. I saw this as an opportunity to correlate sites within the Robledo and Dune Canyon ranges.

The next weekend Doug took me to the small outcrop that he had found. Again I had to laugh. Hunting fossils is so funny sometimes, because to the uninitiated, finding productive fossil outcrops borders on a clairvoyance. This was another rich site.

"So many people ask me, 'How in the heck did you find this site?' because they see nothing interesting," I noted to Doug. "Especially at AF 13. It's not even on the arroyo bottom, there is no telltale debris, it's the 'wrong' color, and it's virtually hidden from view. Well, Doug, I'm not going to ask you how you found this pinprick."

After an unproductive hour of digging at the plant site, we found only a couple of Walchia fronds, I asked Doug to take me to where he had found the petrified wood. We drove north until we approached the sand dunes.

"They're up on this saddle," Doug pointed. We walked around for a while, but saw no petrified wood. "I think I was up here," Doug said a little rattled.

"It's okay," I laughed. "It happens to all of us. Paleontological Field Rule 7 says fossils can sometimes disappear if you leave them unmarked and then try to relocate them. Sometimes you can't find them even when you do mark them! The reason I'm interested in the occurrence is because petrified wood can often be a good indicator that fossil bone may be nearby. The same fossilization processes occur with both."

## Secret Tracks, Hidden Tracks

Since we were so close to Rippletrack Draw, we decided to walk it again. We drove north to the mouth of the draw and parked. I had taken Doug through the canyon a couple of weeks earlier, but now it was noon and there was a cloudless sky. I wanted to walk the drainage when the sun was high and conduct a little experiment.

I discarded my pace map. While we walked through the draw, I wanted to see what Doug and I could observe without my notes.

Just as I thought, Doug and I saw nothing. No *Walchia* plants. No pelycosaur trackway. No water ripple layer. No amphibian tracks. The color of the material, already yellowish in any light, was an entire whitewash in the noonday sun. With no oblique light to highlight the tracks, they seemed to evaporate into thin air.

"Well, Doug," I began, "we've just found out why this canyon is still chock full of tracks. You can't see them after about 9:30 in the morning." Sure enough, Rippletrack Draw, so rich in fossils when I walked it at 6:00 AM, was barren at noon. Disappearing fossils, surprising plant sites, hidden tracks inside slabs, shorelines in the desert. What a life!

I began sampling Rippletrack Draw from that day on, gathering a few key fossils here or there just in case someone else found the occurrence and lifted the one-of-a-kind specimens.

One morning after walking to the rippled pavement in the draw, I became frustrated with a big mesquite bush that was strategically placed in the best spot for taking a picture of the layer. The layer was difficult to photograph in any light, because both the ripples and the tracks were oriented directly toward the morning sun, providing the least relief for casting a shadow.

There at the base of the bush was a hole, about twelve inches in diameter, right through the rock. I thought I saw claws on one side of the hole. "What the heck?" I thought, as I looked at the hole more closely. "Is that a track in there?" I asked myself. I pulled back to get a perspective. There in front of me were eight mesquite bushes, all growing out of holes in the rock layer, all of them exactly spaced in alternate rights and lefts, just like a trackway.

I was staring at what might be the biggest trackway I had ever seen. It appeared to be that of a pelycosaur. I had estimated that the biggest pelycosaur trackways I had found in the Robledos were made by animals about seven to eight feet long. I did find one isolated back footprint of a pelycosaur on a loose slab indicating a track maker that would have been about full size, which we believe to be ten to twelve feet long. But if what I was looking at was indeed a pelycosaur trackway, it was the biggest yet, easily approaching twelve feet. I had another thing to show Nick when he came the following weekend. I couldn't wait.

## Hotton Returns: The Hunt for the Track Makers

Shortly after Doug found the first tracks from the Dune Canyon range, the first honest-to-goodness, full-time scientist came down for the first of two summers of research. At the 1989 annual Society of Vertebrate Paleontology meeting, Hotton had mentioned the Robledo discoveries to Dr. James Farlow, one of the few paleontologists with expertise in trackways. Farlow was immediately impressed, and mentioned that he had a Ph.D. student who was looking for a dissertation topic.

Mark Schult of Indiana University had already made inquiries at the New Mexico Museum of Natural History about the feasibility of doing his dissertation on some dinosaur tracks in northern New Mexico. Farlow asked Hotton if Mark, a sedimentologist, could somehow fit into the ongoing research in the Robledos. Hotton called me and we agreed that we desperately needed a sedimentologist. There was more than enough work to keep several universities and museums busy on a full-time basis.

Mark was with me for about a month before Hotton's visit. One of the crucial research questions I had to resolve was what I needed to look for in order to find the bones of these track makers. The conditions necessary for the preservation of bone are nearly the opposite of those for the preservation of tracks. Trackways need a deformable surface that can be gently buried by overwash sediments, or tracks are made and preserved in softer sediments and then pushed through as underprints on underlayers. With bone, a skeleton must be buried quickly, so that it is protected from predators and the elements. Such quick burial most often comes through dramatic floods.

I held out the hope that somewhere along this broken-up shoreline one could find evidence of catastrophic sedimentation events, like stream channel deposits or flood zones. How could I recognize such occurrences in the field? I needed Hotton's help.

I had so much to show Nick that our days were filled with activity. We first went to AF 2, and the BLM brought a film crew to interview both Hotton and me while we looked at the material. I had so many trackways exposed in place that the impact was overwhelming. Nick and I debated about what animals had created a few of the more mysterious trackways, including a three-toed trackway that ended abruptly. Did it get picked off in midstride by some larger predator? Or did it jump or fly?

"Since we know of no flying vertebrates from the Early Permian, if this thing took off, somebody's got a lot of explaining to do," Hotton chuckled to the camera.

The next day I took Nick to the newest deposit. I didn't want to prejudice Nick any more than I already had when we neared the "mesquite bush" trackway, so I asked him about the lay of the land as we stood on a small saddle above it. I pointed out the symmetry of the bushes just below us. "That's curious," he commented.

I took him down and asked him to examine the hole beneath the first mesquite bush. I was hoping that he would see it right off, and he didn't disappoint me.

"Holy cats!" he exclaimed.

"Holy cats is right," I answered. "All of the bushes here are growing out of the tracks of a pelycosaur."

Nick inspected the occurrence for some time, as he did not want to come to any hasty conclusions. There were stress cracks that broke the layer into a myriad of rectangular pieces. But the holes were not associated with the cracks. The holes were not a result of geological deformation. They were independent from the stress fractures. We measured the holes and found there was indeed a symmetrical progression that could only be explained by the trackway hypothesis.

The next day Doug and Mark joined Nick and me in the Dune Canyon deposit. I had taken Nick up Rippletrack Draw the day before, and it was now time to show him the extent and variety of the fossils in this little corner of the world. I drove past the discovery slope and into the sandy arroyo bottom and then up canyon until we could drive no more. We got out of the jeep, and I started toward the cliff face to show Nick some coalified plant layers. I was only ten feet from my jeep, but Nick never got there. He was on his hands and knees looking closely at a small round lens of rock about dinner table size. "Ha!" he exclaimed. "I think we've got bone."

"You've got to be kidding," I said in amazement. "We haven't even started yet!"

"Well, I can't help that. See these long, slender black streaks here," he said, pointing toward the rock. "Now that's bone. It's broken up all to hell, but it's bone nonetheless. There's not enough here to make a good identification of what animal or what kind of bones we're looking at, but they're long enough to be limb bones."

"Is this the type of rock I need to look for?" I asked Nick.

"Yes, this is the kind of stuff we find bone in in west Texas. There's probably more of it around. Have you seen any?" Nick asked.

Mark, Doug, and I said no. But I had. I just couldn't remember where.

"Look over here," Mark said.

We moved about ten feet to the other side of my jeep. Mark had found some large pieces of petrified wood embedded in the sandstone. There also appeared to be some bone in the rock as well, though it was difficult to tell.

Again, finding the bone slivers and the petrified wood were very good signs. Eventually, we looked at the coal seam with the carbonized plants on the cliff face on the other side of the jeep. We were all certain that this area would be the most likely area for finding bone. We walked around for most of the morning and then headed back to the Robledos. "I'll be back," I told the Dune Canyon deposit. "I'll be back."

# CHAPTER ELEVEN

## The Hunt for the Track Makers' Bones

Nick left for Washington, D.C., two days after our trip to Dune Canyon. The night before he left he gave a talk at Kent Hall Museum on the legitimacy of the trackway finds and the impossibility of fraud. He talked about my upcoming hunt for the bones of the track makers and mentioned the bone slivers we had found that morning. He noted that the hunt would not be easy.

Nick explained the very different processes of fossilization that preserve tracks and bones, and mentioned that finding the two together in the same deposit would be against the law of averages, but as that morning proved to us all, not impossible. If finding productive trackway outcrops in this fragmentary shoreline was a "needle in the haystack" proposition, finding the bones would be like finding the head of the needle. But I was ready to give it a try.

The little lens of bone-bearing rock that we found in Dune Canyon gave me a visual understanding of what I was looking for. Dune Canyon, it seemed, would yield new data, new finds, and new insights that would put the Robledo discovery in a better scientific context.

For the first six months after the Dune Canyon discovery, I saw no reason to minimize the significance of the Robledo deposit. In fact, the difficulty of getting the Dune Canyon deposit to yield good material made me even more impressed with the Robledo treasures. One important difference between the two deposits was "God's saran wrap," the marvelous separation layer that lies conveniently between the rock beds in the Robledos. There was no such layer evident in Dune Canyon, so it was virtually impossible to excavate such well-preserved tracks. The material simply won't split along discrete horizons. I recognized that the significance of the Dune Canyon deposit lay in its comparative value with regard to the kinds of animals and plants found within the two deposits.

Mark Schult was spending most of his days at the AF 2 site, mapping and doing sedimentary analysis of the layers. Nick Hotton had encouraged me to explore the Dune Canyon deposit, but had also strongly advised me not to lose my focus. The big prize in his mind, bones or not, was still the systematic excavation of the faunules at AF 2. It was crucial that these layers be carefully explored and studied.

But there was a direct correlation between working the discovery site and the rapidly escalating number of new trackway sites I was finding. From working AF 2, I had become so familiar with what productive red bed layers looked like on edge, that I was finding more and more tracksites. But still, the bones in Dune Canyon weighed heavily on my mind. I wanted to spend time in the range and ascertain its potential to yield better bone than the specimens we found with Hotton a month earlier.

On June 16, I got the trackway "team" together for the first organized search for bone. Mark Schult, Doug Wood, and I drove back to where Nick found the bone lens. I wanted us all to take another good look at the rock before we began our exploration. Doug was going to take us to a new canyon to the south that contained some track and plant material.

"You mean the next canyon over?" I asked.

"No, not that one," Doug responded. "I walked it earlier, and there was nothing there."

The canyon I was referring to was the one I walked the day after Doug and I first combed the area. I had just finished exploring Rippletrack Draw, and I had high hopes for the canyon to the south, but it was sterile. Much later, as Doug walked it, he too concluded that it was sterile. In any event, we had to walk through a small section of it to get to the next canyon. We would have to take all of six steps before climbing up the other side. We were in that small canyon for less than a heartbeat, but I saw something out of the corner of my eye.

"Whoa!" I exclaimed. "I want to see something." I walked to a little exposure no more than twelve feet wide and five feet high. The strata was very different from the surrounding rock and consisted of the material that Hotton had asked us about.

"Well what do you know," I said. "The canyon I thought was sterile may not be after all. Doug and I had both missed this little spot as we walked it.

"Hey, what's this?" Mark asked.

"It's more petrified wood," Doug replied.

"But what about this?" I said with a start. In my hand was a five-inch-long rock. It was broken in three parts, but the pieces were still together, precariously perched on the side of the outcrop. The next rain would certainly have washed it off altogether. But we were one rain early. It looked like bone. We observed what appeared to be the vascular passages characteristic of bone cortex.

"Hey, here's more," Mark said. What Mark found looked like the conical tooth of a carnivorous pelycosaur. It was about three-forths of an inch long. After about fifteen minutes, we had a couple of handfuls of what appeared to be bone or petrified wood. We were very concerned that we read this material correctly. Our visual identification of bone in the field was seriously hampered by large quantities of petrified wood in the same outcrop. To make matters worse, the wood and the bone were almost indistinguishable in color, both being coal black.

Nick had taught me a little trick for identifying bone in the field. Lick it. If the rock sticks to your tongue, it's bone. If it doesn't, it's either petrified wood or a rock. It was comical to see Nick on his hands and knees with his tongue on a black sliver, but it was effective. This particular morning, all three of us licked a lot of rocks.

Even though some of the specimens stuck to our tongues, the only way to be certain which was bone and which was wood was to perform laboratory studies. We drove to New Mexico Tech to see Don Wolberg. Don visually concurred that some of them appeared to be bone, but we needed objective verification. Mark made a cut of one of the fragments and placed the section under the microscope. The interior of the fragment conclusively showed the vascular nature of bone cortex. It took nearly three hours of driving time for a three-minute lab verification, but it was well worth it. Our hunt for bone had ended five minutes after we left my Jeep. Mark and I cheered.

That night I called Nick. "This is getting to be a regular habit with you, Jerry," he said. "Now what have you found?"

"We've found more of the rock that you told us to look for. I stared right at it a month ago when I walked this canyon, but I did not know it. Since you taught me what to look for, we found it right away. A few fragmentary limb bones, and a couple of teeth, were lying on the surface of a small outcrop. Mark thinks they are preserved in the remnants of a small streambed."

The rest of the story was reported by the Associated Press:

### Dateline: July 2, 1990
### Las Cruces, New Mexico, Associated Press
### Ancient Streambed Found Rich in Bones

Scientists involved in the Las Cruces Paleozoic Trackways Project in southern New Mexico have found the bones of animals that could have made the fossil footprints discovered near Las Cruces, New Mexico, in 1987.

Jerry Paul MacDonald, director of the Smithsonian-based project, announced today the discovery of an ancient streambed that may be rich in bones from the Early Permian period, 280,000,000 years before the present.

"This could be an even more significant discovery than the footprints themselves, in the sense that it is the first recorded occurrence of Permian bone this far south in New Mexico," MacDonald said. "Many of us knew there just had to be bone in the area, since it was so rich in tracks." The question was where.

The big break in the search came in May of this year when Dr. Nicholas Hotton of the Smithsonian Institution's Paleobiology Department came for several days of field exploration with MacDonald. News of a major new trackway deposit discovered by trackway project assistant Doug Wood, a graduate student in education at New Mexico State University, and MacDonald six months ago led to heightened reconnaissance of the new area. MacDonald refused to discuss the location of the new trackway deposit except to say that it is "quite a distance from the Robledo Mountains," site of MacDonald's major fossil footprint discovery which shook the paleontological world in the spring of 1987. . . .

I think this latest discovery vindicates our work once and for all," MacDonald said. "Every step of the way we have proved how rich the paleontology is in southern New Mexico in the face of unceasing local criticism."

"It's sensational," exulted Hotton in a phone interview. "The discovery of bone in association with the tracks makes his discovery a whopping ten out of ten. He now has tracks, plants, invertebrates, and skeletal remains in the same area. It's a paleontologist's dream."

MacDonald said the bones will be studied by vertebrate paleontologists at both the Smithsonian and the Carnegie museums. "I know enough about bones to move over and let the experts have at it," MacDonald said. Dave Berman, curator of vertebrate fossils at the Carnegie Museum, has studied Permian animals from New Mexico for the last twenty-five years. Berman was the first to find bones of *Dimetrodon,* the fierce top predator from the Permian, in New Mexico near Albuquerque in 1977. "At the rate Dave was working, it would have taken him another ten years before he got to Las Cruces to search for bone. We are thrilled to have saved him that much time," MacDonald said.

The numbing series of discoveries made in the Las Cruces area since 1987 include: the world's longest trackways from the Paleozoic era; an ever-growing list of the trackways of over fifty vertebrate and invertebrate animals, of which at least half may be new, undiscovered species; dozens of arthropod and insect trackways never before found; over a dozen species of plants; and now bone, all in an area MacDonald said was ignored by vertebrate paleontologists as "unproductive."

"I have always been a firm believer in second opinions," MacDonald said. "Who was going to believe us this time?" Three years ago MacDonald sought professional evaluations of his trackway finds from both the Smithsonian Institution and the Carnegie Museum of Natural History in Pittsburgh after in-state opinions proved less than positive. Both museums employ recognized specialists in the Permian period. The written opinion of both museums was that MacDonald had uncovered the greatest Paleozoic trackway deposit in the world, surpassing even those found in the Grand Canyon. A short time later the Natural History Museum of Los Angeles County joined the Smithsonian and Carnegie museums in support financially and technically for MacDonald's work. [Footnote: Associated Press Wire Service, July 2, 1990.]

## On My Own Again

One month after Mark arrived, I lost Doug to the Utah public school system. Mark was absorbed in his own research, so I was on my own again. I began to explore additional canyons for more track sites, and even flew over the Robledos on two separate occasions to look for what seemed to be a lifeboat of red shoreline in a sea of gray limestone.

From the air there were entire canyons made up of Abo formation red beds, but that didn't necessarily mean they would be productive. I was most interested in trying to locate a few small outcrops on the ground. The small outcrops are more inviting because they are a manageable size. But three years of experience also told me that small isolated outcroppings hold out more promise for good tracks than do large ones.

Abo formation 10 in Branson Canyon is one of the largest outcroppings in the Robledos, extending nearly one thousand feet, but I haven't found anything of great significance there even though it's five times larger than AF 2. But that would soon change. Just up the canyon is a tiny red bed outcropping (AF 11), only thirty feet long and perhaps ten feet high. It is incredibly rich. I suggested to Mark

Shult that he work the site during his second field season. He found a number of good-sized pelycosaur trackways and a variety of trackways of smaller animals. Further up the canyon is one of my favorite sites, AF 13. I love this site because working it is a challenge, the color matches more closely the Dune Canyon trackways, and it is so remarkably hidden up a steep slope.

AF 13 consists primarily of an overhang of Abo. It must be excavated from the bottom up—very rich, very dangerous. If you try to pry down too much overhang, you could die in a landslide because there is no place to escape. Because of this, it will probably always be safe from exploitative excavation, unless, of course, the entire overhang is dynamited and brought down to the floor of the canyon. Such a thing could happen, as the value of the site is in comparative research, and not unique track assemblages.

Farther up Branson Canyon is AF 15, which is very peculiar. The entire outcrop is oriented sideways. It's very near a major fault that runs through the Robledos from north to south. The layers have been uplifted and turned on end, making it seem as though the track makers traveled straight into the sky. Because all of the layers are the same thickness, it is obvious that they were laid down horizontally and then, after solidifying into rock, set on end by tectonic activity. Although it's not difficult to excavate here, it is difficult to keep the layers intact, since individual slabs are likely to slide down the smooth surface like a guillotine, with the potential to cut off the foot of the one who dislodged it. I walked the entire length of Branson Canyon and plotted all the productive outcrops, sites ten through fifteen. It was now time to move into the next canyon. I was ready because discovery is the greatest natural high I've ever experienced.

## From Pecans to Footprints

My laboratory is located in one of the southern New Mexico State Fair's quonset huts. During the fairs, it was my practice to open my lab to the public. On these occasions, I heard from dozens of visitors that they had tracks on their fireplaces, on the exterior walls around their homes, and on their patios. Hispanic families that had been in the area for centuries, told stories of tracks on Picacho Mountain, just to the south of the Robledos, but in three subsequent years of searching, no one has found them, but this does not mean they don't exist.

During the 1990 state fair, a fellow approached me with a proposition. He suggested that, if I would train him, he would report back to me any possible trackway outcrops that he saw along his regular jogging route through the mountains. Having just had a very successful experience with Doug Wood, and again mired in research and politics, I was in a mood for such a proposition.

We talked for quite a while, and I gave him a private tour of my lab and material. He seemed like a likable guy, and he was as enthusiastic as Doug about the chance to work with me. "Why not?" I said to myself.

That was how Dave Slagle joined my project. I guess he was a logical choice, because he was a pecan farmer. Up to this point, I had enlisted the help of a Tucson policeman and his wife, a graduate student in education, an eighth-grade science teacher, a petroleum engineer, a restaurant owner, and a dentist. Why not a pecan farmer? Help doesn't get any more broad-based than this.

Dave and I hit it off immediately. I found him intelligent, quick to learn, and very dedicated. He was in all respects another Doug Wood. I really considered it a miracle that he made himself known to me. Like Doug, Dave had a nose for fossils, even though he had never gone fossil hunting before. After a few months of training, Dave was prepared to be my scout, anytime he wasn't busy planting and harvesting pecans.

We studied geological maps, and I explained that every arroyo and canyon needed to be searched, regardless of whether or not the map indicated an Abo occurrence. I knew from experience that some small outcrops could be easily overlooked. The entire Dune Canyon deposit was overlooked as far as tracks were concerned.

I had already covered the eastern side of the Robledos for a distance of about one and a half miles into the hills. We needed to walk the entire southern half, because, according to the map, nearly all the Abo was in that part of the range. Since I had found fifteen good sites along the eastern side, I was optimistic that we could at least double that number with a search of the western side.

Dave found an old jeep trail that entered the Robledos from the south and drove to the top of the mountains where he could get a clear view of the western half. There were some big outcrops about one and one-half miles to the north in Cattletank Canyon. Dave parked at the mouth of the canyon and worked his way north until he reached the outcrops. One small outcrop was nestled in a bend of a small arroyo. About three to four feet of trackway of a small-sized animal was exposed. He carefully excavated it and brought it to me.

"This is great," I told him. "It's an amphibian. Look at the rounded tips of his toes. And look here." I pointed to a long line that seemed to bisect the trackway in half from top to bottom. "That's his tail drag," I said with excitement. But the best was yet to come.

As I flew over the Robledos, I marked outcrop locations on a topographical map. This was not so easy in an airplane. We flew east to west over the south-central section of the range, and, after I got my bearings, I was able to pinpoint several good outcrops on the map. Most of the outcrops were large, but there was one that had "Come to me" written all over it. It was significantly isolated from all the others. In fact, it was the most isolated outcrop in the whole range. Just exactly what I wanted.

Now our job was to find it on the ground. The outcrop was about eighty feet long, but buried deep into a complex canyon, with the exposed area facing north, not south. Worse yet, from the ground on either side of the canyon, it couldn't be seen at all. You have to be almost on top of it before you realize its there. It was a tough hike just to get into a position to observe the outcrop. It took two days, but Dave found it. It was in a canyon completely made up of marine sediments. No red debris led into the canyon.

Dave, his daughter Whitney, and I made it to the site in about half an hour from the jeep. I was in for a shock. This new site, which I called WSA 1 because the BLM had designated it a wilderness study area, was the richest I had ever seen. No other site even came close to having such abundant trackway debris, not even Dune Canyon. In about an hour, the three of us, without digging, collected nearly one hundred beautiful trackways, all just lying on the surface of an eighty-foot-long outcrop.

But we had a problem: it was very difficult to get down to the site; with a loaded pack, it was almost impossible to get out. Three big climbs out of this layered canyon made specimen retrieval prohibitive. There was only one thing to do—take out as many of the smaller slabs as we could, then photograph the ones that were impossible to move. And that is what we did. I was convinced that WSA 1 was invincible against plundering. We left WSA 1 as we found it, an unopened treasure chest. Dave and I continued to work our way up Cattletank Canyon.

We hiked from the southern end of the canyon until we came to one of the large red bed outcrops Dave had seen from the jeep trail. It was very impressive, but for much of the length of the exposure, the layers seemed so cemented together that it defied excavation. On the left side there was a cliff of Abo. There was simply no place to get a toehold to begin prying out layers or even slabs. Farther up the exposure and to the right, the canyon sloped a little, so there was a slightly better chance of pulling some slabs out of the canyon wall.

The exposure ended with a waterfall that runs only when flash floods occur. The waterfall was cut in red bed material. The cascading water had peeled back some of the layers as they rested on the floor of the canyon to reveal a small staircase-type exposure covered with various trackways and plants.

The red bed waterfall had been exposed for quite a while, and all of the fossils on the layers were badly ground down, but it did give us a glimpse of what was preserved in the layers on either side of the canyon. We decided to sample the sloped red beds to the right of the falls. The material was rich in new kinds of tracks and traces. But, unlike AF 2, a year's worth of occasional work at this new slope did not produce a single footprint larger than three inches. All of the tracks were made by small animals. Was this meaningful? Probably, but even now I'm not sure why.

I have observed subtle differences in the fauna of several of the sites. My feeling is that they may reveal various microhabitats along the shoreline. Because of the lack of mud cracks and the abundance of water ripples and horsetail reeds, I believe Dune Canyon may have been close to a lagoonal or swampy environment that was wet most of the time.

Some of the AF sites in the Robledos may have been farther away from the actual shore, and so the mud was not wetted as frequently, and a preponderance of mud cracks are preserved. The Robledo outcrops preserve many more tracks of pelycosaurs than either Dune Canyon or AF 13. In fact, after three years of additional exploration, I was ready to call the initial discovery site (AF 2) pelycosaur heaven.

I called the waterfall site the "Conifer Forest," because conifer fronds could be seen on nearly every slab and layer. To put this into context, at AF 2 only two layers out of the twenty-five excavated are made up almost entirely of plants and plant debris. Additionally, most of the plants preserved on these two layers were bits and pieces as opposed to single preserved fronds. But at the conifer forest, the plants were intact; some fronds were nearly five feet long and spectacularly preserved. And there seemed to be a dearth of tracks.

In fact, tracks of insects seemed initially to be more abundant than the tracks of vertebrates, which can probably be attributed to the abundance of vegetation in the immediate area. Yet vertebrates obviously visited the area. Something had to keep the invertebrate population in check, so where were all the footprints?

As stimulating as this vast exposure was (though equal in size to AF 10, it was a hundred times richer), I wanted to find that special site. Walking Cattletank Canyon south from the Conifer Forest outcrop, I turned up a small wash that drained the slopes of the range from the east. The entire drainage was not more than sixty feet from the canyon floor, but I liked what I saw. On the south slope of the wash were a series of grayish white layers that were tilted about thirty degrees from horizontal. These layers contrasted dramatically with the perfectly horizontal (red) layers of the Conifer Forest, just one hundred yards away.

As a paleontologist, I love the exception rather than the rule. And this little spot was another exception: small, manageable, different. Just the way I like it. I'm not exactly sure why, but this insignificant outcrop was where I wanted to spend my day. And it paid off handsomely, for I found the richest concentration of insect trackways I had ever seen, overshadowing all other sites with its abundance of specimens. I called the site Insect Hill. And it was a beauty.

There appeared to be a few vertebrate tracks in this small exposure, but they were overshadowed by the vast array of invertebrate trails. The most common insects represented were centipedes. Since they are forest floor predators, it made sense to find many of them here. Tracks of both beetles and other flying insects were also quite common. But, again, there were no large tracks. When I took *Smithsonian* magazine writer Doug Stuart to the site, as luck would have it, I found the largest trackway from this new area. It was made by a big, lumbering amphibian with footprints about four inches long.

Insect Hill was a tough site to work because of its location. A cardinal rule in hunting for trackways, especially invertebrate trackways, is to study every slab by holding it up to the light in such a way as to get the most oblique illumination from the sun. Only then can the invertebrate trails be observed, for they are sometimes so faint that they are difficult to discern even in low-angle light.

Insect Hill faced north, however, and above the layers there is a hill that effectively hides the outcrop from the southern rays of the sun. There is only about an hour of light that can be used to detect trackways here, and only when the sun is rising. Even then, each slab must be held above your head to catch the eastern rays. Thank God for sunny New Mexico, for it is pointless to hunt trackways, at least small ones, on cloudy days. In fact, I walked these canyons again very early in the morning, so that I could make sure I hadn't missed an outcrop because of poor lighting.

Dave continued to explore Cattletank Canyon north from the Conifer Forest and Insect Hill sites. He found several more small outcrops, and then another mile and a half into the range he happened upon another larger outcrop. This one was exposed on a hillside that was about fifteen hundred feet long. It reminded me of AF 10—a lot of bravado but no substance. We decided to call it Souvenir Canyon, because we could envision dozens of people combing the canyon for an elusive track.

Cattletank Canyon forked at this point, and Dave chose to walk up the western arroyo. The relief in the canyon spread out, and at first, there appeared to be little of significance there. But then he came upon another Abo deposit about ten feet high and 150 feet long. Even though the layers were stacked, not sloped, they could be easily peeled back because the top had all but eroded away, leaving Abo strata, instead of limestone, as the capstone.

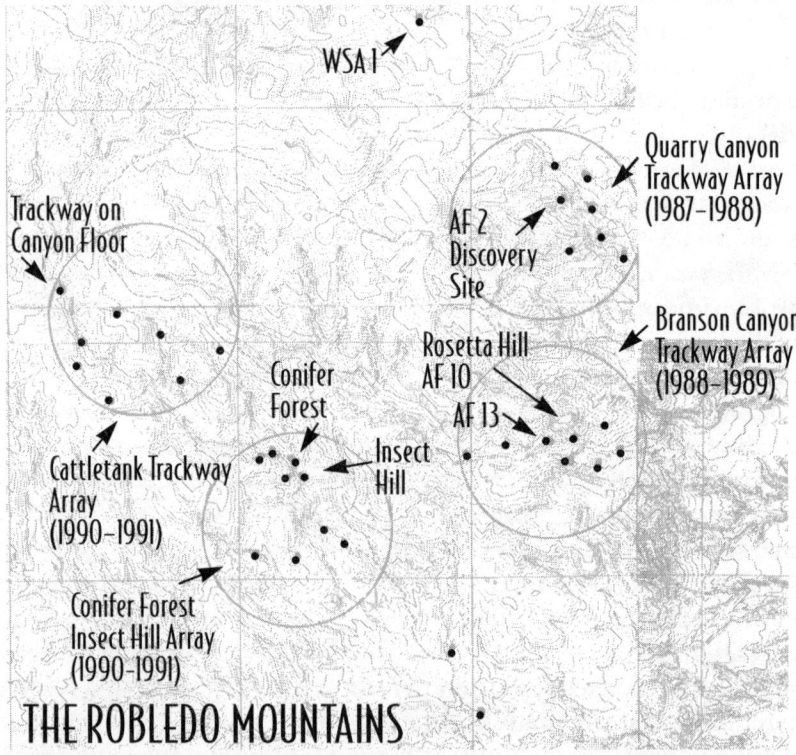

*Large circles represent concentrations of footprints (small dots). Dates are when these track sites were found. Topo map shows maze of canyons and arroyos that need to be searched for track sites. In seven years nearly twelve square miles have been searched.*

Dave found some insect tracks, a few small amphibian trackways, and something spectacular. On the northernmost section of this exposure, he noticed a big pelycosaur trackway marching across the canyon floor. Twelve prints were preserved on one side of the canyon, and then the trackway picked up again on the other side. Unfortunately, the forty feet in between were sand and gravel.

## Windows of Opportunity

What excited us was the notion that in the not-too-distant past, perhaps only tens of years, this trackway was fifty feet long as it bisected the canyon floor from east to west. However, flash floods had destroyed forty feet of trackway. Erosion was our best ally as well as our cruelest enemy, for it allows relatively short windows of opportunity in which to collect the fossils.

Until someone figures out a way to detect fossils underground, which can be done in the case of radioactive bone fossils, but not other fossils, scientists still have to rely on the process of erosion or human excavation activity such as highway construction. But this is a double-edged sword, because the work of winds and rains doesn't stop once a fossil is exposed. Erosion continues unabated, eventually destroying the exposed fossil as well. Thus, the time between the first exposure of a fossil and its obliteration is the paleontologist's window of opportunity.

Scientists are happiest when just a bit of bone is exposed and the remainder of the skeleton is buried below the surface. A talented field man can find these little teasers, but most people need a lot more bone exposed before they can recognize the material as a significant fossil.

Sometimes, initial exposure is a disaster, as the specimen can break up quickly once exposed. Some mastodon bones I found a long time ago are a good example of this. The top hinge of a jawbone was exposed on a slope I was exploring. It was only an inch above the ground and about six inches long. As I uncovered it, I came upon the teeth of the elephant, hidden just below the surface. They were intact, but like a house of cards. They broke apart every time I even breathed. It took a good month of lab work to put all the pieces back together. But if the teeth became exposed on the surface, one good rain would have smashed them apart and sent them on a long trip to the bottom of the hillside as gravel. So even though one good rain might have exposed the fossil, the next good rain would have destroyed it. Talk about a short window of opportunity!

*Pelycosaur trackway from AF 2. The dappled surface in the lower right corner of photo may be a belly imprint of the track maker. Note the lack of tail drag.* Photo by Jerry MacDonald.

On another hillside there was a tusk, half of it exposed at the surface. It was impossible to save. It was like finding a fossil pastry. It seemed to have shape and mass, but the middle was made up of nothing but air. I was a week or a month too late.

So Dave and I were too late to see this fifty-foot pelycosaur trackway. All that remained was eight feet. We learned that trackways are not resilient at all. Once exposed, they erode very fast. A very rich exposure of trackways in situ could be washed out in a few years. The window of opportunity for these trackways, although longer than that for bone, was still short and the material very vulnerable.

The first year I began excavating at AF 2 I decided to do some weathering experiments. I took a variety of tracks made on different kinds of material, for example, sandstones for some, mudstones for others, siltstones for still others, and laid them out on a flat surface just opposite the excavation. Not surprisingly, the mudstones were quickly obliterated, losing their integrity in a matter of months. The siltstone slabs fared the best, but even here the surfaces began to exfoliate (peel away) in a few years. Nothing appeared resilient enough to last a decade, let alone a generation. It is probable that the range changes dramatically each decade, like a snake shedding its skin, and what may appear sterile one decade may appear very rich the next. This may explain why the motherlode was so difficult for people to find.

Walking the Robledos in 1963 may have given a much different picture from that gleaned walking the range in 1987. I thought of the Dune Canyon deposit, and especially the ripple layers in Rippletrack Draw. Based on studying the poorly formed layers, I am convinced that the tracksite that contained the fifty-foot pelycosaur trackway, exposed right on the bottom of Cattletank Canyon, would have entirely washed away in a few years. I am also convinced that the ripple layer from Dune Canyon had only recently been exposed, perhaps only a matter of a few years before I observed it.

I'm equally sure, however, that the trackway debris would have remained constant throughout the range, though locally a site may have fluctuated in terms of the number of specimens exposed on the surface. This is why it is imperative that paleontologists utilize all fossil information, however fragmentary or seemingly insignificant, as indicators of what could be laying below the surface.

I had discovered the motherlode when very little of it was exposed on the surface. I did not discover WSA 1 and its remarkable debris field first, or Rippletrack Draw first, or this wonderful trackway on Cattletank Canyon's floor that Dave and I were now looking at. The motherlode was found on the basis of debris, not exposed faunules. It would have been nice to have found trackways lying exposed in situ on the canyon floor, but this rarely happens. Good fossil hunters should not expect gifts from God, but they should expect to work for the material they are hunting.

Dave and I talked about what to do about the remaining eight feet of trackway exposed on the canyon floor. I called this new locality Cattletank Draw, because there was a rancher's cattle tank nearby. Although a dirt road passes close to the outcrop, most of the trackway lays in a perpetual shadow, so it was probably never noticed.

I was excited about Cattletank Draw because it could be the easiest site to excavate. It was the only site in the Robledos, with the exception of the quarry, that you could drive to. Also, there weren't hundreds of feet of rock above the exposure. Like a stack of pancakes, I could start with layer one and just peel back and peel back for ten to twelve feet before reaching the canyon floor. But I decided against excavating the remainder of the trackway right away, because I wanted Hotton and others to see it when they came for their annual visit. Unfortunately, this was a mistake that I would come to regret.

North of Cattletank Draw, the geology of the range changed. There were no more red bed outcrops. It seemed that we had finally run out of these trackway exposures, but our final tally of productive sites was a respectable thirty-two. I felt that perhaps six of these thirty-two sites were potentially better than the site that started it all, AF 2. And then, of course, there was WSA 1; the stuff dreams are made of.

\* \* \*

Hotton's next visit was in spring 1991, and naturally I primed him for a trip to the new discoveries in the Robledos. For six months prior to Nick's visit, Dave and I studied the best routes and mapped the sites. We found three ways of getting to the Conifer Forest. One was excruciatingly long and involved opening up a bunch of cattle gates, the other was so full of switchbacks that you practically needed to take Dramamine for road sickness (and this road was frequently washed out), and then there was Dead Man's Curve. This last was the shortest and most scenic route, and by far the most dangerous.

Dave was a man after my own heart. When he first showed up for a trip into the Robledos, he was driving a 1951 Willys Jeep CJ. I knew that this was going to be a long and productive relationship, for I owned three Willys Jeeps, two 1951s and a 1958.

When Hotton arrived, we planned a trip to the new sites. My wife and my two sons wanted to go, and Dave took his daughter. We decided to take the Dead Man's Curve route, because, after all, we had two Willys jeeps. Dave led the way. Needless to say, there was general panic when we angled our way across the steep slopes at Dead Man's Curve. My wife said that if the slope didn't kill me, she would when we passed it. Nick was laughing a worried laugh, "to keep from screaming," he told us.

"Don't worry," I said. "It feels much worse than it really is. I've watched the truck cross these slopes, and the chassis stays close to the mountainside. It's only the additional tilt of the body that makes it feel like we are going to roll."

"Try telling that to *my* body," Nick exclaimed.

Adventures aside, we made it to Insect Hill and the Conifer Forest in one piece. The new discoveries did not disappoint Nick. Dave and I asked him many questions about nearly every geological feature we came across. We talked about everything from shorelines to sand dunes. We talked about bugs and reptiles and everything in between. It was becoming obvious to us all that the sky was the limit with regard to these never-ending discoveries.

"You have enough sites to make a dozen museums happy," Nick said. "I think a number of research endeavors could be maintained out here with very little conflict among them. As far as abundance of fossils, this is as close to limitless as they come."

Limitless, yes. But not invulnerable. We had a tiny six-square-mile area with what appeared to be the richest concentration of Paleozoic trackways in the world. But as humankind has proven with the destruction of the rain forests of South America, six square miles of anything can be destroyed in just a few short years if human encroachments are not controlled or limited. These fossils were insufficiently protected under existing laws. It was time for policy making—and some paleontological politics—to enter the picture. We didn't have to wait long. The wheels were already in motion.

# Chapter Twelve

The Sociology and Politics of
Paleontological Discovery

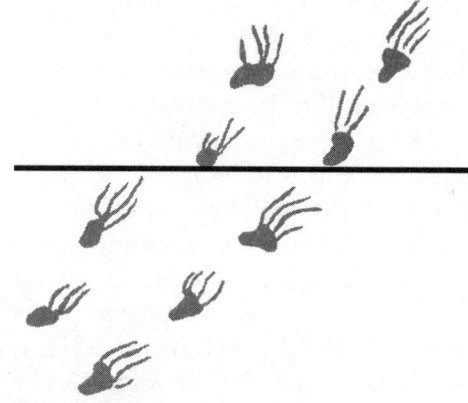

In March 1990, as we were beginning the comprehensive exploration of the Robledos which would result in the discoveries described in chapter 11, the final brick was laid in the wall of criticism and political intrigue which had dogged the project from my first discovery. The *El Paso Times* decided to investigate independently local scientists' reactions to the Robledo discovery. The result of the investigation was a front-page, top-of-the-fold article entitled "Scientist Wins World Acclaim But Is Snubbed in New Mexico." I think all of us, whether pro or con, picked up that paper with a great deal of trepidation.

But the *El Paso Times* article was a blessing in disguise. Coupled with the *National Geographic* report that was just released, the article exposed the serious polarization of opinion that existed within the state of New Mexico. United States Senator Jeff Bingaman (D-NM) had read the two differing reports and he made a special trip down to Las Cruces to inspect the trackway material and talk to me.

When he arrived at my lab on March 15, he had in hand both the *National Geographic* report and the *El Paso Times* article, which appeared only three days earlier. Several BLM officials accompanied the senator, including State Director Larry Woodard. As we walked through the specimens already collected, I described the prehistoric setting in which the prints were made, and discussed the process of trackway preservation. I also pointed out the seemingly endless varieties of trackways of insects and vertebrates that I had found in this little section of earth. I stressed how unique and valuable the fossils were. Bingaman listened intently.

"I've come down for two reasons," Senator Bingaman said. "I wanted to see for myself exactly what you had found down here.

I wanted to see if it was as significant as claimed. To someone who knows very little about fossils, I have to say that I am amazed at what you have uncovered. It's terrific. I want to see if there is anything that can be done to get you the in-state support your work requires," Senator Bingaman continued, "and I want to begin moving to protect these fossils for posterity."

Bingaman asked me what I felt was needed in both of those areas. I suggested that if we could get in-state scientists to come see the specimens for themselves, it would go a long way toward resolving the conflicting opinions over the significance of the fossils and toward obtaining fuller participation in the project.

I gave the senator a packet of letters of evaluation from paleontological experts, and I gave him a packet of newspaper articles, including articles that contained a few statements from in-state scientists questioning the integrity of the find and the quality of the work.

"See if you can do something about this," I said, as I handed him the material.

"Let me look it over," Bingaman said. "I have some ideas that I think can help, and I'm going to talk them over with the BLM. You'll be hearing from me soon." As the senator was leaving, the BLM director gave me the high sign. It looked like soon all would be well with the world. Meeting Senator Bingaman was the end of one phase in the Robledo project and the beginning of a new one. The new phase would bring many changes with regard to my involvement in the project and my work in the field. As I now look back on the *El Paso Times* report, I see that it made everyone on both sides say that enough was enough. New attempts at mutual reconciliation were instituted on everyone's part and this is where the similarity between the bone wars and the Robledos finally ended.

## The Evolution of Discovery

Discovery is both an event and a process. The Robledo discovery took place on June 6, 1987, but something led up to this event: a prediscovery phase. The prediscovery phase involves both the acquisition of information necessary for the discovery process to begin and the explorations that result from the acquisition of such information. The acquisition of reconnaissance material from the Robledos, as well as the interviewing of individuals who had previously collected or seen trackways, was part of the prediscovery phase of the search for the footprint motherlode.

But the prediscovery phase also involves acquiring a certain state of mind, an uncontrollable itch. I call it the bug in the brain. The psychological processes essential to initiating the hunt are centered around the phenomenon of recognition, both of the prediscovery information crucial to the search and of the ability to identify the discovery event itself when it happens.

The trackway evidence that I had gathered from observing specimens in walls and porches, floors and fireplaces, could have led me astray; I could easily have interpreted this footprint material as insignificant on the basis of abundance. I chose to believe, however, that the trackways' apparent abundance meant that there could be a motherlode of trackways in the hills. That is how I interpreted the slab that Mark Torres had brought in with reptile tracks on it. How I interpreted the significance of both Mark's slab and the building stone was very important. Mark's footprint slab was the icing on the cake that I had already begun to bake in my subconscious.

My search was a natural result of the evidence I had gathered, and on June 6 I was satisfied that I had found what I was looking for. This was the day when my work matched the expectations I had formulated years earlier. On this date I had recognized discovery. The discovery event marked the end of the prediscovery phase and the beginning of a new phase in my work. I now had to turn the discovery into an event that had meaning to others besides myself. The significance of the discovery had to be verified. The process had to move from a subjective phase to an objective one.

The second phase in the process of discovery is the legitimization phase, which begins when the discoverer seeks outside confirmation of the legitimacy and significance of his or her discovery from an expert or experts who, in the discover's opinion, can adequately evaluate the find. Though this phase still involves subjectivity, these independent opinions move the discovery event from a subjective one to an objective one. When the discoverer moves the discovery into the legitimization phase, the result may be a number of reactions: confirmation, repudiation, negotiation, compromise, or confrontation.

Initial in-state reactions toward the Robledo discovery were cool. I then had three choices. First, I could agree with the opinion that the discovery slab was insignificant and discontinue scientific exploration in the area; second, I could agree with the opinion and explore and collect for my own enjoyment or to try and find something better; or third, I could disagree with the opinion of insignificance and seek other evaluations. But, even here, there is a limit. Individuals who choose to ignore the conflicting opinions of experts are increasingly likely to be labeled crazy by their peers. In my case, I sought input from outside experts wherever I could get it. I had not intended from the outset to seek an evaluation from the Smithsonian Institution. Rather, I hoped that if I showed the evidence of my discovery to out-of-state scientists, I would at the very least be passed along until I was finally referred to someone with expertise in evaluating this kind of discovery. As it happened, I was passed around for several days until I was caught in the end zone, so to speak, by Nick Hotton of the Smithsonian.

I can say with certainty that if Nick Hotton had dismissed my find, I would never have gone back to New Mexico. I would have completed my Ph.D. work in sociology at the University of Virginia and would probably be a professor somewhere teaching the subject I love so much. But Hotton did not dismiss it, and the rest, as they say, is history. Again, objective recognition of the value of my discovery guaranteed the survival of the fossils. My subjective sense of value of the trackways was exponentially magnified when united with Hotton's firm evaluation. The entire process of discovery is energized and gains momentum through the accumulation of recognition. It is important to stress that in matters of science, announcing the discovery to the press is part of the legitimization phase. Reporting a so-called discovery in the *National Enquirer* does not, as people who read the tabloids believe, legitimize a discovery. Once a discovery is objectively legitimized, the legitimization phase is usually ended by the announcement of the discovery, both to professionals and to the public. Such an announcement describes not only the discovery event but also its immediate meaning and future implications.

When news of discoveries are widely circulated, their significance acquires some political importance, and then the third phase—the politicization phase—in the evolution of discovery begins. News of the significance of the Robledo discovery attracted the attention of New Mexico's senators. Independently, through contact with Smithsonian and Carnegie scientists, as well as discussions with the BLM, New Mexico's senators recognized the legitimacy and significance of the Robledo discovery and sought to become involved. In my case, involvement by the political sector was generated both positively, through becoming informed and accepting the professional reports of the great significance of the discovery, and negatively, through the criticisms of some in-state detractors.

The fourth phase in the discovery process, which usually follows rapidly on the heels of the third, is the enculturation phase. Common responses to this phase from the community touched by the discovery include adaptation, participation, and integration. Economics drive this phase, and the possibilities of a variety of community actions include the creation of visitor centers, museums, local, state, or national parks and monuments, and tourist attractions, as well as novelty shops that sell mugs, posters, track replicas, T-shirts, postcards, bumper stickers, books, videos, and the like.

It should be emphasized that in all discovery phases, the involvement of the discoverer is torn more and more from the activities that initiated the discovery to activities that promote it. In time, the discoverer spends little time doing that which he loves and more time doing that which he feels is necessary for the continuation of the project. This is an ironic double bind, because the discoverer spends so much time seeking grants and other funding, equipment, and sponsorship that he or she has little time to continue the actual work.

The discovery is the discoverer's child. The emotional attachments are quite similar. Yet soon the child grows up. Others want to hold and care for it. The more the discoverer draws attention to the discovery, the more others seek participation in it. Yet if the discoverer keeps the find secret, he or she will not get necessary or deserved support. A world-class discovery belongs to the world, not just to the discoverer. Money, recognition, and support require reciprocity, whether stated or not, as all social interactions do. Speaking engagements, articles, public appearances, press conferences, tours, and the like, are expected from the one who has received the support.

Within all discoveries, there is a period of weaning. In time, the discoverer moves farther and farther away from physical contact with the discovery. The meeting with Senator Bingaman and other government officials was the beginning of official political involvement in the footprint discovery. There was more politicking in my future and even greater excitement for all.

## The Prehistoric Trackways Study Act of 1990

One month after my first meeting with Senator Bingaman and BLM officials, the BLM called with exciting news. Senator Bingaman, working with BLM officials, had drafted a bill to provide money for a preliminary study of the Robledo fossils and to lay the groundwork for federal protection of the trackways. Senate Bill 2684 was born.

Tim Salt, area manager for the BLM, gave me a copy. I rushed home and called Gene Elliot and Thom Votaw. We met that evening and reminisced over the long, sometimes painful road we had traveled during the early stages of the discovery. We had come a long way in just a few short years. The footprints had moved from interesting curiosities, languishing from neglect, to the best Paleozoic trackway deposit in the world, attracting great interest. But I also couldn't help but feel more than a little melancholy. The trackways had been my "babies" and now it was time to wean them from my own little incubator and pass them into the care of others.

The fossils, covered almost instantly after formation, had been buried under millions of tons of rock for over a quarter of a billion years. Now, this mass grave was again exposed at the surface, and my frequently solitary efforts at protecting nature's tomb were being transferred to a wider administrative jurisdiction. The fossils would now be taken care of by the government of the United States. Senate Bill 2684 described the significance of the fossil footprint discovery in dramatic terms:

**101st CONGRESS**
**2nd Session**
**S. 2684**

**To authorize a study of methods to protect and interpret the nationally significant fossil trackways found in the Robledo Mountains near Las Cruces, New Mexico.**

---

**IN THE SENATE**
**OF THE UNITED STATES**
**May 24th (legislative day, April 18), 1990**

**Mr. Bingaman (for himself and Mr. Domenici), introduced the following bill; which was read twice and referred to the Committee on Energy and Natural Resources.**

---

The Congress finds that fossils are important for scientific studies of prehistoric life on earth. On lands administered by the Bureau of Land Management in the Robledo Mountains in New Mexico contain one of the most important fossil discoveries of the 20th century. Discoveries have included prehistoric tracks of amphibians, reptiles, arthropods, and insects; extensive plant fossils; and clues to the weather and climate of the period. Fossil footprints that form trackways help scientists recreate the environment and habitat that supported prehistoric life. Nearly 100 trackways from the Permian age have been uncovered in the Robledo Mountains. The trackways are over 280,000,000 years old, and they document the emergence of life from water to land. The trackways are unique in length and represents most taxonomic groups, including many prints of previously unknown animals. The trackways and other fossils are being lost for scientific study through unsupervised collecting and commercial quarrying.

The bill went on to describe the need for proper study of the fossils, and the need for a facility in the immediate area where the fossils could be curated, exhibited, and studied. It also requested that the fossil deposit be appropriately designated by Congress.

The bill was exciting to read, and I thought of the fact that eventually, if it passed both houses of Congress, the President of the United States would have to sign it. It was simply too much for me to grasp.

## Sociology as Prediction

Sociology is sometimes like prophecy. You first interpret the vision and then wait for it to happen. A good sociologist is trained to analyze human organizations as well as other human collectivities, whether big or small. Sociologists must learn not only to describe human behavior but also in some cases to predict where such behavior will lead. When asked, they must be able to predict with accuracy what the results of some interactions may be.

I had analyzed the Robledo discovery as events were taking place. I tried to predict what the community responses to the discovery would be, both initially and when it gained in importance. Some of this early research prepared me for the initial skepticism.

In the spring of 1988, I had four discovery phases laid out for the trackways discovery, complete with a tentative timetable. But my timing was way off. By the summer of 1990, the discovery was significantly ahead of schedule. I thought that the politicization stage of the discovery process would be about six to eight years into the project. Government bureaucracy moves slowly, I reasoned, and prior history of discoveries such as mine indicated that it takes nearly a decade of involvement before the politicians enter the picture.

As I look back on it now, I can see why my estimates were off. The significance of the discovery was never in doubt for a moment. The evaluations we received from a number of world-renowned experts spoke straight-forwardly to the significance of the trackway deposit. The critics' complaints and allegations, though as troubling as a slew of gnats, were ignored by both the politicians and the scientists who were involved in the project. Since ascertaining the significance of the deposit was completed relatively quickly, years of debate over this point was eliminated. The only thing left to do, a monumental task in itself, was to write up the research and begin protecting and preserving the discovery.

I also did not anticipate participation by the United States Congress. My thoughts on political involvement went no further than the state of New Mexico. I thought that the only federal involvement would be from the Bureau of Land Management and the the Smithsonian Institution. Having Congress jump into the project within three years of the discovery event was a shock to me, as were the discussions about making the Robledos a national monument. I felt that it would take ten years before there was movement by politicians to make the area a national monument, yet discussions about just such a thing were taking place in the summer of 1990. The BLM even secured the services of an architect to draw preliminary plans for a museum and visitor center for the prehistoric trackways deposit. The political train left the station quickly, and I had to race to catch up with it.

By analyzing these events, I was able to predict and prepare for future developments. I believe that the main reason a discovery of this magnitude was still being worked single-handedly by an amateur paleontologist was that with my sociological training I was able to steer clear of many of the pitfalls that have plagued similarly significant discoveries. Also, great emphasis on communication with the scientists and officials involved in the discovery probably saved the project a number of times.

## "How Much Money Do You Want?"

At the beginning of summer 1990, the project was well into another banner year. The interest of Senator Bingaman and Congress gave me a long overdue second wind. I had more trackways exposed on the various layers at AF 2 than ever. I wished that I could leave the site just as it was permanently, so that everybody could see more than a dozen trackways marching in and out of solid rock. But that would never happen. These trackways had to be removed before the rainy season commenced, which was about the Fourth of July. They would not be able to survive the forces of nature without man's help. If they were to lie exposed on the surface, the trackways would need the protection of a pavilion, like the one at Dinosaur National Monument.

One day, after having explored the southwestern canyons of the Robledos, I arrived home to find a blinking red light on the answering machine. With trepidation brought on by past experiences, I pushed the button.

"Hi Jerry, this is Pat Montoya from Senator Bingaman's office. Senator Bingaman wanted me to tell you that Senator Dale Bumpers will be in Las Cruces tomorrow and we want to know if you can give him a special tour of the trackway site before ten o'clock. This is very important, because Senator Bumpers is chairman of the Senate Committee on National Parks and Forests. To have him view the fossils firsthand is going to go a long way toward getting the kind of money and protection that is needed for the project."

A flashing red light with good news! I confirmed the meeting with Bingaman's office right away. Bumpers was scheduled to speak at the Las Cruces Hilton at 9:30 AM I was to take him to the site at 8:15. We didn't have a lot time.

I arrived wearing my best-looking fatigues and in my fire engine red 1951 Willys. My wife followed behind me in her two-door coupe. Senator Bumpers and Pat Montoya were already waiting in the lobby. Senator Bumpers was wearing a pin-striped suit and dress shoes. "Can we do this thing in an hour?" Pat asked. "The senator is very pressed for time."

"I'll do my best," I said, but I had my doubts. I led the party out to the parking lot, and then Senator Bumpers saw his transportation to the track site. I opened the door to the jeep and sheepishly began wiping the dust off the front seat. Bumpers looked on in disbelief. It looked like the trip was in some jeopardy until Pat asked if there was another way to get to the site. My wife suggested her car.

"Where is it?" Pat asked.

"It's parked right over there," Pearl said. She pointed to her little red coupe. "It needs to be cleaned, and it's a little dirty inside . . ."

"We'll take it," Pat interrupted.

I told Pearl to leave right away and that I would follow in my jeep. I told Pat we would still have to ride in the Willys for about a fourth of a mile, if we were to complete the tour in time for the senator's speech.

"We'll worry about that when we get there," Pat said with a huff.

When we arrived at the gate to Quarry Canyon, it was already 8:40. With some concern for the safety of his suit, Senator Bumpers gingerly rode with me until we arrived at the base of Devils Postpile.

"We can go no farther, sir," I said. "We have to walk the rest of the way."

"How far is it?" Pat asked.

"It's about a half-mile walk," I answered. "It'll take about twenty minutes."

Pat and Senator Bumpers looked at each other as if to say, "What on earth have we gotten ourselves into?"

I was very concerned about the senator's shoes. I had visions of his tripping on the loose rock and spraining an ankle or worse. I could see the headlines in the next morning's paper: "Senator Bumpers Injured on Way to Fossil Site."

We walked up Quarry Canyon to the site, and the longer it took, the more concerned Pat and the senator became. Around each bend was another two hundred feet of canyon, and the site seemed longer to get to than ever before.

By the time we finally arrived at the site, the senator had broken into a good sweat. It seemed as if all he wanted to do was to take a quick peek before rushing back to more familiar surroundings at the Hilton.

But Senator Bumpers could not have visited the site at a better time. The excavation had never looked any better than it did that morning. I had been "housecleaning" for nearly three weeks. I cleaned all the debris from the exposed layers, cleaned and prepared all the trackways, and laid out some great loose material on the flat slope on the other side of the excavation.

As we walked on one of the most impressive layers that I had exposed (I called it a feeding frenzy because it preserved fifteen different trackways of predator and prey) the transformation in Pat and Senator Bumpers's countenances took all of five seconds. Senator Bumpers was clearly impressed. I took him over each layer, explained what kinds of animals probably made the trackways, and pointed out how the area was once semitropical, the shore of a vast inland seaway.

He was so impressed that he actually got down on his hands and knees to see some of the very tiny tracks exposed on some of the layers. And he sat down on a rock—in his suit.

"I've never seen such a thing in my life," Bumpers exclaimed. "I never imagined that such a thing could have been preserved like this. To see these footprints going right into the bottom of this mountain is amazing. And how old are these footprints?"

"The party line is that they are over a quarter of a billion years old," I said. The Senator just shook his head.

"Dale," Pat said. "We have to head back. We have less than twenty-five minutes before your talk."

"Oh, they can wait," Bumpers replied. "I'm not done yet."

*Senator Dale Bumpers (right) discusses the discovery at the AF 2 site with MacDonald (center) and Pat Montoya (left). The bipedal-like trail can be seen in the lower right corner of the photo.* Photo by Pearl MacDonald.

He turned to me with genuine enthusiasm and asked, "What do you need? How can I help? I want to do everything I can to keep this thing going."

"This is it," I said to myself. "The best chance I'll ever have. Go for the whole enchilada."

"I'm doing this whole thing on my own, sir," I began. "Don't get me wrong, that's okay, but I do need money. And we need more professional involvement."

"You dug all of this out yourself?" he asked with surprise.

"Yes, sir," I answered. "I've moved about 120 tons of rock and carried out about 32 tons of rock out on my back."

"That kind of dedication is going to get a lot of notice," he said and gave me a pat on the back. "So it's a one-man operation. That's incredible. Nobody does work like this without compensation any more. You're one of a dying breed."

All my aches and pains and heartache were nothing in light of this kind of praise. "Who's involved now?" he wanted to know.

"The excavation is sponsored by the Bureau of Land Management and is hosted by the Smithsonian Institution," I answered. "It's entirely federal, since the material is on federal land. We thought that keeping it federal would minimize any political hangups that may result if it was spread around. Those two agencies have given me real support, not token support, but what the project needs goes far beyond what those agencies can offer."

"How much do you need?" the Senator asked. "How much money do you need to get this thing going?"

I was afraid to say. What if he thinks it's too much? What if I turn him off? What if I back down and give a figure that's less than I think I need?

"One hundred fifty thousand dollars," I said under my breath.

"What? How much?" Senator Bumpers asked.

"One hundred fifty thousand dollars," I said a little louder.

"One-hundred and fifty thousand dollars!" he exclaimed. "Is that all? You don't even need to make a speech to get that kind of money."

"Really, is it okay to ask for that much?" I said with excitement. "The site has two major needs. It needs to be extensively studied, and it needs to be adequately protected. I think it should be a national monument. The money should be under the joint control of the BLM and the Smithsonian. We need the money to solidify the research so that a decision can be made with regard to how to adequately promote and protect the fossils."

"Okay," Senator Bumpers said. "You can definitely count on my full support. Let's get this study going, and then once it's over, we can go for the millions needed to make this a national monument, build a museum, and make it into the kind of thing it deserves. I'll be in touch with Senator Bingaman, and we'll get this thing rolling. Now we have to get out of here fast!"

We walked hurriedly back to the Willys and drove out of the canyon to where Pearl's car was parked. Senator Bumpers transferred over and Pearl sped away. Since Senator Bumpers was a former governor of Arkansas, Pearl told him that we had honeymooned at Eureka Springs, Arkansas, in 1974.

"You're kidding," the senator said. "My wife and I honeymooned there as well. That cinches the whole thing," he continued with a laugh.

Senator Bumpers opened his speech at the Hilton, dusty suit and all, by noting that he had just met a couple who had also honeymooned in Eureka Springs as he and his wife did. Pearl seemed to have made an even bigger impression on the senator than the trackways did. Every little bit helps.

## The Senate Field Hearings

In late June 1990, Senator Bingaman invited me to testify on behalf of the trackways at the field hearings of the Senate Subcommittee on Public Lands, National Parks, and Forests in Las Cruces. He felt that holding the hearings on the significance of the discovery near the site would not only allow politicians a chance to view the excavation first-hand, but would also provide an opportunity for locals to hear expert scientists testify about the credibility of the discovery.

Senator Bingaman was able to bring nearly all of the in-state critics to the hearing. They participated in the field trip to the excavation and in the hearings that commenced soon afterward at the lecture hall at the Doña Ana Community College. Bingaman achieved in two months what we hadn't been able to achieve in two years. After just three hours of testimony and visual inspection, the criticisms ceased and there was universal acceptance of the significance of the discovery.

The next day, reports of the Senate hearing reached the papers nationwide:

**Dateline: July 7, 1990**
**Albuquerque Journal, Associated Press**
**Solitary Scientiest Shows Off Tracks**

Jerry MacDonald labored alone for months, stripping away ancient mud flats to uncover animal tracks that predate dinosaurs by millions of years.

He knew his discovery was significant. Each layer revealed abundant tracks, some from previously unknown species, and out-of-state scientists later called his find the greatest animal trackway of its era in the world.

Yet MacDonald could muster little academic or governmental support within New Mexico for his research.

But on Friday, MacDonald's solitary world was crowded as more than two dozen politicians, bureaucrats and journalists trekked into a narrow canyon northwest of Las Cruces to view his find. Later in the day, during a Senate subcommittee hearing in Las Cruces, people packed into a lecture hall broke into applause after he described his work.

In the two years since the 38-year-old sociologist announced the discovery, he had gone from outcast to celebrity.

"I am a little sensitive to criticism," MacDonald told Senator Jeff Bingaman, D-NM, as the two stood in the canyon beside tracks left by animals and insects 280 million years ago. "I didn't appreciate hearing over and over, 'We knew it was there all along.'"

After carrying slabs totaling 20 tons using a harness strapped to his back, MacDonald said he is tired, sore, and nearly broke.

Hints that he might be a fraud were not appreciated either, he said later.

Many disbelievers got the faith after Bingaman announced he would hold a hearing on the bill he introduced with Senate colleague Pete Domenici, R-NM, to protect and study the area, he added.

Witnesses at Friday's hearing uniformly praised MacDonald's work, and several testified the area should be declared a National Monument.

"This is a world-class resource no less significant than Dinosaur National Monument," said Bruce Craig, cultural resources manager for the 150,000-member National Parks and Conservation Association. . . .

Some scientists, shocked at the first news of MacDonald's discovery, warned of a possible hoax. The Robledo Mountains had long been a resource for geology students hunting fossils, but scholars dismissed the few animal tracks found there as insignificant.

MacDonald upset that premise by showing that layer upon layer of ancient tidal flats contained plant fossils, insect trails and the tracks of more than 50 types of animals, many never before known to paleontologists. Some of the trackways extend more than 40 feet, allowing scientist's to study how the expanding reptile population lived and moved in the Paleozoic Era. . . .

Unable to find support at home, MacDonald attracted the attention of the Smithsonian Institution in Washington, D.C., the Carnegie Museum of Natural History in Pittsburgh and the Los Angeles County Museum of Natural History. The Smithsonian appointed him field director of what is now called the Las Cruces Paleozoic Trackways Project.

A few weeks after the field hearings, I received another letter from Senator Bumpers:

Dear Jerry: On July 26th, the Subcommittee on Public Lands, National Parks and Forests will conduct a hearing on Senate Bill 2684, a bill to authorize a study of methods to protect and interpret the nationally significant fossil trackways found in the Robledo Mountains near Las Cruces, New Mexico.

The purpose of this letter is to invite you to testify at the hearing. You are requested to bring 10 copies of your written statement with you to the hearing. Please be prepared to summarize your written remarks so that there will be time for questions and discussion of the issues.

Although Congress invites an individual to testify at a congressional hearing, the U.S. government does not pay for the transportation of witnesses. I needed $500. It was money I did not have. Bingaman twice sought the money from NMSU, but the university was unable to come up with the funds. Unknown to me, the BLM found a Las Cruces businessman who was willing to pay my way. It was a wonderful gift. It even worked out so that I would be able to stay over a couple extra days to do research at the Natural History Museum at the Smithsonian. I wanted to look at Gilmore's Grand Canyon collection one more time.

I did not go to Washington unarmed or without support. I knew that a variety of experts and government officials were going to testify in favor of the trackways study act. But would the testimony be unanimously favorable?

The hearings began on Friday morning at 10:00 AM in the Senate chambers. I knew nothing about how hearings were held, or what I was supposed to do. A dozen senators came out of a door behind the committee bench and sat down. When Senate Bill 2684 came up, Senator Bingaman opened the hearing by reading his statement about the trackways. When Bingaman was done, Senator Pete Domenici (R-NM) asked for the floor. Senator Domenici looked right at me.

"I want to take this opportunity," he began, "by emphasizing that I am very proud of what you have done with these fossils from New Mexico. And I want to assure you that all of New Mexico, and the nation, are proud of you as well. I want you to understand that we are very supportive of your solitary efforts and we are solidly behind you and your work. I want to congratulate you."

After the opening remarks were completed, several individuals testified on the importance of the fossils, the need to adequately study and house them, and the need to develop the site both scientifically and publicly, including its designation as a national monument.

Nick Hotton testified on behalf of the Smithsonian, and his testimony was read into the congressional record:

> I am pleased to testify on Senate Bill 2684 concerning the fossil trackways near Las Cruces, New Mexico.
>
> The Robledo Hills trackway locality is of great scientific significance. From what I've seen of it . . . the Robledo Hills trackway locality

is probably the best of its kind of Permian age. The only one that can be compared with it is in the world-famous Coconino sandstone, in the Grand Canyon, which, however, includes mostly tracks of small animals. The Robledos tracks, by contrast, include large as well as small animals and probably represent all major taxonomic categories of Lower Permian tetrapods otherwise known only from bones. The Robledos quarry also yields tracks of otherwise unknown arthropods, and good impressions of plants, each of which will provide invaluable information regarding the environment of the time.

Permian fossils, bones and tracks alike, are about 270 million years old, and they represent our first detailed view of terrestrial life not too long after it had emerged from the water. There are older terrestrial fossils from various places in the world, but none known in such detail over such a broad area—bones of these animals are found all the way from Arizona to central Texas. . . .

Bones . . . tell us what the animals looked like, and with luck where they died and how they came to be preserved. Trackways, however, tell us what they were actually doing during life—each one is a little snapshot of what some Permian reptile or amphibian was up to on one day in the far-distant past. Both of these lines of evidence, bones and tracks together, are essential for proper scientific grasp of what life was like so long ago. However, I think that trackways offer a much more dramatic illustration of such life, and will be correspondingly more impressive to the public if they have controlled access to the Robledos locality.

My testimony would not be complete without reference to the work by Mr. Jerry Paul MacDonald at the Robledos locality, work which has been executed in a thoroughly professional manner. Mr. MacDonald deserves full credit for this work, which he initiated and has carried out virtually single-handed. . . .

In conclusion, I must express my appreciation of the cooperation afforded by . . . the Las Cruces office of the Bureau of Land Management. This cooperation has provided encouragement to a talented young man when he needed it most, and in doing so has given paleontology a rich source of data that will continue to be useful for generations to come.

My testimony was last. I thanked the committee for their interest in the bill and for their kindness in inviting me. I spent the first few moments describing the events that led up to the discovery, and briefly commented on their significance. Then, I spent the remainder of my time urging Congress to take strong action to both protect and exploit the footprint deposit:

Today, in the waning years of the twentieth century, these footprints are in trouble, not only from the unstoppable forces of nature, but also from the ravages of man. Already, a rich fossil plant layer, preserving much of the semi-tropical environment these exotic animals inhabited, was totally destroyed, their remnants now comprising the floors in a one-half-million-dollar house in downtown Las Cruces, or in the exterior walls of homes and businesses in the area. Already, small footprint slabs can occasionally be seen within the rock walls of suburban Las Cruces, and some collectors used trackway debris to line their fireplaces.

Such exploitation of fossil occurrences is not unique, and even in the Robledo Mountains can be excused. We just didn't know better. We had no idea of their incalculable value to science and history. But we know better now. We must take strong action now to protect a valuable natural resource that has miraculously survived into our lifetimes.

The suggested similarity of the Robledo track site with Dinosaur National Monument is an excellent one. Though dinosaur bones are found in many places throughout the United States, such a phenomenal concentration of skeletal remains within such easy reach of scientists and the public made the national monument designation logical. There, in one spot, was a concentrated representative example of everything great about the United States' rich fossil history with dinosaurs. In this one site alone was the dinosaur hunters dream come true, as well as the dinosaur lovers' heaven.

The Robledo trackway deposit is as rich in tracks and trackways as Dinosaur National Monument is in dinosaurs. In the Robledos, we have a concentration of tracks that is indeed representative of the best of several lesser sites in North America and the world. Here, in one spot, are preserved the life traces of dozens upon dozens of new and exciting animals, as well as plants, insects, and even skeletal remains. One could spend their whole life in the Robledos and still come away with a broad and formidable understanding of the Permian period. There just simply isn't any better pre-dinosaur trackway site to be found anywhere else in the world.

Needless to say, the Permian trackways of the Grand Canyon indirectly survive today in part because of the protection national park status has afforded them by the United States government. What the Robledo Mountains lack in beauty compared to the Grand Canyon, it makes up for in the haunting beauty and abundance of these ancient trackways.

For the above reasons, I suggest that the Robledo trackway deposit eventually be considered as a national monument, so that all of the authority and respect that such a designation carries with it can be in force. While it is true that the number and variety of trackways seems almost endless within the proposed study area, the deposit itself is fearfully small, just over four square miles.

Considering the past history of the area in terms of indiscriminate collecting, quarrying, and the fact of a major trackway theft that occurred during the present excavation, [September 1988], as well as numerous unsupervised trips and activity that increase by the week, a failure to adequately protect the area could result in tragic losses of irreplaceable material.

I believe that the suggestion by a few that the Robledo area be designated as a national natural landmark is inadequate for such a rare and vulnerable national resource. To date there are well over five hundred such designations, but I am aware of only two stellar world-class pre-dinosaur trackway sites, the aforementioned tracks protected in Grand Canyon National Park, and the unprotected Robledo Mountains Paleozoic trackways of New Mexico.

In conclusion, the Prehistoric Trackways National Monument will undoubtedly be a source of local, state, and national pride as a showcase for a long-lost community of courageous life forms. A lasting legacy of such a monument will be a renewed commitment to try our best to protect this fragile planet and all of the marvelous creatures it contains.

Again, thank you for your commitment to developing this remarkable national resource.

Additional support of Senate Bill 2684 was subsequently submitted by several more paleontologists, including Doctors Spencer Lucas and Adrian Hunt of the New Mexico Museum of Natural History. Both concurred that the Robledos deposit was a world-class find. This testimony was crucial in bringing around other scientists from New Mexico who may have had doubts in the past.

Later, two of the foremost trackway experts in North America, Dr. Martin Lockley, of the University of Colorado at Denver, and Dr. James Farlow, of Indiana/Purdue University, contributed evaluations on the Robledos which were read into the *Congressional Record*. Dr. Lockley's evaluation was particularly authoritative, since he had seen firsthand hundreds of sites around the world. When I read Lockley's comments I had the same excited feeling I had when I read Hotton's first evaluation three years earlier:

The Paleozoic (pre-dinosaurian) fossil footprint sites of the Robledo Mountains, New Mexico, are undoubtedly the largest, most exciting and scientifically most important fossil footprint discovery ever made in the western United States, even in the world. Not since the 1920's discovery of Paleozoic tracks in the Grand Canyon has anyone come close to matching those discoveries. The Robledo discoveries surpass the paleontologically famous Grand Canyon sites and well deserve the widespread international acclaim that they have generated.

As a specialist in the field of fossil footprint research I have studied and observed hundreds of sites in North America, Europe, and Asia. I can state that I know of no other Paleozoic site that displays so many scientifically valuable features. For example the trackways are extremely diverse and varied, evidently representing a very broad spectrum of ancient animal life, ranging from large fin-backed reptiles through medium- and small-sized amphibians to insects and other invertebrates. In addition the preservation of tracks and other features, such as rain-drop impressions, is exquisite.

This is what paleontologists call a "window into the past" and we count ourselves lucky to record a few such high quality windows every generation. Finally I would add that the Robledo trackways sites are distinguished also by their abundance (over 30 sites), and potential for excavation of large exhibit-quality specimens, found in association with many other fossils.

The Robledo Mountains trackway sites are a prime candidate for study and protection/preservation so that future generations of scientists and lay persons may have access to the valuable information encoded in these fabulous fossil footprints.

I support any efforts made to research and protect this unique natural resource. Mr. MacDonald has so far done a remarkable job in bringing these sites to light and undertaking initial excavations almost single-handedly.

With these evaluations coming in, I couldn't help feeling like a heavyweight boxer who had won a unanimous decision. My body and mind, bruised and beaten for so long, finally sensed that I could let my guard down. My wife hugged me and said, "It's over now, Jerry. You're not alone anymore. You've done it. You can rest now."

# CHAPTER THIRTEEN

## The Sociologist Under My Hat

Before the expansion of modern technology in the last century or so, there was primarily a single "arena" in which both the process and the event of discovery could take place, and that was the geographic world. Discovery, for the most part, was tied to a definite geographic location. For example, the search for sunken ships, lost cities, buried treasure, tombs, burial mounds, dinosaurs, and the like can be done only in the field, and the event itself is permanently tied to one specific locality. In this context, discovery is immobile, since the geographic world cannot be replicated in a lab, broken down, isolated, or manipulated.

Additionally, with the rapid development of technology, much science has changed dramatically. Another arena now exists in the mobile world of the laboratory. For the first time in history, scientists around the world can study the same phenomenon at the same time with either the same or different approach, and even the same material.

In a laboratory context, the discovery process is not tied to a particular geographic location. Discovery is mobile. Discovery in this context could and does take place in virtually any country and in any adequately staffed and equipped laboratory in the world. In medicine, for example, the call for a cure for cancer has already sounded numerous times throughout the world. As a result, there are thousands of experts seeking the "cure." Naturally, everybody wants to discover it first.

While field discoveries can only occur in one specific locality, in the laboratory arena, both the quest and the subsequent discovery can occur virtually anywhere. The vast bulk of laboratory discoveries are in the realms of medicine, physics, and chemistry. Yet the laboratory is not without its drawbacks. Laboratory studies have major limiting factors that separate them from work in the field. In most cases, laboratory work requires significant economic and technical support. In fact, laboratory work leading to discovery often requires a background of particular expertise in order to initiate the hunt. Not only does one need to have a well-funded lab, but one must also have the ability to run a variety of technical equipment such as computers, microscopes, atom smashers, lasers, and medical tools. Consequently, laboratory discoveries are, for the most part, high tech.

Discoveries performed in the field are not as restrictive with regard to such socioeconomic-technical factors. Geographic field work, by its very nature, can be done with a limited amount of funds and status. The primary limiting factors are free access to possible search localities and awareness of discovery when it happens. Field discoveries are, for the most part, low tech.

Discoveries in the field have another advantage: many times virtually anyone can make one. At the most basic level, all that is required of the discoverer is awareness and recognition of what they have found. The history of paleontology is rife with examples of serendipitous discoveries, proving that in some cases pre-discovery training in the field is not required. This is not to say that field discoveries are easy or require little training. As I said in an earlier chapter, paleontologists are rigorously trained to recognize the most scant piece of evidence as important when they are in the field, and years of field work experience increases the odds of discovery significantly. They are also trained to follow through with their discovery from it's excavation and removal, to its analysis and curation. The serendipitous discoverer can't do that. If we made a contest of it by putting a trained field paleontologist and an average person off the street in the same fossil bed, the paleontologist would be the clear winner 99 percent of the time.

Although a few field discoveries occur as "accidents" by the untrained, accidental discoveries are almost non-existent in the laboratory. There are exceptions, however. One of the most prominent (and high tech) discoveries of recent years was Robert Ballard's discovery of the *Titanic*. This was without question an incredibly technical field discovery. United with the Woods Hole Oceanigraphic Institute, the hunt for the *Titanic* cost millions of dollars and required the most up-to-date submersibles, sonar, and video equipment. Ballard found the ocean liner in 1985. While most of the information Ballard utilized in his search was available to anyone from the time it sank, Ballard was the only one to find the ship.

Still, the *Titanic* discovery brings up a few more important ingredients in the process of discovery: opportunity and resources. By opportunity, I mean that the hopeful discoverer has the time available to pursue his quest; by resources, that the hopeful discoverer has the financial and logistical support to begin his search. Many have the opportunity to make a discovery, but lack the resources to do so. Ballard was able to pull these two ingredients together.

Because the discoverer must learn to recognize the exception, whether in a laboratory or on a hillside, it is imperative that the scientific method be taught in the schools and universities. A strong grasp of the scientific method will ensure that discovery will continue to be the catalyst for advancement and progress. Awareness must lead to recognition.

There is a story, perhaps apocryphal, about some fishermen who moored their boat year after year to a strange rock jutting out from a small promontory in the lake near Elephant Butte, New Mexico. They were aware of the rock, but they did not recognize it as a *Triceratops* skull, which it was later found to be.

Indeed, many discoveries can be entirely serendipitous. The only prerequisite for discovery in such a case is that the discoverer have enough prior knowledge or awareness of the thing observed to recognize it as important. He or she must be able to make an on-the-spot diagnosis of possible significance, to contrast what he or she has found with what came before. For example, in March 1991, a man bought a painting at a rummage sale for $4. He bought the painting for the frame, and when he removed the back to throw the painting away, he found an original copy of the Declaration of Independence, worth over $1 million. Fortunately, the man had enough knowledge to recognize the hidden parchment for what it was.

Yet few discoveries are this serendipitous. Most major discoveries are well thought out and planned. All the available information is gathered, regardless of how that information has been interpreted in the past. In paleontology, for example, leads from amateur collectors are probably the most important avenues to discovery. Leads often come from gem and mineral shows, swap meets, and casual discussion. Farmers often find fossils in their fields, and hikers come across material during their walks.

Discoveries can also occur months or years or even decades later when someone acquires new knowledge about a curious object collected years before. In this case, their curiosity is rewarded retroactively. Awareness gives way to recognition. Not only is new value placed on the object but if, for example, it is a fossil or an archaeological artifact, new value may even be bestowed on the place where the object was found. At this point, a return to the discovery site is accompanied with new knowledge, and all subsequent fossils or artifacts collected there are recognized as significant. This is what happened with the dinosaur nesting sites discovered by amateur paleontologist John R. Horner in Montana.

John Horner's discovery of the first dinosaur eggs in the Western Hemisphere and the nesting clutches that held and protected them in life was triggered by an amazing string of "what ifs." Horner was working as a paleontological preparator at Princeton University. He says that he twice applied to every museum in the country looking for any kind of work that would bring him and vertebrate fossils together. Princeton accepted him. If that had not been the case, he would not have had the opportunity to work under Dr. Don Baird. Baird allowed Horner to participate in his research and encouraged him to work on his own. Baird took Horner with him on trips to every natural history museum on the East Coast.

Horner became curious about why so many dinosaur fossils were found in marine sediments. He also noticed that most were the bones of duckbilled dinosaurs. Furthermore, he discovered that there was a dearth of juvenile dinosaurs in all of the museum collections he had visited. Yet his curiosity seemed to lead nowhere.

Then Horner found out that one of the best collections of juvenile dinosaur bones came from the Bear Paw shale near Billings, Montana, not far from Horner's hometown. During a vacation, Horner and his friend, Bob Makela, decided to poke around the Bear Paw shale beds where paleontologist Earl Douglass had found the juveniles so many years ago. They never had the chance. It rained for three days. They were knee deep in mud. Collecting, let alone even reconnaissance, was impossible. The trip was a bust.

Horner and Makela drove down to the Milk River badlands near Rudyard, Montana. Makela and a teacher, Larry French, had found some mammal fossils and wanted to show them to Bill Clemmens, a fellow paleontologist. Clemmens was impressed with the fossils and in turn told Horner and company about the owner of a rock shop in Bynum who had some dinosaur fossils he wanted identified.

Horner and company reached Bynum on a Sunday morning, when the co-owner, Marion Branvold, was running the shop. As they were identifying fossils in the shop, Mrs. Branvold went into her house and brought out a jar full of other bones. Horner recognized immediately that they were the bones of a juvenile duckbill. It was exactly what he had come to Montana to look for. Two and a half weeks later, the Branvolds took Horner and Makela to the place where the juvenile bones had been found. Horner and Makela collected very quickly and noticed a clear demarcation line between green mudstone with juvenile dinosaur bone and red mudstone. They soon realized that they had found the nesting place of a duckbilled dinosaur. The rest is history. Horner had discovered dramatic new evidence on the social behavior of dinosaurs.

Here, too, the "what ifs" are endless. The greatest "what if" of all was why did these coincidences happen to the man perfectly suited for the task? A man who already had a "bug in the brain"? Only Horner could have been able to string together these varied events into the pre-discovery phase that led to one of the greatest paleontological discoveries in North America.

Coincidentally, the area where Horner found the dinosaur nesting sites, the Willow Creek anticline, was studied, mapped, and walked over for decades by professionals just as the Robledos were. In less than ten years, two tremendously important paleontological finds were discovered in areas that had appeared to be overstudied. One man's curiosity is another man's treasure.

## The Seedbed for Discovery

There are three kinds of research settings in which discovery can occur: pristine settings where no prior work has been done, on-going research settings where an area is currently being worked, and completed research settings where the major work is already done. In a scientifically pristine context, there is no consensual diagnosis concerning the possible productivity of the area. A discovery here becomes the prime catalyst for developing such a diagnosis. In areas that are the focus of ongoing research, discovery events usually help to support or modify the developing diagnosis of significance of the area being formulated by the scientific community. In areas so well known that a completed diagnosis of significance has become well established within scientific circles, very few, if any, subsequent discoveries occur. One or two that may occur are expected to reinforce the existing evaluation of significance.

Discoveries that take place in unstudied areas are the most easily received and developed. But here the work is poorly funded, if it is funded at all. And discoveries made by amateurs are generally soon taken over by experts more qualified to exploit the occurrence scientifically. Discoveries made in areas already undergoing research are usually funded, and there are usually one or more experts on site and sometimes research assistants and volunteers. There is a clear agenda of research already defined and a number of search plans or experiments in progress. Discoveries in areas of completed diagnosis are just as poorly funded and manned as if the area was brand new to science. Nobody likes to fund replicative endeavors. It is assumed that "everybody" has done "everything" that can possibly be done in the area. Discoveries in these contexts can be more problematic because they force reevaluations of conventional wisdom.

Some discoveries that occur in an area that is already well-studied inevitably challenge the previous diagnosis and, in some cases, imply a misdiagnosis. A variety of attendant considerations are added to the discovery which may involve the discoverer. His or her skills, qualifications, character, and experience become intertwined with the discovery. In extreme cases, rumors or even allegations of fraud, deceit, or ignorance may be initiated, especially by the authors of the original diagnosis.

It is in this third context that the Robledo discovery event belongs. The history surrounding the trackways from the Robledos suggested that the region was overlooked, indeed in a sense misdiagnosed, and some of the resultant behavior surrounding the Robledo tracks was consistent with defending mistaken assumptions.

## Galloping Paleontologists

James Farlow, Mark Schult's advisor from the University of Indiana, visited the Robledo sites in June 1991. Also present was Dr. Steven Buchmann, an entomologist with the U.S. Department of Agriculture and an amateur paleontologist with expertise in terrestrial invertebrates. After we visited the main excavation site, AF 2, I wanted to take them to the new discoveries in the western canyons of the Robledos.

Dave Slagle and I met Steve, Jim, and Mark at the Quality Inn at 6:00 AM, so that we could catch the oblique rays of the sun when we arrived at the site. We made it to Dead Man's Curve at 6:45. Although I knew intellectually that it was impossible to roll, it still felt like the Willys was tilting too much toward the canyon below. Jim and Steve grew equally nervous.

"Is there any other way out of the mountains besides this curve?" Steve asked.

"Yes, there is," I answered, "but it takes a lot longer and it's not as exciting."

"Well, I think we've had enough excitement for one day," Steve noted. I had no idea that I would have to leave the mountains by way of the other road, or that, like it or not, Steve was in for more excitement.

My Willys worked its way up two mountains until we reached our destination, a flat mountaintop overlooking Insect Hill and the Conifer Forest, about a quarter of a mile below us.

"I am really interested in your reactions to Insect Hill, Steve," I said as we walked down the mountainside. "My sense is that a lot of the invertebrates that left those trails are similar to insects living in today's high desert environments, but a lot of others are semi-aquatic to apparently fully aquatic."

As we walked toward the sites, a lizard or skink would dart out in front of us when we ventured too close to their hiding places. And every time one did, Jim was off and running, chasing the poor thing from one mesquite bush to another, leaping over rocks and shrubs to observe these frightened reptiles.

"I don't get enough of an opportunity to observe lizards in Indiana," Jim explained, "and so every chance I get, I follow them to see how they run."

He wasn't kidding. I had seen Jim do the same kind of thing in a documentary on dinosaur trackways presented on PBS's *NOVA*. The segment showed Jim chasing emus across a wetted surface, so that he could calculate the speed versus the stride of emus and by extension that of long-extinct dinosaurs. I realized that all of us who study pre-historic trackways are in a sense "galloping paleontologists." We love to watch and study the movements of animals, whether the jerky movements of a spider, the speed of a lizard at full throttle, or the grace of an emu gliding across the mud.

Paleontologists are a strange lot. We engage in seemingly strange behaviors as we try to understand ancient life. On any given day you might observe one of us licking rocks, digging holes, or chasing lizards, or you might see us walking and running across muddy sur-faces, scientifically working with plastic dinosaurs, building models of clay, using toilet paper to wrap our discoveries, studying birds, pho-tographing seemingly insignificant rocks, sand, and mud, and spend-ing hours over a slew of broken bones. And we like doing these things. We do these things to identify, preserve, and interpret the evidence we dig out of the ground.

When we reached the Cattletank Canyon, we walked north a few hundred feet to the Conifer Forest. Lying everywhere were the spectacular *Walchia* fronds, and the specimens were subjected to photo shoots for most of the day. We also looked at the Abo formation waterfall and did some collecting on the eastern slope of the red beds.

When the sun was high enough, I took the group back to the south until we reached Insect Hill. It didn't take long to hit pay dirt. I pulled out a slab with almost a dozen centipede trails on it. The widths of the trails were varied, which indicated that at least some of them were made by a variety of centipedes. Steve confirmed that the trails did indeed look similar to those of centipedes, but they were pretty big.

You haven't seen a centipede until you've seen one of ours. New Mexico is blessed with an abundance of them. The larger ones can be eight inches long, and nearly two inches wide from leg tip to leg tip. Many of the old Hispanic families in the area consider the large ones as evil (*Santopies malditos*). And why shouldn't they. The old timers say that they can embed their legs into your skin, leaving a stitched-like scar that would make Dr. Frankenstein proud. They give me the creeps.

But having to deal with a live eight-inch centipede is nothing compared to the chills I get when I think that the centipedes from the Early Permian were over three feet long with a girth the size of a man's fist. And I know this is true firsthand. I uncovered a full-sized imprint of a centipede, a *santopies malditos*, that was twenty-one inches long and four inches wide.

As we poked around on Insect Hill, I suggested that we go north to the Cattletank track site. I told the others of the big pelycosaur trackway that was lying across the canyon floor, the middle of which had been recently ripped out by the action of flash floods.

"I definitely want to see it," Jim said. "But is it far?"

"Yes," I said.

"No," Dave said.

"I think we ought to drive there," I suggested.

"Oh, it's not that far," Dave said. "We can walk it easily. It's only a mile at most."

"No, Dave," I said. "It's got to be closer to two miles."

After this exchange of contradictory recommendations, we decided to walk. After an eternity, and nearly two miles later, famished and dying of thirst, we reached the spot.

"Oh no," I exclaimed.

"What's wrong," everybody asked.

"Dave, our eight-foot trackway has become a four-foot one," I said.

"What?" Dave exclaimed.

Apparently, more of the trackway had been torn away in the spring rains, proving once again how extremely vulnerable these trackways are once exposed. This was not good news.

"Is this it?" Jim said. "We've walked all this way to see this? It wasn't worth it."

Now all we had to look forward to was the two-mile walk back to Conifer Forest, and the quarter-mile hike up the mountainside to the Willys. As we walked back, Steve became interested in the bees we occasionally encountered. He told us to go on while he spent time with the bees. We told him that we would wait for him at the jeep.

When we made it to the Conifer Forest, we picked up the rest of the gear, rested for about ten minutes, and then made the climb to the jeep. The minutes began mounting until it was close to an hour, and there was still no sign of Steve. We talked amongst ourselves about the impossibility of getting lost, since you just stay in the canyon. We decided that something was wrong. Dave volunteered to run (that's right, *run*) back up the canyon toward Cattletank Draw.

While Dave ran up the canyon, I had the brilliant idea of moving the jeep about ten feet so that all of it could be visible from the canyon below. I drove the ten feet and we all heard it at the same time—the wonderful and unforgetable sound of air rushing out of a tire.

"I think we've got a flat," Mark said.

"We've got to act fast," I said. I pulled a canister of liquid tire out from under the seat. "I'm always ready for anything."

"Is that why you don't have a spare?" Jim asked.

"I'm getting it fixed. It's flat," I answered. "But don't worry, this stuff will work."

I sprayed the can into the tire, and the rush of air slowed but did not stop. Jim and Mark stood there as I moved the jeep the ten feet back down to the trail. Then they yelled "Stop! Stop!" But it was too late. Another leak began in another tire.

"I think we're in trouble," I said. "We have got to get out of here before all the air leaks out and we really have a problem."

"How many cans of that stuff do you have," Jim asked.

"Three," I answered, "and I've already used one."

I shot a can into the other tire (it wasn't as bad as the first one), and we sped out of there like a bat out of hades. We drove the trail to the south, because we could get closer to civilization that way and even I didn't want to try Dead Man's Curve with two leaky tires. We drove about three-quarters of a mile and then I shot the remaining cans into both tires. When we were about to turn east out of the canyon, we met up with Steve and Dave. Steve had just kept going south in the canyon; he had forgotten to turn east up the mountain when he reached the Conifer Forest.

"Dave! I have no time to talk," I yelled. "I'm getting two flat tires. I've got to drive as far out of the mountains as I can. Can you go back to your truck and drive the rest of the people out?"

"Bueno," Dave said.

We made it out of the canyon and waited by the gravel quarry. But it looked like the tires were going to get the best of us at last. I left Jim at the pit to wait for Dave and Steve to come along, and I drove on about ten pounds of air till I made it to the convenience store a couple of miles away. It was without a doubt the worst field day I ever had. It sure made an impression on Jim.

"Look at it this way, Jim," I said later while we were having lunch, "you've had a day you'll remember for a long time. Imagine what you could tell your grandchildren. You made it over Dead Man's Curve, a four-mile hike to see a trackway that for all intents and purposes no longer existed, a fellow scientist getting lost in the hills, and two flat tires in the middle of nowhere. Yes, what a day!"

## Reading Some of the Pages

Safely back at Jim's hotel, we agreed to meet that night to view slides of hundreds of the specimens. It was great fun to see professional paleontologists oooh and ahhh over the material I had uncovered.

"I just can't get over the fact that very few of these trackways preserve tail drag," Jim noted. "We are so far back in time that we're close to actually seeing these primitive animals emerge from the seas, and yet the trackways are dramatically narrow in gait, and even among the small animal trails, there just isn't tail drag."

"That's exactly the point, Jim," I answered. "I've uncovered perhaps two dozen big pelycosaur trails, and in every instance the width of the trails are narrow, which means that these animals, once thought to be so sprawling as to leave tell-tale tail drag are holding their bodies well off the ground.

"There is one exception," I continued. "At AF 2 I've discovered one big pelycosaur trackway that does have a heavy and continuous tail drag. On layer twenty-five the trail is still as narrow as the others, but it does preserve tail drag. I believe that this trail was made by the herbivorous pelycosaur, *Edaphosaurus*, with its long and heavy tail. The thing that excites me, though, is that this exception proves the rule. It clearly shows that the abundant trails without tail drag are legitimate gait patterns, and not just anomalous traces."

While Jim and Mark were dumbfounded by the vertebrate trails, Steve Buchmann was excited about the invertebrate trails, especially the insects.

"This is as staggering a collection of invertebrates as the Burgess shale," Steve said, "and just as bizarre."

Steve had no idea what had made most of the invertebrate trails, and some of the trails were so strange that we could not even conceive of the kind of locomotive scheme, let alone morphology, that could be responsible for them.

"This is a once-in-a-lifetime opportunity to study terrestrial invertebrates with statistically significant sample sizes," Steve wrote to me later in June when he returned to Arizona. "I am so stumped that I'm going to have to do a ton of experiments with living insects to see if I can even come close to what I saw at your discoveries."

After about one-half hour of slides, I came to one of my favorites—one that I was convinced preserved what I believed to be evidence of one animal gobbled up on-the-hoof by another. I was very curious to see if Jim agreed. As Jim viewed the slide, he could re-create the entire scene. A small amphibian was still for a moment as a beetle-like insect ventured perpendicular to the amphibians orientation. In a moment the amphibian struck, and the beetle was lifted off the mud. The amphibian struggled with its prey, losing it perhaps twice, before disabling it enough to eat it. There are several invertebrate trails that are not only intermittent but oriented in the opposite direction of the preceding trail. The amphibian tracks show slide marks, sweeping tail drag, skitter prints, and tracks that could only be made in a wrestling match.

"I've been shown a lot of tracks that have been touted as terminations, and they were not," Jim said when he viewed the slide. "I've been very hard to convince, not only because the actual preserved termination event has to be such an incredibly rare occurrence, but also because I could always come up with an alternative explanation other than that of a termination. But here, I have to agree. This is the

### DIMETRODON
### OLD STANCE

*The old stance of* Dimetrodon, *based upon skeletal reconstruction alone, pictures it as a clumsy semi-sprawler with a very wide stance and constant belly and tail drag. The first trackways of these predators, found in the Robledo Mountains, consistently show narrow trackways with no tail or belly drag marks. It was clearly much more agile than originally thought. The difference*

NEW STANCE

*in stance can be illustrated by the technique of two freestyle swimmers, one whose stroke is wide and to the side of the body, and the other who pulls his arms and hands underneath his chest with a hand-over-hand motion.* Drawings by Noah MacDonald.

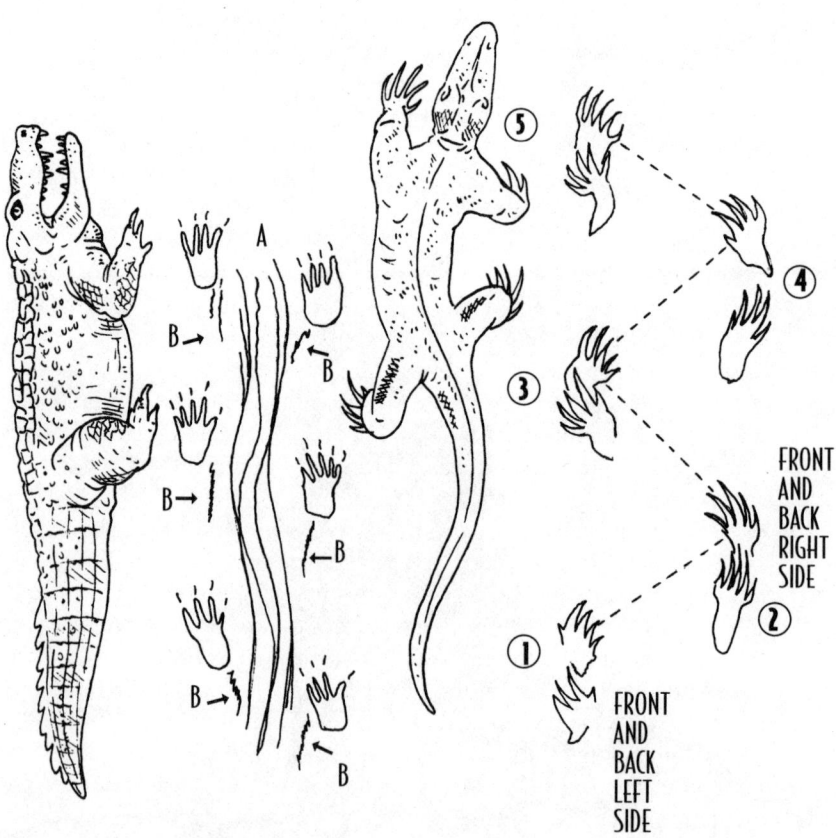

*The trails of a present-day alligator and an Early Permian pelycosaur. The alligator trail (left) is wide and cumbersome, with heavy tail and body drag (A) and even toe drag (B). The pelycosaur trail is narrower, preserves no tail or body drag, and is represented by alternating pairs of tracks, such as the front and back left feet (1), front and back right feet (2), and so on. Drawing by Noah MacDonald.*

closest thing to a termination other than being right there to see it happen with your own two eyes."

Later that month, I received the evaluation of the Robledo trackways that I had requested from Jim when he left for Indiana. Fortunately, he omitted reference to our event-filled field day:

"... I have a great deal of experience working with fossilized footprints at sites in Texas and New England, and I have also visited many dinosaur tracksites in Arizona, Colorado, and Utah. Although the Abo formation tracks are considerably older ... I nonetheless believe that my experience with fossil vertebrate tracks qualifies me to offer an evaluation of the quality of the New Mexican material.

The Permian tracksites . . . represent one of the most remarkable trace fossil assemblages anywhere. There is an astonishing abundance of footprints, crawl marks, and burrows, many preserved in exquisite detail. Furthermore, the ichnofauna includes traces of an amazing diversity of creatures. . . . If that were not enough, at some of the sites . . . are great quantities of fairly well-preserved plants.

In the abundance and diversity of its trace fossils, the Abo formation is reminiscent of the much younger Newark Supergroup sites (Late Triassic-Early Jurasic) in eastern North America. However, many of the most important specimens from these sites were collected more than 150 years ago, before the advent of modern collecting and analytical techniques. In contrast, Mr. MacDonald's Permian sites have barely begun to be worked. The Las Cruces fossil fauna presents a unique opportunity to reconstruct a set of ancient ecosystems. . . .

It will be many years before the potential of the Abo formation sites is fully realized, but it is already clear that they are of enough scientific importance to warrant protection of some sort. I therefore enthusiastically endorse efforts to protect these sites as a national monument, so that any excavation or other development will proceed under the direction of qualified personnel, and not at the hands of rockhounds or commercial collectors.

Mr. MacDonald deserves the gratitude of the paleontological community for his strenuous efforts in making the initial finds, and in bringing these spectacular fossils to our attention, often in the face of considerable obstacles and local intrigues. The fauna is very much his discovery, and his self-described role as scientific midwife is an apt description of the great service he has done for paleontology."

As more and more scientists were visiting my sites, and writing up their opinions of my discovery, I could see that for the most part my solitary efforts were coming to a close. In fact, the whole face of the project was changing. It was obvious to all that it was time for serious paleontological science to take over. We were all amazed by the amount of significant material that had been amassed almost single-handedly in the last six years, but it was now time to produce the professional research that would forever preserve these discoveries within the annuals of science. From this point on, the research could never be conducted solely by me, no matter how competent a paleontologist I had become. And what I had come to recognize was that my role as fossil midwife was over. It was time to pass my knowledge on to others, and begin plans for my future role in the Paleozoic Trackways Project.

# Chapter Fourteen

## Putting It All Together

Day after day, 280 million years ago, when the tide drew back the sea, a menagerie of animals foraged at the water's edge, following the tide as it receded and returning to dry land ahead of the tide as it returned. Even though tidal flats and mud flats along river courses can be very good pickings for foraging animals, the receding tide, for the most part, does not leave exposed organisms squirming and writhing on the surface. Many tidal organisms live just below the surface, which in fact is almost featureless, and their presence is revealed to foragers by depressions in the surface or by bubbles breaking on the surface. But the activity of foraging itself places the foragers in danger of being caught and eaten by still bigger predators. The bill of fare at this Paleozoic "restaurant" was extraordinary, and the list of "guests" quite long. There was more than enough of the main course to satisfy a goodly number of larger bellies. The trophic structure along this vast mud flat simply fell together in this manner, settling a number of bio-ecological issues by unplanned but constant interaction among all of these animals. Still, while all of this was taking place, the shore itself was quietly recording the entire scene with the uncompromising diligence of a religious scribe. When the day was over, the next blank page of the diary, carried by the encroaching sea, fell gently over the page just finished, burying the events in what time would make a rock-hard tomb.

Our goal is to get an accurate understanding of this "restaurant." We want to know who came, what they ate, who they fought, where they rested, and as much of their daily routine as we can observe. Trackways enable scientists to *observe*. We can't observe activity from bones, no matter how articulated or complete. We can only observe activity through footprints.

The Robledo discovery gives us our best opportunity to interpret an Early Permian terrestrial ecosystem. Additionally, diverse evidence from several other volumes from the earth's encyclopedias covering other areas around the world help us read the pages found in the Robledos. Volumes found in the Grand Canyon, west Texas, northern New Mexico, South Africa, and Europe, and now the Robledo Mountains, enable scientists to better reconstruct what life was like during the Early Permian in specific localities and to generalize what the larger environmental and ecological conditions must have been like throughout much of the Early Permian in central and western North America and in other parts of the world.

The high concentration of living things preserved in the Robledos indicates a large number of environmental and topographical factors that allowed for the formation of well-vegetated inlets, lagoons, embayments, and lakes, and included vast areas of low relief that frequently swelled with water and took weeks to dry up. This ecological setting was highly favorable for supporting an abundant and diverse fauna and flora. The repetitive nature of the evidence from site to site and from layer to layer suggests that these favorable ecological conditions remained the same for a considerable period of time.

Earth was kind to leave us an encyclopedia by which we are privy to many of the secrets of the Paleozoic. To be sure, key chapters and volumes are still missing, and although we have found hundreds of "pages," many organizational clues, the chapter and volume headings, have long since disappeared. While it will take years of painstaking research to organize the Robledo volume into the earth's encyclopedia, the pages from the Robledos do provide us with a useful regional census of the numbers and varieties of animals known to frequent the area during the Early Permian.

## The Vertebrates

Nearly all of the vertebrate trackways found in the Robledos were made by reptiles and amphibians. The exceptions may be the discovery of flapping-like trails that may have been made by foraging fish in very shallow water, and the intermittent trails of creatures like mudskippers. Most of the layers within the AF 2 excavation preserve approximately equal numbers of both reptile and amphibian tracks, but there are a few notable exceptions. For example, layer ten (the discovery layer) preserves only trackways of large predatory reptiles, while layer four preserves trails of small insectivorous amphibians.

Many of the small reptile tracks were made by animals that looked like living lizards, although they were not closely related to them. These animals were small, lightly built reptiles with long slim shanks and forearms, and ranged up to two feet in length when fully grown. These animals appear to have been very abundant in the Robledos, and their presence along the shores suggests a warm and at least partially wooded environment. Body fossils of similar animals have been found in Kansas in association with such wooded environments. Interestingly, no body fossils of these animals have ever been found in New Mexico. The only evidence we have that these animals lived in the area is by the discovery of their tracks in the red beds of New Mexico.

Many of these small reptiles were very active and agile. They were built for speed, an asset they undoubtedly used to run down small prey and to escape from being eaten themselves. Among these small reptiles (diapsids) were the remote forerunners of dinosaurs, and it is interesting that they were so inconsequential here in the Late Paleozoic, and yet were dominant sixty million years later, in the Mesozoic. Other small reptiles that frequented the Robledos area were more primitive in form. Of these primitive reptiles, nearly all would become extinct by the end of the Paleozoic, and only a very small number of species would survive into the beginning of the age of dinosaurs.

In the Early Permian, nearly all of these small reptiles were apparently insectivorous, and they found a plentiful bounty of food along the shores of the seaway. Modern reptilian insectivores drink as they eat. For example, 80 percent of a cricket's body weight is fluid. This ability to meet its water needs from its prey allowed insectivores to venture far from areas with abundant standing water. Modern reptiles do the same thing.

The Robledo mud flats were also densely populated with amphibians. The ubiquitous tracks and trails of amphibians suggest abundant bodies of fresh water close by, though the land must have lain close to the Early Permian seaway. Few living amphibians tolerate salt water, and instead are river, pond, and lake dwellers.

Nearly all of the amphibians in the area were small, stocky, salamander-like animals. Some, the microsaurs, fed primarily upon both terrestrial and semi-aquatic invertebrates. Others, like the lepospondyls, signal that shallow waters near the seaway were well stocked with a variety of fish which provided a rich food source for a large number of semi-aquatic to fully aquatic amphibians. Some of these amphibians also fed on invertebrates, and would have found

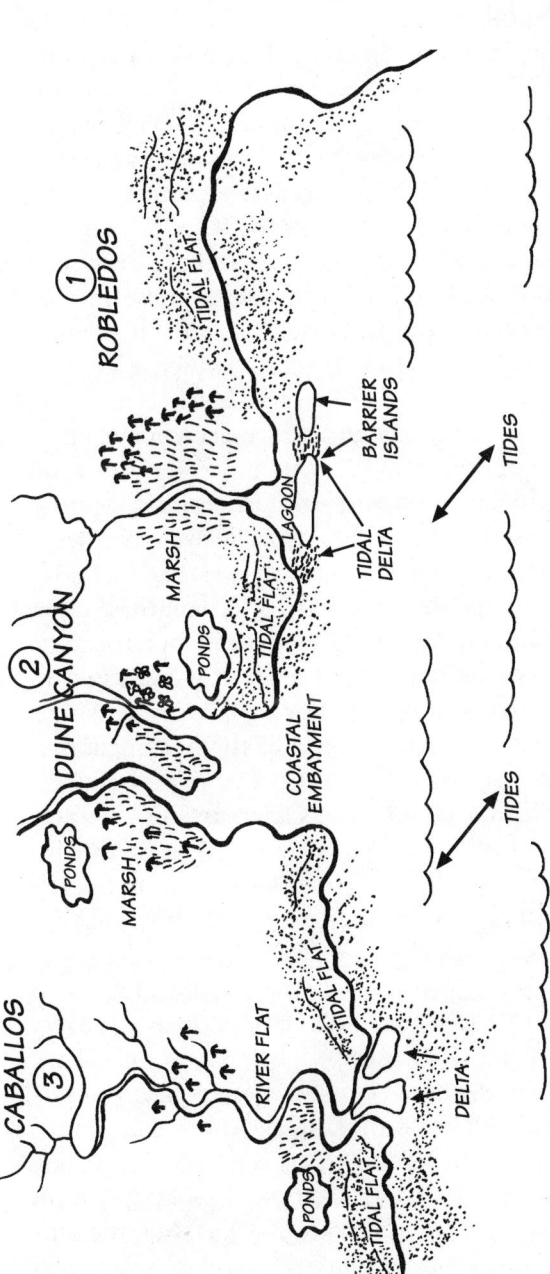

*A re-creation of the southern New Mexico shoreline, showing a variety of local habitats presumed to have existed at the time. The Robledos trackway deposit (1) appears to be predominately tidal flat, but punctuated with conifers (Conifer Forest/Insect Hill) and partial lagoonal/marsh areas (AF 13). Numerous large pelycosaurs roamed the flats, as did a seemingly disproportionate number of amphibians. AF 13 and Insect Hill are perhaps transitional sites between tidal flat to coastal embayment-like environments more characteristic of Dune Canyon. No bones have been found in the Robledos.*

*Dune Canyon, on the other hand, appears to preserve a more deltaic swamp or marsh deposit (2), with areas representing both salt and fresh water, with a high proportion of amphibians and greater varities of plants like horsetail reeds. Very few large-sized predators roamed the area. A few bone sites have been found, but not as many as in the Caballos.*

*The Caballos trackways (3) appear to be further from the shoreline, and there is an absence of the intertonguing sequences between marine and terrestrial sediments characteristic of the Robledos. The Caballos most likely preserve a river flat environment, with predominately fresh or brackish water, and a high proportion of both small reptiles and amphibians, as well as several bone sites of the track makers.*

ample food along the Robledo mud flat. It is estimated that upwards of 60 percent of these amphibians, especially the microsaurs, were fully terrestrial as adults, and could easily hold their own with comparable-sized reptiles.

The most impressive trackways of amphibians are probably those of *Eryops*, an amphibian that was probably fully terrestrial as an adult. *Eryops* attained a maximum length of six feet, in contrast to the largest amphibians alive today, the Japanese salamander, which can attain a length of two and one-half to three feet. There have been several impressive single tracks of adult eryopids found at several sites in the Robledos, but successive tracks of adults are very difficult to find. Curiously, this is not the case with juvenile eryopids, which appear to be very abundant.

The lack of abundance of trackways of mature eryopids is curious. When fully grown, *Eryops* spent most of its time close to fresh water, perhaps even occasionally slopping around along the mud banks. But at AF 2, only two mature *Eryops* trackways have been found, and they have been very difficult to excavate.

*Eryops's* head was enormous, nearly one-half its length. *Eryops* probably captured prey with a grab-and-gulp strategy, not unlike a large bull frog. It probably was an opportunistic feeder—if it moved, he ate it. *Eryops's* tail was short and stiff, and it was probably slow out of water. It had a row of very impressive conical teeth which held the prey while *Eryops* maneuvered it for swallowing. *Eryops* body fossils have been found in New Mexico as well as in Oklahoma and Texas.

## The Pelycosaurs

During the Early Permian, land faunas, including those of the Robledos mud flat, were dominated by big, agile, predatory reptiles—pelycosaurs such as *Dimetrodon* and *Sphenacodon* (closely related to *Dimetrodon* but without the sail), of which the largest were more than ten feet in length. The Robledo trackway assemblage contains the best tracks of these animals found anywhere on earth. For example, layer ten alone produced four trackways of these animals. One twenty-foot trackway is now housed at the Natural History Museum at the Smithsonian Institute. Two side-by-side trails twenty-five feet long are exhibited at the Carnegie Museum of Natural History in Pittsburgh, and one twelve-foot trackway is now exhibited at the Natural History Museum of Los Angeles County. Each of the three preserves dozens of consecutive prints.

In the Early Permian there was no animal that could compete in strength and agility with *Dimetrodon* and *Sphenacodon,* who had no effective enemies save for their own kind. All other predators were too small to offer a challenge. At the front of their jaws these animals were armed with large, dagger-like teeth, which were separated by a step-like feature from a more posterior set of flattened shearing teeth. The skull was narrow and long, with strong jaw muscles that allowed for a wide gape and fast "snap" during jaw closure. The design of their jaws suggests that *Dimetrodon* and *Sphenacodon* could seize active and vigorous prey of large size and dismember it in the process. These animals were probably very fast moving but, like living reptilian predators, probably only for very short distances. Some argue that *Sphenacodon* was the more deadly and dangerous because its lack of a sail allowed it more agility in the underbrush and more secretive stalking habits.

Though *Dimetrodon* and *Sphenacodon* were comparable in bulk to the lions of the modern savannah, not all of the predatory

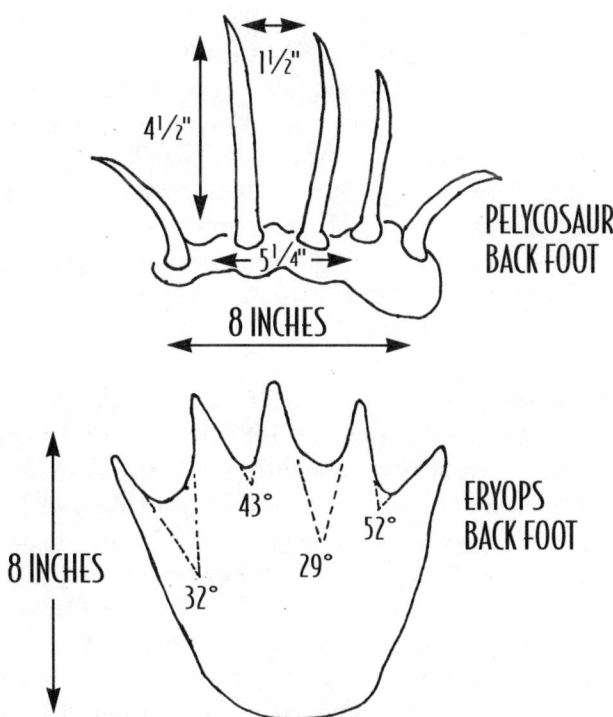

*Differences in the back feet of two Early Permian predators. Pelycosaurs, like* Dimetrodon, *possess long and gracile digits while the amphibian* Eryops *has short and robust digits and a massive pad.*

pelycosaurs were large. *Varanosaurus,* for example, attained a maximum length of about three feet and weighed about forty pounds. Like *Dimetrodon* and *Sphenacodon, Varanosaurus* was a high-level predator that could subdue prey approximating its own size.

Although these prehistoric animals were dissimilar in many respects to anything alive today, they were probably comparable in behavior to the living giant lizards of the island of Komodo, in Indonesia. These animals, the so-called Komodo dragons, lurk in ambush, well hidden but just off the well-trodden paths of potential victims. When the prey is near enough, the Komodo dragon lashes out, aiming for the limbs so as to lacerate muscles and tendons. This strike disables the victim, and the dragon kills by hanging onto the legs, allowing its teeth to cut arteries while the prey struggles to free itself. A mature Komodo dragon can kill and eat a deer in fifteen minutes. So also must have been the style of hunting and feeding of predatory pelycosaurs of the Early Permian.

Big pelycosaurs also fed upon large amphibians like *Eryops,* as well as occasionally on smaller animals. My guess, however, is that eating smaller prey was hardly worth the effort needed for their capture by a full-sized *Dimetrodon,* and probably many of these small animals were simply too fast to hunt down, and even if caught, provided a poor compensatory meal for a ten-foot, three-hundred-pound reptile. Still, they undoubtedly ate what they came across. Continuous small meals are just as good as a feast. The Komodo dragons are a good example of contemporary reptilian agility. A mature Komodo dragon holds its body well off the ground, as well as all but the final six inches of its tail. It's fast (for a short distance) and lethal.

Herbivorous pelycosaurs such as *Edaphosaurus* also appear to be represented in trackways from the Robledos, but only rarely so. The largest *Edaphosaurus* attained a length of ten feet and weighed about three hundred pounds. Only one trail from the Robledos can be assigned to this pelycosaur with any degree of confidence.

From studying *Edaphosaurus* skeletons, most paleontologists expected *Edaphosaurus* trails (none had ever been found before) to be fairly wide, with a heavy tail drag down the center. The Robledo evidence partially confirms their expectations, as just such a trail with tail drag has been found at AF 2. This ten-foot trail contrasts sharply with the abundant trails of presumed carnivourus pelycosaurs which are narrower, with no hint of tail drag. The tails of *Dimetrodon* and *Sphenacodon* were not as heavily built as their herbivorous cousins, and, true to form, nature granted that the more streamlined tail be attached to the predator rather than to the prey.

The skull of *Edaphosaurus* was small in proportion to its bulky, slab-sided body and the marginal teeth were shorter and blunter than those of *Sphenacodon* or *Dimetrodon*. On the inner side of the upper and lower jaws of *Edaphosaurus* were broad plates that bore numerous small teeth. Hotton believes that edaphosaurids utilized a diet of tough vegetation which he suggests was probably well laced with abrasive dust.

Perhaps the reason that very few trackways of herbivorous pelycosaurs have been found in the Robledos so far (another herbivourus pelycosaur, *Casea*, also appears to be rare in the Robledo ichnotaxa) is that they may have munched their way through lush foliage further inland where food was plentiful and vulnerability to predators was lower. More likely, however, is that trackways of herbivorous pelycosaurs are scarce because they themselves were scarce. Herbivorous pelycosaurs are rare even as body fossils in the Early Permian in North America.

There was a third kind of pelycosaur that lived along the Robledos mud flat. These animals, of which *Ophiacodon* is an example, were probably semi-aquatic reptiles. *Ophiacodon* was a long and slender high-level predator (up to nine feet long, four hundred pounds) that probably fed on fish and other prey smaller than itself.

Though skeletons of *Ophiacodon* have been recovered on both sides of the seaway (in New Mexico and also in west Texas), tracks of these animals may be difficult to distinguish from those of *Dimetrodon* and *Sphenacodon*. We are probably safe to infer that these pelycosaurs were present in the area, but fossil trackway evidence remains poor.

The fully terrestrialized predatory pelycosaurs, on the other hand, probably prowled the gently fluctuating mud flats, since the shores did not lack in abundant food sources for small- to mid-sized carnivores. These pelycosaurs, like the biggest fish in the sea, so to speak, came after and swallowed everything smaller than themselves within their grasp, including any small- to mid-sized predators they were lucky enough to catch.

Still, it was probably not uncommon that an occasional full-sized *Edaphosaurus* fell victim to a well-hidden *Dimetrodon*. Such a large carcass would provide food for a considerable time. Large carcasses were fought over and ultimately eaten by several pelycosaurs in addition to the initial slayer in much the same way as groups of Komodo dragons consume large prey.

Perhaps predatory pelycosaurs approached today's numbers of the Komodo dragon on Komodo Island in the Japanese Sea. Free from predatory mammals, the Komodo dragon has abundantly multiplied and has successfully filled the top predatory niche on the islands. A large population of Komodo dragons means that battles for space and food sources, as well as territorial squabbles, are common. It is likely that the same kinds of behaviors occurred with a comparable population of predatory pelycosaurs

## The Predator and the Prey

Scientists estimate that among terrestrial faunas of the Late Paleozoic, the numbers of predators to prey was about 30 percent. The Robledos ichnofauna does not dispute this high ratio, and perhaps even exceeds it.

Though the footprint evidence suggests perhaps ten carnivorous pelycosaurs to every herbivorus one, it's certain that this ratio is not indicative of predator/prey percentages throughout the area, or that this ratio is even close to that of other Early Permian communities in the southwestern United States. The ratio of prey to predator was probably closer to three to one. The problem is that the herbivourous pelycosaurs are under-represented in the ichnotaxa of the Robledos, probably because they did not forage along the flats.

Uneven faunal representation through preserved fossils is one of the main problems paleontologists encounter when doing census work. The abundance or paucity of species at any one locality is very hard to determine with any degree of accuracy. Yet paleontologists are not entirely handicapped by lack of data. In the Robledos, we can at least build a census showing what animals lived together in one locality (the footprints tell us that), and as such, fairly confident food pyramids can be deduced. From the "guest list" of animals dining at the Early Permian restaurant, we can get a good idea of the relative number of animals in the region at any one time.

One thing we can determine right off when considering the census of the area is that the mud flat reflects a trophic structure that was in balance for a very long time. Layer after layer reveals the same kinds of animals over and over again. Lots of plants, for example, mean a lot of consuming insects. Lots of insects mean lots of small insectivorous tetrapods. Small insectivores mean plenty of mid-sized predators. And lastly, a lot of mid-sized reptiles and amphibians mean plenty of top predators—in this case, large pelycosaurs. A top predator can be defined in this way: He ate everybody and nobody (save perhaps its own kind) ate him. But the fact that nearly every layer is punctuated with tracks of big pelycosaurs indicates the long-term stability of lower trophic structures.

So even though only one trackway can be ascribed to *Edaphosaurus* with any degree of certainty, we can be assured from the stability of the trophic structure that there were probably quite a few more edaphosaurs roaming the area. Perhaps a more accurate ratio of herbivores to carnivores will be obtained as more trackway sites are worked in the Robledos.

It is clear that the pelycosaur footprint percentages (especially of herbivores) are nowhere near representative of the region, and it is therefore inaccurate to draw inferences for the whole of the Late Paleozoic along the North American seaway. Yet it is fascinating to see so many top predators competing for the rich food source this shoreline paradise preserves.

Compare the predator/prey ratios of prehistoric mammal faunas throughout the Cenozoic, which at their best only produce a ratio of 2 to 5 percent predator and 95 to 98 percent prey. In the fossil mammal beds of the southern Rio Grande of New Mexico, for example, on average only two bones out of one hundred can be attributed to predators, such as tigers, bears, or canids (wolves or dogs). The rest are of herbivorous mammals like elephants, camels, horses, deer, bison, sloths, rabbits, etc. But not so in the Late Paleozoic. And not so on the mud flats of the Robledos. So, why were there so many predators among the Robledos ichnofauna?

The conventional wisdom is that Early Permian predators were cold-blooded and ate less than their warm-blooded descendants; therefore, the ecosystem could support more predators without depleting the supply of non-predatory animals. Also, because they were cold-blooded, all of the animals had to divide their time between sun and shade to maintain a proper body temperature. As a result, they were limited in long-range mobility (in other words, everybody had to hang around the same places). The sail on *Dimetrodon* probably partly compensated for cold-bloodedness by enabling it to both warm up and cool down faster than its reptilian contemporaries, increasing its range of mobility.

With fearsome predators like *Dimetrodon* roaming the flats, significant adaptations of defense among all other reptiles and amphibians continued. Defensive adaptations include speed, agility, concealment, visual and audio enhancement (like shaking the tail, puffing up the body, snapping, or hissing), and armor. And, indeed, the animals of the Early Permian are showcases for many such adaptations, some quite ingenious. Skeletal recovery preserves armored adaptations, and track-ways preserve adaptations of speed and agility.

I believe the sail on *Edaphosaurus* was just such a defensive adaptation. What better way to protect yourself from threatening predators than by looking like a *Dimetrodon*? The bull snake and a diamondback rattlesnake are an excellent case in point. As I was walking to the site one day, I was stopped in my tracks by what I thought was a rattler. As I peered into the bushes to get a look, I could see it clearly. The snake was coiled up, its head about a foot above the ground, and its tail about two inches in the air, rattling to beat the band. The markings on the back of the snake were just like those of a diamondback. The tail had the tell-tale (pardon the pun) black stripes and the head was hissing and puffing. Believe me, it was a scary sight.

But this snake, upon closer examination, had no rattles. The head, though puffed up as large as it could be, was still too small to be that of a viper. What was scaring the heck out of me was not a rattlesnake, but a bull snake. The bull snake is a perfect example of mimicry in nature. The bull snake had taken on the disguise of a rattler, to make itself look like the poisonous predator. It was mimicking the king of dangerous reptiles, the diamondback. The bull snake uses such a disguise to perfection, fooling and scaring me just like it would with any other animal that the snake felt threatened by. It was even shaking the weeds with its tail to sound like a rattler. It worked. Even after I became convinced that the coiled creature in front of me was not a rattler, its disguise was so convincing that I found myself constantly doubting my inspection.

Mimicry is a very important defensive adaptation that many animals use to protect themselves against predators. The eye spots on the back of some caterpillars make them look like a snake, likewise, the eye spots on the back of some species of frogs. Certain fruit flies look for all the world like spiders (especially to other spiders), and these flies have even learned how to mimic a spider's visual displays as well. And the kings of disguise, the insects, mimic and camouflage themselves as plants.

What better way to protect oneself as a gentle plant-eater than by not only looking like the king of beasts, but by acting like one, too? I can see a threatened *Edaphosaurus* flashing its sail from side to side, moving its body up and down like it was doing push-ups (many reptiles do this today), and puffing and hissing, trying to scare the heck out of the intruder. I'm sure that this display worked more than it failed. Nature is full of examples of mimicry like this. Of course none of this would be preserved in fossil evidence, but nature often appears content to stay with defensive adaptations that work, regardless of what animal or what period they come from.

When I excavate, if I'm really lucky, I uncover a few of these encounters, and I am allowed to view the final moments of the prey. It is remarkable to me that after both the slayer and the slain have long since died off, I can still view their encounter. Their steps are recorded on the layers as faithfully as a choreographer would lay out a dance.

## The Invertebrates

The invertebrate population that inhabited the Robledos mud flat is no less interesting or compelling than that of the vertebrates. Abundant invertebrate trails of both terrestrial and semi-aquatic and aquatic animals have also been preserved throughout the area. Their tracks, as if recorded on the finest rice paper, preserve the daily wanderings of a great variety of animals. In fact, before the Robledo discovery, New Mexico's insect record was strictly limited to a few isolated localities found in Pennsylvanian (not Permian) sediments.

The likelihood of an animal being fossilized depends upon two things: the structure of the organism and the environment where it died and was buried. These factors, however, are not uniform. The physical make-up of animals and plants varies considerably, as do the environments in which they existed. As a result, the paleontologist sees a view of ancient life that favors animals with hard parts (shells or skeletons) over those that possess only soft parts, like jellyfish, a caterpillar, or a fly. This bias also favors lowland environments over continental deposits, which have a tendency to erode faster than coastal areas. The result is an unequal representation of species within the fossil record.

Nowhere is this bias more apparent than with the Robledo collection of invertebrate trails. Globally, more than any other category, insects are the most under-represented of all fossil groups, due to both structure and environment. Only a very small percentage of prehistoric insects have been recovered around the world (representing about one thousand families), and based on the fact that 75 percent of all present species are represented by this group, we can see that insects are very

under-represented by this group. Additionally, we also discover that insects are in fact very under-represented in the entire fossil record.

We know that many present-day insects are found exclusively in certain localities with specific environmental conditions. The knowledge gap between what the paleontologist suspects existed in the Paleozoic and what has actually been recovered is huge. At best, the insect record is fragmentary and incomplete.

Present-day numbers of known living insect species exceed 1.5 million and the number of species suspected to exist exceeds four million. Even if we assume that insects have reached an evolutionary peak in their abundance and diversity, there still must have been many multiple thousands of species that existed in the Paleozoic. The staggering variety of the Robledo invertebrate ichnofauna dramatically proves this point. Invertebrate trails include the tracks of scorpions, centipedes, millipedes, cockroaches, arachnids, silverfish, beetles, various other arthropods, and even annelids (sandworms). Also there are tracks preserved of flying and hopping invertebrates, such as dragonflies and mayflies, among others. All of these forms have been found prior to the Robledo discovery in close proximity to dense plant layers, which were built up over time around swampy lowland environments.

Some arthropod trackways match very closely the trails of trilobites (which became extinct by the end of the Permian), and of a variety of eurypterids ("water scorpions"). Though fossil evidence suggests that eurypterids began as exclusively marine animals, their body fossils have since been primarily restricted to fresh or brackish-water environments. Also, eurypterids in New Mexico had previously been found in conjunction with dense plant layers as well as with other insects. It is not surprising, therefore, that just such associations have been observed along the Robledos mud flats.

Several trackways have been found that probably pertain to crustaceans, a diverse group of primarily water-dwelling arthropods, which had not previously been found in the Permian sediments of New Mexico. Many of these invertebrates were inexorably tied to the daily tides and were the main staple for fully terrestrial to semi-aquatic vertebrates. Just like Biloxi beach today, the retreating tides doubtless exposed a marvelous and abundant variety of animals.

This abundance (and variety) of invertebrate life is not only consistent with the discovery of extensive plant-bearing deposits along the Robledos mud flat, but the local abundance of semi-aquatic to aquatic invertebrates, including sandworms (annelids), is added evidence that the area was once a coastal wetlands environment with abundant fresh water nearby.

## The Plants

Finally, where there are abundant insects, there are abundant plants, and, indeed, the Robledos are locally rich in fossil plants. Much of the area around the seaway was covered by low-lying tropical swamplands. From these swamps rose coniferous trees and seed ferns. The setting was perfect for supporting a wide variety of insects. Centipedes and millipedes, along with spiders and other insects, lived in the rich plant litter that covered forest floor habitats that were undoubtedly sprinkled throughout the whole of the shoreline.

Yet 98 percent of all the plant fossils recovered from most sites in the Robledos, including AF 2, are of primitive conifers. In fact, there are whole layers comprised of plant material, and one site, the Conifer Forest, preserves endless layers of conifer fronds. In some areas there appear to be forests of conifers with eight-inch girths that stood fifty feet high. Close to the shore was an undergrowth of lush ferns and other plants that provided good cover for predators and perches for flying insects, perhaps like *Meganeura*—a carboniferous dragonfly with a wingspan of up to two feet five inches.

It is only when we leave the Robledos that the plant picture changes. The Dune Canyon deposit, twenty miles north of the Robledos, preserves considerably more varieties of plants. This is probably because the Dune Canyon region appears to be host to more high energy settings from rivers and embayments, as opposed to the gentle deposition of the mud flat in the Robledos. The proportions of conifer branches in Dune Canyon is significantly reduced, while other plants, like horsetail reeds, increase dramatically. There must have been a variety of small habitats that sprang up around the rivers, ponds, and bays near the mud flats, and these spots must have been bristling with horsetail reeds and other swamp plants. All of this helped support a thriving semi-aquatic population that lived there.

One of the most exciting discoveries found in the Dune Canyon area is the fragmentary remains of a small swamp-like wetland, complete with carbonaceous plants. These swampy areas suggest that the region, at least locally, was perpetually wet. This is certainly the opposite of the shoreline evidence from the Robledos, which confirm that significant periods of drying often occurred before the area was soaked again.

There was probably quite a bit of plant debris along the boundaries of the shore, sometimes enhanced by storms and floods. And under the conifer canopy was probably a decent forest litter which was home to both rummaging invertebrates and small carnivorous reptiles. One such invertebrate was a centipede-like carnivore that grew to a length of nearly a meter.

## The Climate and Weather

Traces of the weather and the physical environment of the area have also been preserved along the Robledo mud flat. There is evidence of times of drought, periodic dust storms, small movements of the shoreline, and traces of rapid water run-off.

For example, perfect raindrop impressions often punctuate the trackway layers. Layer eight of the AF 2 site preserves so many raindrops that I can almost feel the rain on my face. Sand ripples formed by prevailing winds are also preserved, as are the gentle ripples caused by winds lapping the shallow water along the seashore or in ponds farther inland. Raindrops are more common in the Robledos, and wind and water ripples are more common in Dune Canyon.

Fanned by gentle breezes and nearly imperceptible wave motion, the soft muds registered these tiny movements as accurately as a seismograph records a tiny tremor. In fact, it's possible that the effects that resulted from the daily tidal action along the shore of the seaway was greater than those generated through constant wave action. Wave action had very little effect on this year-round Early Permian resort. There was no surfing here.

Also preserved are the desiccation cracks formed when recently water-saturated areas began to dry out in the sun. The trails of animals wandering in and out of mud puddles as they foraged along the mud flats are also preserved. I can almost feel the warmth of sultry air as it begins its never-ending job of drying the mud for preservation before the next page is laid by the encroaching tide or the seasonal rains.

There is also some evidence of storm and flood events. There are a lot of complete conifer branches strewn across some of the layers. Were these complete fronds evidence of annual shedding or were these branches torn from the trees by a wind storm?

Also likely to have occurred are Santa Ana-like winds that blew in from the upland and more arid areas, sweeping with them dust storms that may have contributed to the saran wrap layer, the delaminating layer that now separates 50 percent of the track-producing layers.

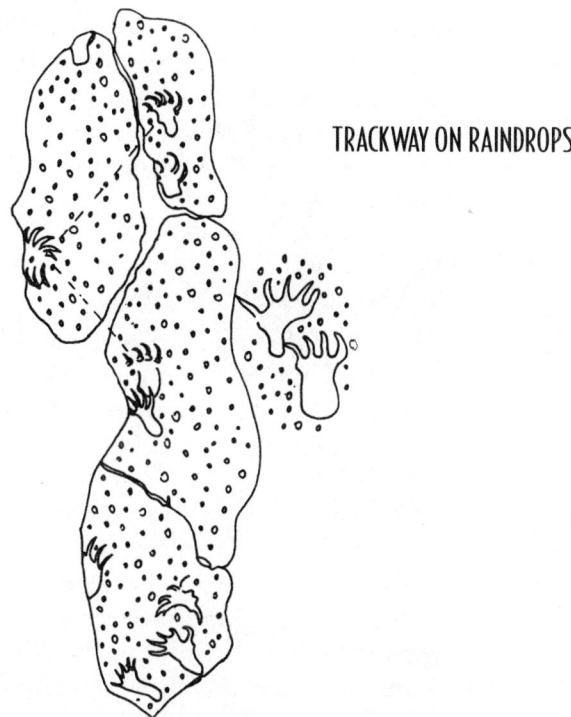

TRACKWAY ON RAINDROPS

*A pelycosaur wanders through mud imprinted with raindrops. Since there are no raindrop craters on the footprints themselves, the rain must have stopped before the prints were made.*

This semi-tropical paradise apparently underwent annual dry and wet seasons, and was subject to warm temperatures all year. Undoubtedly, larger than normal storms deposited rapid sedimentation along the shoreline, either from hurricane-like storms from the seaway (not unlike the storms that form over Lake Michigan) or dramatic floods from off the upland environments to the west. Algal mats also could be found in isolated areas, and portions of the mud flats were probably characterized by pockets of sticky ooze and soft sediment.

I envision a situation not unlike regions along the American coasts of the Gulf of Mexico—places where a swimmer can wade out into the sea for nearly a quarter-mile and the water is still only chest-high. I feel certain that a variety of small animals frequently checked the fluctuating perimeter of the seashore, hunting for food as deftly as the present-day sand pipers of Padre Island.

Conditions apparently remained constant for a considerable period of time, when the area was presumably part of an established feeding ground. Maybe these animals basked on the shore because they were cold-blooded, and then swung into action, hunting and feeding, when they warmed up. For example, it is surprising how warm a mud-cracked surface can become. It can get as warm as asphalt, upwards of 150 degrees Fahrenheit, if solar conditions are right. If you're lucky, you can sometimes observe present-day reptiles doing the same thing on recently "reformed" Paleozoic muds. The fine-grained mud layers, when fully dried, can attain a temperature as that of baked clay. In the absence of any substantial rock formations near the mud flats of 280 million years ago, the best "electric blanket" around was the hardened mud surfaces near the shores of the seaway.

## Trouble in Paradise

This is not to suggest that all is well with the Paleozoic window that the Robledos preserves or that there are no problems in relating the Robledo trackway evidence to current scientific thought on the Paleozoic, evolutionary sequences, and fossil formations. On the contrary, there are quite a few problems. And, there are quite a few surprises.

The Robledo trackways have generated debate on a number of levels. The size of individual footprints has reached the upper limit of the size of the animals known from bones from the Late Paleozoic. Ten- to twelve-inch tracks have been uncovered from layer twenty-five of the AF 2 site. Also, of the dozen pelycosaur trackways found so far, only one is wide with continual tail drag preserved. All the others are surprisingly narrow with no evidence of tail drag. Since most paleontologists have assumed these primitive reptiles were sprawlers, it is curious to find only one trackway of a sprawling pelycosaur with tail drag from all that have been found. This observation may call for modification of a long-standing belief and suggests that many museum reconstructions may be incorrect.

The lack of tail drag also suggests that much of our work on modern reptile locomotion may not apply to these ancestral creatures. One Robledo trackway appears to be bipedal, despite current theories on locomotion that reject any bipeds in the Paleozoic.

This brings up the question, how does science tackle problematic evidence? First, science must explore the range of explanations from least to most controversial. This is perfectly illustrated with the debate over possible bipedalism in the Early Permian. Since present theories on the evolution of terrestrial locomotion suggest that true bipedalism did not emerge for at least fifty million years after these trackways were formed, there must be some other explanation for the apparent bipedalism preserved in this trackway. For example, a quadruped could have, for some inexplicable reason, stood up on its back legs for a time, perhaps, as some have suggested, while in the water. Or the front feet of the quadruped may be obscured by larger back feet which overprinted its front feet. The most controversial, of course, would be that the trackway was indeed made by a biped.

It will take time to resolve these mysteries, the best evidence for or against the bipedal nature of this trackway is if we can find another one. If another one is found, we can compare stride and pace of the new trackway with the old, as well as comparing foot morphology. If these variables are similar in nature to the bipedal-like tracks from layer twenty-five, then the question of gait can be resolved.

A large enough sample of trackways make questions about anomalous gaits disappear. For example, at the AF 2 site I found a trail that looked for all the world like it had been made by a one-legged horse. There were successive horseshoe-like marks touching each other all in a row. There were no corresponding parallel marks on either side of the trail. The trail was comprised of just one line of tracks, strongly suggesting some kind of invertebrate with one foot, like a snail. But alas, after watching snails in the mud all day, I had to conclude that the trackway was not made by a snail, at least not any similar to contemporary ones.

I kept the specimen and did not refer to it for quite a while until I found another at AF 13. All of a sudden I began to see that perhaps my "one-legged horse" trail is indeed a legitimate trackway and not some anomalous sedimentary structure. A few months later I found another one in the Dune Canyon deposit. Three similar specimens from three different locations clinched it for me. The "one-legged horse" is a legitimate trail of some as yet unknown animal. Now, if we can only find another bipedal-like trackway.

Other problematic traces include the following: A few trails seem to have been made by three-toed (tridactyl) animals. As such, these possible three-toed trackways threaten the assumption that three-toed forms such as birds and certain dinosaurs first emerged in the Mesozoic era. Some of these newly uncovered trackways seem to disappear into thin air. So the same kind of debate has occurred with this trail as with the bipedal-like trackway. Perhaps the animal was running and only the middle three digits of the foot were impressed in the mud, granting the illusion of tridactylism. Perhaps the three-toed trackway is an underprint and not the actual trackway surface. The digits of animals often impress differently during a walk, as opposed to a run. The middle digits are often deeper than the outside ones. If one excavates the layer directly below the actual trackway surface, it is not uncommon to find this phenomenon. But the layer preserving the three-toed trail *is* the actual trackway surface.

The presence of many amphibians is another of the great mysteries of the Robledo ichnofauna. If the Robledos indeed preserve a marine tidal flat, why are there so many amphibians present on the tidal-formed layers? At the AF 2 site, some layers of tracks are almost entirely composed of amphibians, yet the environment proposed for the site is a sandy shore along a saltwater sea. We also are not sure if the red beds were fully a tidal flat or a river flat. The trackways are definitely not emplaced in marine sediments, although marine sediments are abundant.

The abundance of amphibians is difficult to explain if the Robledo/Dune Canyon environment was indeed a large tidal flat. The evidence of marine invertebrates, in most cases just below the appearance of the first trackway layers, makes the presence of amphibians even more problematic. Doubtless there must have been large freshwater sources throughout the region from rivers, small lakes, and lagoons.

Some have proposed that the amphibians of the Late Paleozoic were more tolerant of marine environments than they are today, and there is some skeletal evidence to support this hypothesis. Many of these early amphibians were fully terrestrialized as adults, and behaved in every fashion like the small reptiles in the region. But these amphibians were still tied to freshwater for reproductive purposes and this fact alone restricted their ability to move further inland away from fresh water. So why are so many of them here on the apparent shores of the Permian seaway?

The abundant footprints of amphibians in the Robledos may put the seal of authority on the debate, unless, of course, everybody is wrong and the Robledos do not preserve a tidal mud flat. Or, more troubling, maybe the tracks we perceive to be made by amphibians were in reality made by reptiles. I don't think this possibility is true, since skeletal evidence of amphibians, and especially of their foot morphology, matches many of these trackways perfectly, and does not match the skeletons of reptiles. Also, historically, many of these Robledos footprints have been found at other sites both in North America and in Europe, and have been identified for decades as amphibian tracks.

*(Top) A portion of the bipedal-like trail from layer twenty-five of AF 2, and a single track (bottom) from the same trail.* Photos by Pearl MacDonald.

And what of the abundance of invertebrates, both marine and terrestrial, that has been found in the Robledo deposits? There are very few sites devoted to terrestrial Paleozoic invertebrates. The world-famous Burgess shale is probably the best locality for studying marine Paleozoic invertebrate life. But what about terrestrial invertebrate life in the Paleozoic? Mazon Creek in Illinois preserves scores of terrestrial and marine species together in a coastal environment. Like Mazon Creek, the Robledo tracks may prove to be one of the best Paleozoic windows into the terrestrial invertebrate realm.

There are very few papers on the tracks and trails of prehistoric terrestrial arthropods, including myriapods and insects as well as other terrestrial invertebrates. It is probable that in this area significant scientific rethinking will be required. These gaps in our understandings of terrestrial invertebrates have up to now been filled in by generalized inference based on other related paleontological evidence. Such extrapolations, no matter how carefully constructed, will inevitably be challenged by the discovery of empirical evidence on the lives and habits of these creatures.

My own research with invertebrates on mud surfaces has convinced me that many of the trails made in the Abo of southern New Mexico are indistinguishable from the trails made by the invertebrates of today. This further poses the question of what are so many typical modern trials doing in the Permian? Is this just more evidence that we know virtually nothing about the evolution of these forms?

Another problem is the abundant evidence of primitive conifers (*Walchia*) that populated the entire coastal region within the Robledos and Dune Canyon. The conifers left their fronds up and down the shoreline, and some of the Robledo sites, like Conifer Forest, are predominately made up of *Walchia* plant layers. The problem is that *Walchia* has historically been considered a plant found in stressed environments. Their long needle-like fronds make them good candidates for marginal environments with low rainfall and poor soil development. So what are they doing here in a tidal flat? Tidal flats are not considered stressed environments.

At AF 2 the presence of *Walchia* is preserved through plant debris. A complete *Walchia* frond is very rarely found. Needles and other frond parts can be found in three layers at the site, and they appear to be debris washed up on shore, probably during storms. So the *Walchia* found at AF 2 may not be indigenous to that locality, but were swept in from source areas somewhere else.

At the Conifer Forest site, however, the situation is different. Though there are some layers that preserve predominantly plant debris, most of the plant fossils are of complete fronds of *Walchia*. Conifer Forest may be the local source area of a conifer settlement. Explaining the plant evidence both at AF2 and at the Conifer Forest is difficult, but the evidence does not support the idea that the Robledos shoreline was a stressed environment.

Additionally, stressed environments are considered to be low diversity regions, where only the heartiest faunas and flora exist. These areas are frequently populated by *Walchia*, but in the Robledos the quandary is compounded. The Robledos is a high diversity environment, which brings us to our third problem.

Tidal flats are historically considered low diversity environments, with perhaps a handful of vertebrates at the most dominating the area. For example, the fossils found up and down several dinosaur track sites that were one-time coastal regions only preserve two or three distinct species of dinosaur. Yet in the Robledos coastline the diversity, as we have seen, is phenomenal. Why?

The fourth problem is perhaps more serious: present-day tidal flats are significantly bioturbated by a plethora of burrowing animals. Yet there is a striking absence of bioturbation in the Robledo track sites.

Clearly the axiom the "present is the key to the past" does not perfectly apply to our little corner of the world. Yet these problems can be partially explained. There is no question that the actual shoreline of this vast sea was daily searched, if not trampled, by scores of animals. But the daily tides would wipe out these tracks, and we know of no way that shoreline tracks along a sea can be preserved, except in extremely rare cases such as a volcanic eruption, landslide, or earthquake where the sea suddenly retreats to form a new shoreline farther out.

What we need is a region that was both frequently wetted and allowed to dry for days at a time. A right-on-the-shore habitat would not allow for such conditions because the daily tides would wipe out all trackway traces every day. But there are areas just offshore that do qualify for producing long wet and dry periods. During the rotation of the earth, the moon forms a tidal bulge that literally follows the earth's rotation. One bulge is always facing the moon and one is always opposite. At any one time around the earth, the successive lunar tides pass at intervals of about twelve and one-half hours, producing daily tides. But, additionally, the gravital attraction of the sun also raises two tidal bulges, although they are only about one-half as strong as the lunar tides. Solar tides travel around the earth every twenty-four hours. When the sun and the moon are aligned, the two tides coincide, producing high (spring) tides every two weeks at full or new moon, and low (neap) tides when minimum tidal amplitude is reached when the earth and moon are separated in longitude by 90 degrees. Every two weeks, the spring tides encroach onto dry flat areas that the daily tides, for the most part, do not reach. As a result, new areas of the mud flat are wetted and then allowed to dry twice a month. This region farther landward is called the supratidal mud flat, and the conditions necessary for the continued preservation of footprints seem optimal. This is not to say that the actual daily shoreline was not just as densely populated with foraging animals as the supratidal region was, but it is just that no evidence of their movements was preserved.

The Robledos trackways were probably preserved at least a mile or more from the daily shoreline. (A one-foot rise in sea level can shift a flat shoreline fifteen to twenty miles landward.) This explains the near wholesale lack of bioturbation of the muds that would have overwhelmed any footprints made right along the shoreline. The abundance of amphibians would logically increase the farther inland from shore, where fresh water pockets could form and be maintained. And the frequency of the trails of scattered marine life, such as arthropods and other invertebrates, can also be explained as displaced fauna move landward due to high tide. The trackway preservation window may be helped even more in storm events, especially when they occur at high tide. Further research is needed to explore this possibility fully.

In every respect, whether it be of flora or fauna, the records are there to be read. Every slab comes with a variety of information. Together, such information allows us to pull out a picture of both the organic and the inorganic world of 280 million years ago. The now environmentally stressed Robledo Mountains were once a steamy, semi-tropical coastline of great diversity and vitality.

## Peeking at True Miracles of Nature

Over the last seven years, my assistants and I have found nearly fifty Paleozoic track sites in New Mexico. I have collected samples and surveyed track sites in five different mountain ranges in New Mexico, and I have viewed other sites in the Paleozoic of North America. Additionally, I have examined Paleozoic collections in museums as well as some private collections. I have compared and contrasted these sites and collections with one another. After doing this, I believe that there is no question that something unique happened to preserve the tracks in the Robledo Mountains. Some environmental situation, some depositional occurrence, some fossilization process; something that made the Robledo's so fabulously rich in footprints.

Even trackways found only twenty miles from the Robledos pale in comparison to the Robledo occurrence. The Robledos are distinct in terms of diversity, the dramatic size range in footprints, the numbers of new taxa, and the seemingly unending faunules stacked one on top of the other.

But there is one important distinction that I see. In all the other sites I have found, collected, and observed, the "saran wrap" layer does not occur with the relative consistency, about 50 percent, that it does in the Robledos. In my opinion, the saran wrap is a key feature that sets the Robledo trackways apart from others, and so enhances the quality of footprint preservation.

It is true that the Robledos preserves more trackway layers in sequence and in abundance per meter than almost any other trackway site in the world, including dinosaur sites. But without the saran wrap layers, broad excavation of these sequential layers would be impossible. For example, the size and continuity of the Caballo Mountains Paleozoic red beds exceed by a thousand times those found in the Robledos, yet the Robledo track layers seem to be a thousand times richer than those found in the Caballo Mountains. If this is true, then perhaps the delaminating layer must be more developed in the Robledos than elsewhere.

It would be a great irony if we knew from hit-and-miss collecting that sequential layers in the Robledos contained abundant tracks and trails, but that we could not excavate them for any distance. Such is the case in the Caballos. It would be like Howard Carter finding King Tutunkhamen's tomb and having no chance at all of opening it without destroying its contents. Without the saran wrap the Robledos would tease us, but never produce. If there are such things as miracles in paleontology, this is without question one of the biggest. This is the biggest "what if" of all: what if there was no delaminating layer separating these superposed bedding planes?

Another miracle of nature emerges when we consider the length of time each trackway layer preserves. Jack Horner's research on prehistoric dinosaur nests convinced him that his excavated layers represented no more than perhaps ten years, and he believes that as little as one year may separate some of these layers. To confidently attach only a ten-year time span to the formation of a fossil layer is extremely rare, and to narrow it down to a year or less is almost unheard of in paleontology.

But the Robledo layers aren't measured in years, but in days. Layer twenty-one, for example, preserves the trails of twelve different track makers, from big pleycosaurs to small reptiles and amphibians, as well as a few invertebrate trails, all on a layer no more than twenty-five feet long.

In all probability these track makers walked across this layer in a span of no more than a few hours or days. After longer time spans, the mud hardened and no tracks were preserved. By analyzing the depth of the tracks, proportionate to size and weight, it is likely that all but two trails were made within hours, if not minutes, of each other. In fact, some of the pelycosaur tracks show unusual movements, such as slide marks, sudden turns, and exaggerated strides and tail marks that are better explained by predation encounters than by business as usual. Remember the modern trackway analysis that can reveal exactly what an animal is doing as it made its trail? Well, layer twenty-one would give a modern tracker fits with all the subtle "nuances" preserved on the layer. It is indeed remarkable that some of Horner's nesting layers took no more than a year in formation, but what of layers that can be narrowed down to be no more than a day or two in formation?

The data for analyzing each particular layer compositionally for reference work and also for dating has just now been gathered. Within the next few years a clear picture will emerge that will give us both an accurate picture of the time interval by which the trackways were formed, and the depositional environment by which they were preserved.

## An Incomprehensible Discovery

There are other miracles of nature that I have observed. One concerns the remarkable richness of the trackway faunules. Some of the layers have preserved over fifty tracks per square foot. If the deposit was any richer it would be too rich, as tracks would overprint each other, making a trampled sea of tracks. Many dinosaur track sites are like this, and such a site is called dinoturbation.

Trackway specialist Glen Kuban summed up the richness of the Robledos by noting that stellar claims of trackway significance are inevitably met with skepticism by the scientific community. So few sites ever match up scientifically to the popular claims:

When I first came across accounts of Jerry MacDonald's work, I was immediately impressed by what appeared to be a veritable menagerie of amphibian, reptile, and invertebrate tracks from the Early Permian. I was further intrigued that the tracks were presented not as exceptional, isolated finds from the sites, but rather as typical examples of the hundreds of exquisite tracks and trails already excavated.

At the same time I was a little skeptical that any trackway site could be that rich. Although I've had the privilege of working on several remarkable dinosaur track sites and museum track collections, even the best of these would not match the diversity, density, and quality of track material claimed to have come from the Robledo sites. I have firsthand experience of the fact that sometimes the press embellish discoveries, and I have often read or heard of many enthusiastic reports of track sites that subsequently disappoint me when I visit the sites in person.

On the other hand, occasionally the opposite is true. That is, sometimes a site turns out to be all that it is claimed to be, and more. This was the case with MacDonald's discoveries. During my visits to the site in August of 1993, it did not take long to confirm that even the most glowing reports about the trackways were accurate, if not understated.

The interesting scientific question that has subsequently popped into all of our minds is this: Was life this abundant throughout the whole of the one-thousand-plus miles of shoreline, or was this a tiny center of activity in an otherwise sparsely populated habitat? If it was the latter, then indeed finding this spot was as fortuitous as finding the needle in the proverbial haystack. We were soon to have our answer.

In New Mexico, because there is so much empty space, there are legions of contemporary trackways preserved for a moment in the sand on any given day. In the fossil mammal bone beds of Tunuca, for example, I can come across the freshly made tracks of deer, wolves, coyotes, rabbits, birds, lizards, snakes, mice, spiders, along with a few insects. I'm very lucky to find all of these trails in a week, let alone in one day. And my search area is a lot bigger, four square miles bigger, than a hundred-foot scar at AF 2.

Continuing the comparison, I would not only have to find a small section of sand preserving scores of trackways from terrestrial animals, but also scores of trails from semi-aquatic to fully aquatic animals. We would have to add the trackways of animals like crabs, fish, frogs, crustaceans, and turtles, among others. In the Robledos, such is the blessing of this gently prograding and receding, quarter-of-a-billion-year-old shoreline; stacks of terrestrial and marine trails are intermixed over and over again. There is no comparable situation anywhere on earth today.

*The eight-foot section of layer twenty-one shows a multitude of animal trackways. Shaded tracks are those of predatory pelycosaurs. Numbers denote different trackways of non-pelycosaurs.*

Few other paleontological sites have yielded so much data in such a short time interval on so many species except perhaps for a few world-famous sites like the Burgess shale. But the Burgess shale preserves only fully aquatic animals. The Robledos claim to fame is in its abundant record of *terrestrial* invertebrates as well as terrestrial vertebrate fauna. And there is a smattering of aquatic life to round out the whole picture.

Another miracle is this: How could these trackways remain preserved for a quarter-billion years when they can't survive exposure to the elements for more than a few years? At first, when I excavated at the main site, the trackways seemed to be nearly invulnerable. It took weeks, sometimes months, to get some of the layers out of the hillside. Sometimes some of the individual slabs would crack as a result of my efforts, but these times were rare when compared to how many times the layers broke my tools. Pry bars broke in half, the heads of many five-pound hammers flew off, and more than one head on my fifteen-pound sledge came off. My levers bent from the resistance of the slabs. When I did find a layer with God's saran wrap the work became a joy and I excavated with ease and confidence. The rest were stuck together like cement.

The difficulty of excavation deluded me somewhat. I interpreted my excavation difficulties as indicative of the fact that the layers were safe from natural erosion. After all, they were one-quarter of a billion years old. They had to be resilient to survive for that long. But my assumptions would soon wash away in a twenty-year flood.

## A Crash Course in Nature's Fury

In September 1992 there came a deluge. A slow-moving thunderstorm parked itself right over the central part of the Robledos. Estimates of the amount of rain that fell varies somewhat, but the evidence suggests that it was at least three inches. In some places, that is not a lot of rain, but in the arid mountains it can be devastating. Having no place to go, the water cascades off the mountainsides and funnels into the arroyos, rushing down the canyons with fearful power.

The strange thing about this September storm was that I was not even aware that it rained at all. Twelve miles away in Las Cruces the weather was crystal clear. So, one morning late in the month I was off to the trackways again. I wasn't going alone. CBS *News* had sent a film crew to do a story on the discovery. We left at 6:30 in the morning so we could catch good sunlight when we reached AF 2. I had a feeling something was wrong when I reached the public quarry. The road to the quarry had been dramatically rearranged. Several places where the road crossed the drainage were washed out and destroyed, and had since been regraded so the dump trucks could get through. I had not seen this before.

"Man, it must have really rained out here," I said as we struggled through the soft mud and sand. Yet I had no thought of concern over the trackways.

I reached the gate that guarded the road to the trackways and, after unlocking it, drove through Quarry Canyon to where I planned to stop at the base of one of our local volcanic wonders, Devil's Postpile, an exposed neck of a long since dead volcano. We never got there. If I thought the public quarry road was bad, the road through Quarry Canyon was totally destroyed. Thousand-pound rocks were strewn everywhere like wooden blocks. The drainage had entirely changed, and it was not in the road's favor. Several drainage scars cut right across the road, leaving canyons twelve to fifteen feet wide and two or more feet deep. I had never seen this before either, but still, I had little concern for the trackways.

This did create problems for CBS. It meant that our one-half-mile hike with equipment was now a mile. We walked up the first arroyo and, although there were fairly big puddles of muddy water, I was still not concerned until I came to the limestone platform mid-way between the jeep and the site. The pits in the limestone on the floor of this portion of Quarry Canyon often look curiously like the tracks of dinosaurs, elephants, humans, gorillas, and about anything else your imagination dreams up. When Glen Kuban, an expert on, among other things, "odd" tracks, saw this section of canyon, he noted that the limestone pits preserved better looking psuedo "man tracks" than the world-famous (or infamous) "man tracks" he studied in the Paluxy River of Texas. Glen used up a whole roll of film photographing them all.

When I reached this spot, I knew that something was terribly wrong. The trunk of a large tree that had been prostrate on the canyon floor for the five years I had walked Quarry Canyon was gone. Not displaced, but gone. I used this tree trunk as the fourth of my six resting points when I carried out heavy footprint slabs. Now, I would have to walk from the third resting spot to the fifth, a daunting distance with a heavy load.

When I made it to the third resting spot, about a hundred yards upstream, I started to get scared. This was my best and favorite resting spot of all because there was a big juniper tree here that provided the only shade between the site and the truck. It is a wonderful spot in the dead heat of summer. The tree was still there, but other things were also there. Jammed into the branches of this tree, a good eight feet up, were rocks, bushes, cacti, and a large section of my tarp. It was ripped in half, and was interspersed with mud and rock and plant debris. It was like the torn and forelorn flag of a defeated army.

I was prepared to encounter some minor damage at the site, but I was still confident that by-and-large the layers were still intact. But as I made my way the last eighth of a mile the magnitude of what I was about to discover hit all at once. Strewn along the arroyo bottom were the spoils of my excavation; big slabs with tracks on them strewn along our path. Slabs so big that I left them at the site. I had believed that these slabs were eternally safe because thieves or vandals would never be able to lift them and carry them out. I did not anticipate that Mother Nature would do what mere mortals could not.

When we were about two hundred feet from the excavation, CBS wanted to wire me for sound. The camera man and the sound man moved ahead to film my approach to the site. They got their money's worth, for as I approached, I entered a state of shock.

"Oh my God, no," I began. "I can't believe this. This is not happening. It's destroyed, it's destroyed."

"Is something wrong?" the producer asked.

"Yes, the site is at least one-half destroyed," I said. "A flash flood has come in and ripped layers out like coupons from a payment book." Work that took me years to perform was undone in minutes by the flood. At the northern end of my excavation, a deep drainage gorge had formed right through the heart of the layers. It was three feet wide, perhaps four feet deep, and about forty feet long. In the middle of the excavation was a small lake, and the bottom of the lake was what was left of layer twenty-five, a layer that had preserved a mysterious bipedal-like trackway. My tarp was designed to protect it from the rain, but nothing could protect the layer from a flood. The first seven feet of the trackway were destroyed, and the final fifteen feet were badly damaged.

CBS didn't know what to do. Do they film me "oh my God-ing" my way across the site, or do they (and I) pretend that nothing had happened and do the shoot as they had originally planned? They chose the latter. It took me a good half-hour to regain my composure and emphasize with excitement the layers that were still there.

In this regard ABC had scooped CBS. An ABC *News* crew had come a few weeks before the flood and filmed the site as I had intended it to be seen, swept clean and chock full with trackways of all kinds and sizes running everywhere. The only silver lining to this mess was that we now had great before and after film of the excavation.

I was brought face to face with the real vulnerability of these tracks and trails. They were fearfully vulnerable to such thunderstorms. I had found them and excavated them, but I had very little power to protect and save them from the elements that had helped expose them in the first place. My nightmares changed from that point on. Instead of dreaming of missing the motherlode or of losing tracksites altogether, my dreams were now full of deluge and destruction. The earth had given, and now the earth had taken away.

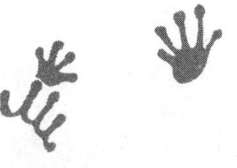

# CHAPTER FIFTEEN

## The Paleozoic Trackways Project

The destruction that occurred at AF 2 that day in September 1992 was a benchmark for me and the project. The flood was so intense that it destroyed half of layer twenty-five, which included the bipedal-like trail and the only big pelycosaur trackway with tail drag. The flood also ripped through my tool stash. Humans were not the only ones who occasionally deprived me of tools. Now it was Nature's turn. I found bits and pieces of tarp strewn for a quarter of a mile down the wash. My tools were probably buried under tons of rock, where they will stay until one day they become someone else's discovery, perhaps thousands of years from now.

The flood triggered a new phase in my research. New Mexico State University had provided me with two graduate students from the Earth Science Department to help me for a semester, Gary Olmstead and Chris Whitman. Their job was twofold. First, they were to prepare a new section of AF 2 for excavation which entailed eliminating the overburden, cleaning off the various layers, and removing any loose trackway material. Layer twenty-five had become the last layer of my original quarry. I wanted to study the lower layers, those below twenty-five, by excavating just to the right of where I stopped working after the flood. Their second job was to begin a systematic analysis of the trackways already removed. I trained them to reduce each trackway to mathematical information, which included the lengths of stride and pace, angles of rotation of the feet, width of trackways, pace angles, and estimates of the size of the trackmaker.

While this went on, my field work changed. Dave Slagle really got the footprint bug for the Caballos and began to spend his time exploring the range for more track sites. I approved of the effort because new sites forty miles from the Robledos and Dune Canyon would give us more information with which to evaluate the Robledo's motherlode. Dave and I made several trips into the Caballos, which were entirely a sea of red. There was little or no Abo tongue at all. It was obvious that only terrestrial sediments would be found in the range. There was little evidence of alternating terrestrial and marine sediments that so characterized the Robledos research. The question we posed to one another was this: In the absence of a clear shoreline environment, would trackways still be preserved? If so, how good would they be? We would soon find out.

Dave spent a lot of time in the Caballos, and he managed to find several track sites, although the quality and quantity was lacking. It seemed clear from what Dave had found that faunules would never be excavated in the Caballos; the layering was not as clearly defined as in the Robledos and God's saran wrap was either non-existent or very poorly developed where it was observed.

What we were doing was kind of scary. What if we found that the Caballos were just as rich as the Robledos? Or richer? It would not only diminish the significance of the motherlode, it would probably kill our arguments that the rare Robledos trackways had to be protected at all costs. We had to confront this possibility head on and I encouraged Dave to scout for more sites. We decided to hunt for the Caballo sites that were discussed nearly thirty years ago by Dr. Peter Vaughn, a paleontologist who was probably the premiere expert on the Abo of New Mexico. Vaughn was the mentor of Dave Berman, who inherited Vaughn's field notes and whose museum, the Carnegie, inherited Vaughn's specimens. Vaughn had mentioned two sites in the Caballos where he had observed not only tracks, but Permian bone as well. I needed a break from pure trackway work and hunting for more bones again would be just the ticket.

We ended up in a real maze. In a sea of red, we had a difficult time finding our bearings in the mountains. Over and over again we searched for landmarks, anything that we could latch on to. The roads were different than they had been in the 1960s, and Dave and I started to pinpoint windmills as our only markers. Dave tried to go out at least once a month, and if he did find something that warranted my attention, we would go out together. Finally, Dave hit a bit of excitement in the summer of 1992. "I think I've found bone," Dave told me excitedly. "It looks like foot bones with complete claws intact."

"Are you kidding me?" I shouted. "I'm coming right over." Then I sped the twenty miles to his farm.

Dave teased me for a few moments by talking and not showing, but then he pulled out four rocks with bone clear as day. This was not an iffy proposition where we had to section the specimens to verify them as bone. We didn't even have to lick them. It was obviously bone.

"Dave," I said. "It's bone, but it's not a foot with claws, it's part of a jaw. Those claws of yours are teeth. Big teeth. It's pelycosaur, carnivorous pelycosaur. Like *Dimetrodon*."

We were smiling big time. The obvious question was if there were any more. "There's got to be," Dave said. We went out the next day and even though we searched the area over and over, we found nothing more. It was heart breaking. We were so pumped up, but Mother Earth withheld any more of her riches. In a full year of hunting in the Caballos, we found no more bone. Nick Hotton confirmed that the bones Dave had found were jaw bones of a sphenacodont (a carnivorous pelycosaur like *Dimetrodon* or *Sphenacodon*).

My attention, though momentarily preoccupied with the Caballos, soon shifted back to the Robledos with a vengeance. Congress had finally allocated money for the trackways. The Paleozoic Trackways Project was not a one-man show any more. There was now a project team which included Dr. Nicholas Hotton of the Smithsonian; Dr. Spencer Lucas of the New Mexico Museum of Natural History; Dr. Adrian Hunt of the University of Colorado at Denver; and Dr. Martin Lockley, also of the University of Colorado at Denver. Additionally, it involved specialists in several areas: Dr. Barry Kues of the University of New Mexico for invertebrate paleontology and Gary Morgan of the New Mexico Museum of Natural History for organizing and computerizing the vast collection of trackways that we had moved up to the museum.

We began the study of the trackways in earnest during January 1994. At this time Hotton, Lucas, Lockley, Hunt, and I met with BLM officials to plan out both a strategy for the Robledos research as well as a timetable for the completion of each of the research tasks that we had been commissioned to undertake. I was soon out in the field again, this time with Adrian Hunt, with the task of pinpointing all thirty-two trackway sites, as well as a half-dozen invertebrate fossil sites that I had found to be especially rich. Modern technology has helped paleontology come a long way since the days of Cope and Marsh, and we used a Global Positioning System (GPS) unit to pinpoint the locations. GPS units send signals up to orbiting satellites, which compute the exact latitude and longitude of the earth-borne signal. I was worried that I had confused the locations of my sites, all

*The trackway team meets together for the first time at the AF 2 excavation as the Congressional study begins. From left to right are Dr. Martin Lockley, Dr. Adrian Hunt, the author, Dr. Spencer Lucas, and Dr. Nicholas Hotton.* Photo by Pam Smith.

of which I had identified using a topographical map and common sense. Most turned out to be surprisingly accurate, but I had made one glaring error—WSA 1 was off by a good half-mile. I wasn't surprised since it had been so difficult to find on the ground in the first place. Hunt and I would also use a GPS unit in Dune Canyon, and, eventually, we were to use it in the Caballos—thank God!

## The Oldest Megatracksite in the World

In late May of 1994 the project team, led by Spencer Lucas and Adrian Hunt, began the imposing task of correlating all of the sites with one another. We measured the layers at the AF 2 site, and then continued up the mountain. This measured section was then added to a section found to the south of the AF 2 site, containing sediments observed to be above the AF 2 site. We were performing sedimentary surgery, grafting layers from diverse sites to one another.

What we wanted to do was to build one reliable sequence of strata from bottom to top; a sequence into which we could then plug all thirty-two trackway sites. In order to do this, we measured the thickness of every sedimentary sequence and took samples of each sedimentary series in order to study their compositions. Thickness, composition, and sequence are the three variables that sedimentologists use to match sedimentary layers with one another. Unfortunately, in nearly every case, AF 2 included, we had to take a section from one area and insert it above or below another section from somewhere else, since the entire sedimentary sequence was rarely found intact from bottom to top at one site.

In Branson Canyon, where sites ten through fifteen are located, we did find a remarkable occurrence. There, stacked like Paul Bunyun's pancakes, was what Spencer heralded as the "Rosetta stone" that would provide the key to the sedimentary sequences in the southern Robledos.

It was a mountain that had no faults or folds, no debris obscuring the exposed beds, and very little dip. It was as near to a perfect sedimentary sequence as one could wish. Nestled neatly at the bottom of the series was AF 10, rising fifty feet high and bristling with hundreds of layers. Adrian had surmised that AF 10 was at the base of the Abo/Hueco tongue. Resting just below AF 10 was a thick series of limestone.

Spencer and Adrian began to measure the Abo tongue series at the limestone base. We then moved into the heart of AF 10 to take samples, climbing the steep embankment and slipping on the laminar beds that had already broken away from the layers.

"I dug six recon pits," I told them. "Three low, three high. The best tracks were found in the lower portion of the outcrop, where these nice red beds are."

The nice red beds I was talking about were about twelve feet thick and fully intact. They make a sharp distinction from the broken red bed layers just above and below them.

"I excavated over on the left end of AF 10, right where these intact red beds meet the bottom of the arroyo."

"What were the tracks like," yelled Spencer, about sixty feet away perched on a red bed ledge.

"They were real good. They reminded me alot of AF 2 material," I yelled back.

"Do you know what we've found?" Spencer said excitedly as he crawled back up to my perch. "We have the world's oldest megatracksite!"

"You're right," exclaimed Adrian. "We really have. This is amazing."

"Now will you please let me publish this, Adrian," Spencer said, tongue in cheek. "You guys (referring to Adrian and Martin Lockley) publish so fast."

"Of course," Adrian replied with a twinkle in his eye.

Martin Lockley recently came up with the term "megatracksite" and it refers to a region of track sites that are preserved together as an aggregate all at the same level. In other words, if we could find AF 2's specific layers at a lot of other sites, it would prove that a large region of mud flat was exposed and trampled on at the same time and then preserved. This is exactly what we found.

"That nice series of beds here," Spencer said pointing to the layers we were standing next to, "the ones you said reminded you of AF 2, well it *is* AF 2. AF 2 is right here—a twelve-foot section of layers laid down both here and a mile north, at AF 2, 280 million years ago."

Adrian began to note that some of the other sites, especially those in the Conifer Forest/Insect Hill region nearly two miles to the west, fit nicely into the model. "They fit perfectly," Adrian noted. "Conifer Forest sits at exactly same level that AF 10 sits, right on the limestone base."

"So we're talking about potentially a six-square-mile region, all exposed and trampled on at the same time," Spencer said.

"Yes, indeed we are," replied Adrian.

"Wow!" Will discovery never end in the Robledos?!

### Dateline May 17, 1994
### Las Cruces, New Mexico
### El Paso Times, Associated Press
### Fossil Footprints Walk Deep into History

The animal track fossils discovered seven years ago near Las Curces are part of a six-square-mile megatracksite—the oldest such site in the world, scientists have determined.

The 280-million-year-old fossils reveal that a rich diversity of reptiles, amphibians and insects roamed a prehistoric, pre-dinosaur shoreline in what is now known as the Robledo Mountians, about eight miles northwest of Las Curces.

Las Cruces paleontologist Jerry Paul MacDonald discovered the first tracks in 1987. Many belonged to beasts never before known to science.

Last weekend, MacDonald, along with scientists from the New Mexico Museum of Natural History, the Smithsonian Institution, and the University of Colorado at Denver, concluded that 32 track sites in

"At least a dozen species of animals have been discovered so far, and there are dozens more of them," said John Arnold, spokesman for the Museum of Natural History in Albuquerque.

The discovery gives scientists a picture of which animals lived together and over how vast a region.

"I think you could say that it's globally significant," Arnold said.

The scientists, along with a number of assistants, are working on the federally funded study of the site.

Until now, the oldest known megatracksite was the Entrada dinosaur site in eastern Utah, about 150 million years old.

The Robledo Mountain site is nearly twice as old and dates to 60 million years before the emergence of dinosaurs.

MacDonald already has collected nearly 2,000 trackways of a variety of creatures.

"Even though the Robledo Mountains preserve at least 32 fossil footprint sites, no one was able to actually follow the same footprint layers throughout the entire range," MacDonald said. "We have now been able to tie the sites together to show that several square miles of shoreline were exposed and trampled on by all of these animals at the same time."

The scientists will present their findings to Congress at the end of the year.

I couldn't wait to call Nick Hotton with the news.

"Hotton speaking," killed the silence.

"Hello, Hotton speaking," I laughed. "Adrian and Spencer believe that what we have in the Robledos is the world's oldest megatracksite. How's that for news? They think it's the only one known from the Paleozoic. All other five known to exist are dinosaur sites."

"Holy Christmas," Hotton blurted. "I'm especially thrilled for you, Jerry," Nick continued. "You're finally beginning to see the fruits of your solitary labors out there for so many years."

"Well, Nick," I told him somberly, "it would have never happened if you hadn't supported me on my dream seven years ago."

Later that day, Hotton was interviewed by the Associated Press:

I am tremendously thrilled at this announcement. I cannot say enough about the significance of the Robledos footprints. This area supported one hell of a population of reptiles of all sizes. It seems to be the same layer cropping out over six square miles, and every place it crops out is just as rich as the next. That's extraordinary. We now have a picture of a large prehistoric shoreline habitat at one instant in time. We not only know which animals were co-habitating, but over how vast a region. It opens up a whole slew of information that was not available to us beforehand.

The Robledo saga was leap-frogging from one significant discovery to another. Who could keep track of all that we were learning? In 1987, placing isolated track debris into layers in situ increased the significance of the track sites considerably. Now, being able to place these isolated track sites into one megatracksite increased the significance of the area once again.

All other megatracksites discovered previously, although larger, appear to have been populated by only a very few different kinds of dinosaurs. Yet one of the significant characteristics of the new Robledo megatracksite is that it contains the footprints of scores of different species. It is easily the most diverse megatracksite, as well as the oldest. For the first time, the trackway team led by Spencer Lucas and Adrian Hunt were able to find the layers that correlated discovery site AF 2 with layers from other sites in the Robledos. I began to think of the Robledos as one big book on fossils, lying on its side, with each layer as a page, and each sequence as a chapter. What Spencer and Adrian did was literally find the same page and chapter throughout the mountain range, even though most of the "book" had been destroyed by erosion. They began to piece the fragments together like archivists would treat an ancient scroll to get a broad picture of what was happening over a large area of the Robledos at the same time.

Now, instead of just thinking about the incredible concentration of assorted tracks on layer twenty-one of the AF 2 site, we were all contemplating the incredible assortment of tracks over a six-square-mile area. We had answered one question: AF 2 was not an anomaly. AF 2's high level of activity and diversity as revealed through footprint density and variety was not an isolated occurrence. Paleozoic life was rich for miles and miles along this long-lost shoreline. The puzzle had come together at last.

Further excavation at the Robledo trackway sites should continue to unravel the unanswered questions concerning the diversity of life, and the proportions of terrestrial, semi-aquatic, and fully aquatic animals, as well as answer why the latter appear to be conspicuously absent from the list of track makers.

Additional evidence will presumably emerge that can help determine patterns of socialization among various track makers and grant a perspective on the make-up of the animal community and the food chain. A concerted effort should be made to understand why the Robledo Mountains preserves such extensive trackways; what conditions were unique to the area?

It certainly seems that a unique set of environmental and depositional circumstances occurred in the Robledos of which there is no contemporary example. The Robledo trackways do not fit well within traditional views on the formation and preservation of trackways. And, as we saw earlier, the Robledo deposit does not compare well with present-day tidal mud flat settings. Likewise, the high ratio of invertebrates to vertebrates also appears to be unique.

What we can say is that the Robledo discovery will fill in significant gaps in our understanding of the fauna and local environments of the Late Paleozoic. It will add a good number of new track types to an Early Permian fossil list that, up to this time, was very sparce in most areas of the world. The Robledo fossil fauna will also show that development of certain species existed for a longer time than was at first supposed, and that prehistoric food pyramids from the Late Paleozoic may have been much more elaborate than previously thought. It will challenge our understandings of the locomotive capabilities of animals in the Late Paleozoic. And most of all, it will write the story of numbers, habitat, and activities of terrestrial invertebrates, a story that in large part has remained unwritten.

The Robledo discovery has challenged us to rethink our understanding of the Late Paleozoic. Such is the potential of a treasure trove of fossils like that found in the Robledo deposit. Such is the reward when inquisitive scientists and bold amateurs are persistent enough to climb through open paleontological windows that they encounter, no matter where they find them.

Undoubtedly, further work in the Robledo Mountains will considerably enrich our understandings of the Permian age and will be of major paleontological significance in a number of related fields for a long time to come. Because there are so many good track sites in the Robledos, the opportunity is there for a comparison of the variety and abundance of trackways from site to site. Additionally, now that the "Rosetta stone" has been found, a comparison of the trackways found in the youngest and the oldest of the sites is possible, as we begin the task of fitting sites into the complete sedimentary sequences found in Branson Canyon. If there were changes in the Paleozoic population of the region, a comparative analysis of the trackways gleaned from each site would offer important evidence of such change.

As other discoveries from the Permian are made in areas far removed from the Robledos, the picture will become even clearer and more complete, as scientists build bridges linking the information together in a consistent and logical way. With each new volume collected, with each new chapter deciphered, we will take another step closer toward a fuller understanding of the perennial struggle for survival that faced our distant ancestors.

Finally, what do the Robledo fossils contribute to our knowledge of earth's evolution? First, they underscore the great antiquity of the first terrestrial reptiles—distant ancestors of contemporary species. Second, they reveal a remarkably diverse parade of animals that we know very little about. Third, they remind us of constant change, both gradual and abrupt, that has punctuated the history of life on earth. Fourth, they remind us of the durability and persistence of life; that such ephemeral footprints can paradoxically be set in stone and preserved for eons is a reminder of the tenacity of life in our vertebrate lineage. Fifth, they remind us that the extinction of species is an inevitable occurance in the gradual scheme of things on earth, and that no species is invulnerable to it. And lastly, the footprints, as well as the layers preserving them, reveal a marvelously wonderful order to everything—sequences, arrangements, classes, and ranks—with some of it sorted and organized as efficently as a librarian would their library.

If you were to ask me what indelible marks the Robledo discovery has left on me personally, three points would stand out both from the loneliness of the early years working single-handedly in the desert to the satisfaction of seeing the Paleozoic Trackways Project making great scientific strides.

The first is that a big part of discovery is attitude and perspective. Just because you may be thinking differently than everybody else does not necessarily mean that you are wrong. Follow your hunches. Many discoveries are made by following one's intuitive gut feelings. The world is full of armchair philosophers, but it's those who go out and seek—in whatever arena their desert may be—who find the rewards over the next ridge.

Second, remember the paleontological field rules. They are good advice in any vocation: Abundance or scarcity does not necessarily mean insignificance; never take anything for granted; always expect to discover something; and work hard and cover a lot of ground.

Finally, be prepared to pay a certain price. Be persistent and let the evidence lead you, not the armchair pronouncements of skeptics or the political agendas of others. Don't give up. The world is full of people who stopped just short of the mark.

Soon after the discovery layer at AF 2 was exposed, in a quiet, reflective mood, I let my imaginings of that ancient world surround me fully, and I fantasized about how startling the discovery would have been if it had been found by settlers one hundred years ago. They may have thought the tracks were those of giant lizards that perhaps still lived in the area. And what of the Native Americans who lived in the area for hundreds, if not thousands of years? What did they think when they encountered, as I'm certain they did, a rock-hard trackway marching blindly across a canyon, only to disappear at the base of a hundred-foot-tall mountain?

There are legends in the area, and in other regions of the American Southwest, of the "spirit animals that walk through mountains." I identified with this phrase immediately when the legend was told to me by a seventy-six-year-old Comanche Indian. In my soul, the trackways I was finding did possess an overwhelming spirituality. Indeed, they are like spirits that walk, even now, through mountains. For one-quarter of a billion years, they have walked through every obstacle that Mother Nature (or the Great Spirit) could place before them. I had found in Native American lore the banner phrase for my quest, for I too, with a little help from a hammer and chisel, was walking through mountains searching for eternal spirits.

# SUGGESTED READING

If you are interested in additional reading about fossil footprints, the Permian, the Paleozoic, or paleontology in general, here are some suggestions for the popular science reader as well as the scientific investigator.

If you love paleontological detective stories, two books come to mind. John R. Horner and James Gorman have written a wonderful story about Horner's discovery of dinosaur eggs, nests, and herding behaviors among the dinosaurs of North America. *Digging Dinosaurs* (Workman Publishers, 1988) appeals to both popular and technical readers and serves as a companion volume to my own story, as Horner, an amateur paleontologist at the time, encounters a few of the same circumstances I did on the way to his "discovery of the decade."

Another good detective story is Louis Jacob's *Quest for the African Dinosaur* (Villard Books, 1993), an enjoyable story that reads more like a novel than an exposé. Jacobs takes the reader through the ins and outs of paleontological discovery, specifically as it relates to his research on the dinosaurs of the African continent.

If you are interested in reading more about life in the Paleozoic, and especially on the Permian, there are many books available on these subjects in popular style, but nearly all are at least fifteen to twenty years old. One of the best is John McLoughlin's *Synapsida* (Viking, 1980), a readable treatise that gives an overview on the evolution of the mammal-like reptiles, from the pelycosaurs to proto-mammals.

For the more advanced reader, Nicholas Hotton's edited volume, *The Ecology and Biology of Mammal-like Reptiles* (Smithsonian Institution Press, 1986), is a Permian-lovers gold mine. With contributions from the best experts in all aspects of vertebrate paleontology as it relates to mammal-like reptiles, you'll find some of the book accessible to the layman, but there is plenty for the professional to chew on as well.

If you want the best reference on prehistoric life in general, and you are more interested in paleontological appetizers rather than a six-course meal, I have a great book for you. The *Macmillan Illustrated Encyclopedia of Dinosaurs and Prehistoric Animals* (1988) is the best illustrated and most concise of the compendiums available today. With good synopses on all of the major animal groups from the Paleozoic to the Pleistocene, you will marvel at the phenomenal variety of life that at one time graced our planet.

If you are interested in becoming a fossil hunter, or are already one but want to refine your skills, there are two good books recently released on the subject. Alan Cvancara's *Sleuthing Fossils: The Art of Investigating Past Life* (John Wiley and Sons, 1990) and Steve Parker and Raymond Bernor's *The Practical Paleontologist* (Quarto Publishing, 1990) are great for the paleontological beginner. These books cover nearly everything, from designing a fossil search, to the excavation, removal, and curation of specimens. Paleontological ethics are also discussed, including what kinds of fossils can and cannot be collected and how to report your finds to the appropriate authorities.

If you are serious about studying fossil footprints, the best books for you are Martin Lockley and David Gillette's edited volume, *Dinosaur Tracks and Traces* (Cambridge University Press, 1989), and Martin Lockley's *Tracking Dinosaurs* (Cambridge University Press, 1991). *Dinosaur Tracks and Traces* is an excellent source book for the very latest findings in the science of ichnology, and the contributors are the best in the field. In addition to articles by Paleozoic Trackway Project scientists Martin Lockley, Adrian Hunt, and Spencer Lucas, other scientists published in this volume include James Farlow and Glen Kuban. Most of the volume is accessible to laypersons, but *Tracking Dinosaurs* is specifically designed for the uninformed reader. It is really a book on the A to Z of footprint knowledge, written by arguably the foremost expert on dinosaur footprints in the world. While the book covers dinosaur tracks, and does not discuss findings of tracks and traces from the Paleozoic, some of the research is applicable to non-dinosaur tracks.

# INDEX

FRANKLIN PIERCE COLLEGE LIBRARY

00091064

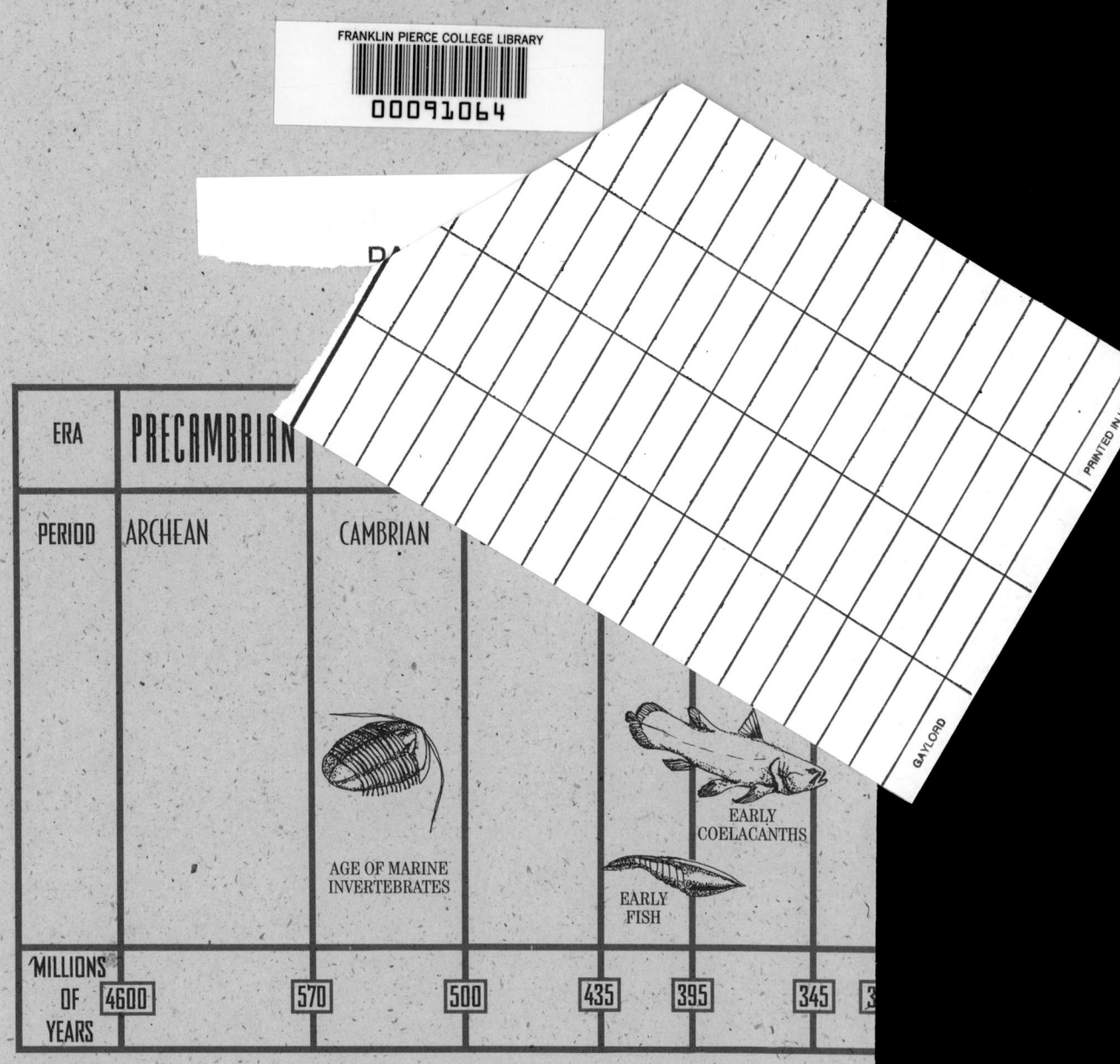

| ERA | PRECAMBRIAN | | | | | | |
|---|---|---|---|---|---|---|---|
| PERIOD | ARCHEAN | CAMBRIAN | | | | | |
| MILLIONS OF YEARS | 4600 | 570 | 500 | 435 | 395 | 345 | 3 |

AGE OF MARINE INVERTEBRATES

EARLY COELACANTHS

EARLY FISH

GAYLORD

PRINTED IN U.S.A.